Shipwreck
or
Shangri-la?

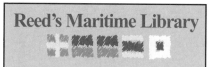

Reed's Maritime Library

Shipwreck
or
Shangri-la?

Peter Lickfold

SHERIDAN HOUSE

This edition published 2001 by
Sheridan House Inc.
145 Palisade Street
Dobbs Ferry, New York 10522
www.sheridanhouse.com

Copyright © 2001 by Peter Lickfold

First published in Great Britain 2001
by Thomas Reed Publications

A Cataloging-in-Publication record of this book is available
from the Library of Congress, Washington, DC.

Edited by Alex Milne
Series Consultant Tony Brunton-Reed
Design & Layout by C E Marketing
Produced by Omega Profiles Ltd.
Printed and bound in Great Britain

ISBN 1-57409-142-5

AUTHOR'S NOTE

MY PURPOSE IN writing this book is to publicly thank the people who helped when our venture to follow a dream turned into a nightmare.

I set out to introduce each of them at appropriate places in the narrative and describe their acts of generosity, but found it an impossible task. In the first place simply to list all the incidents would require a book too heavy to lift and, at the end of it, still only be a list. To add to the difficulty there were many kindnesses we cannot attribute to anyone; we simply found things done without a hint as to who had done them. Then there are people we have never met, and are never likely to meet, whose assistance was invaluable, but we don't even have the privilege of knowing their names.

What is more so many things happened that my memory confuses them, so I have cut the 'list' to the bare bones and told the story as it came back to my mind. Each person involved will, I'm sure, recognize the events even if I recall the details differently and, I trust, know in their hearts how grateful my family and I are to them. They are, in no particular order other than that their boat names are arranged alphabetically:-

Aradonna, Adele & Rodney; *Avon Grace*, Jim & Joy; *Aztec Lady*, John, Joan, Steve & Grant; *Banana Moon*, Didier & Pom; *Beaudacious I*, Joel, Hilary & Ryan; *Betong,* Jeff & Juan; *Bob*, Russell & Liz; *Born Free*, Brian & Trine; *Broomstick*, Joe, Alice & crew; *Brumby*, Humphrey & Claire; *Cairngorm*, Kay & Clive; *Cicada*, Marty & Steve; *Cillim II,*, Ed; *Con Brio*, Gert & Annita; *Cremona*, Berndt & Gunwhal; *Cruise*, Ian & Chrissy; *Cyrano de Bergerac*, Gordon, Jenny & crew; *Dalkiri*, Brian, Gwen, Craig, Candice & Mark; *Darius*, Geoff, Penny, Haley, Kobe & Daniel; *Delight*, Chris; *Dionysus*, Stan & Jenny; *Dawn Treader*, Adrienne & AB; *Eclipse C*, Massimo, Cris & Julie; *Enigma*, Paul, Helen, Georgina & Adam; *Edelweiss III*, Alain & Claire; *Finnegan*, Derek & Hilary; *Glee + 2*, Glynn, Lee, Matthew & Megan; *Harmony*, Chris & Louise; *Hasty*, Tom, Lynn & Tim; *Heather*, Eric & Robin; *Ikarus*, Heinz & Lona; *Imagine*, Alan, Linda &

Zoey; *Inga Viola*, Mike, Gitta, Frog & Anne; *Jonathan*, Thierry & Laurent; *Kekeni*, John & Sue; *La Bamba*, Allesandro, Regina & Franco; *Le Cajun*, Ted; *Malgre Tout*, Adela & David; *Mamaru*, Patrick & Nicole; *Mara*, Jim & Jean; *Maupiti*, Owners & crew; *Mission*, Kim & Gary; *Mystie*, Roger, Jacqueline & family; *Nicola*, Ellard & Eileen; *Paquita*, Terri, Marc & Jack; *Pizzaz*, Mireille, Lothar & family; *Retingy*, Alex & crew; *Revielle II*, Tony & Marjory; *Rouet des Jours*, Paula & Rodney; *Silence*, Frank; *Sgothlong*, Peter, Wendy & Troy; *Stepping Stone*, Mike & Rae; *Summerwind III*, Yoav, Pnina, Bar & Netta; *Sumurun*, Alan, Philippa & Heidi; *Tamar*, Carl; *Targa II*, Manuel, Patrick & Lorenzo; *Tasman*, Gary, Gerry, Akiko & Leon; *Tatanai*, Rita & Enzo; *Toani*, François & Phillipe; *Toti*, Frederick & crew; *Vakuta*, Roger & Milanka; *Veron*, Raoul & Danielle; *Waiari*, Sandy & David; *Wahoo II*, Joel & Frederick; *Wanago*, Lowell, Bea & Jack; *Yebisah*, Knut & Renata; *Ystar*, Marc, Pauline & Family; Cdr. Paul Baker, British Representative on Diego Garcia; David Smith, British Indian Ocean Territory Administrator, Foreign & Commonwealth Office; Members of the Royal Navy and Royal Marines who comprise N/P *1002,* Diego Garcia; Master & crew of the Fisheries Protection Vessel M/V *Northern Desire;* Master & crew of the M/V *Anderson*; Master & crew of the M/V *Henry J. Kaiser*; Master & crew of the M/V *Cpl. Louis J. Hauge, Jnr.* and other members of the American services stationed on Diego Garcia; Members of the 1996 scientific expedition to the archipelago; numerous Sri Lankan fishermen; the site engineers for the satellite communication station on Gan, Addu Atoll; and, very specially, **Five Zulu Four Foxtrot Zulu** – Tony the radio ham in Kilifi, Kenya, and his wife Daphne.

Thank you and God bless.

In terms of producing the book I am deeply indebted to Vanessa for providing the haven in which to finish it, Patrick and Nicole of Mamaru for access to their personal diaries, Dave Hallam, Kay, Philippa, Eric and Robin for their photographs, and to my lovely wife Tina for her forbearance with my ill temper while writing. Special thanks are also due to Jim and Alex Cooper: to Jim for creating the link between writing and publication; and to Alex, whose gentle and perceptive editing transformed the manuscript into a book. However, any remaining malapropisms, unruly grammar or other derelictions are entirely my own.

BOOK ONE

THE ISLANDS ANGLAISE and Boddam are part of the tiny, uninhabited, Salomon atoll in the Indian ocean, and so small and insignificant that few maps show even the surrounding archipelago, yet they have profoundly affected my life and I have been racking my brain how to tell of it. I suppose it's best to start at the beginning, probably when our dream of sailing in search of paradise was first voiced, at a boat show in London's Earls Court more than thirty years ago.

Like most dreams it burned bright and strong through bad times and merely warm and mellow when things were good, but the essential fire survived raising a family, emigrating to a new country and the turmoil of a chequered career. What's more, it survived most of that time without nourishment as twenty years passed before so much as a dinghy came into our lives.

To this day I'm not sure whether it was playing with that dinghy on the local dam or reading a magazine article describing a lone sailor's visit to Salomon that fanned the flames to forging heat but, while still somewhat committed on the domestic front with one daughter yet to complete her university studies, we started the search for a cruising boat. A vessel that would take us in reasonable comfort to wherever we wanted to go but at a price we could afford. We soon learned that those requirements were mutually exclusive.

In fact the dream nearly foundered at that early stage as the search dragged on and on. We drove thousands of miles to see boats we couldn't stand up in, boats that were too big, too ramshackle or too ugly; boats that were ideal but too expensive and boats that were simply wrong before realizing that, in the real world, even dreams have to be compromised – or forgotten.

Eventually *Vespera* came to light to tempt us. She was

substantially more expensive than we could afford and substantially less than we wanted, but out of all we had seen she was the least difficult compromise to accept. She was about the right size, large enough to walk around in yet small enough for the two of us to handle on our own. Most important she had a good 'ambience'. The decision was taken, the cheque written, and from that moment we had a new head of the family.

The dream was a giant step closer, or at least we thought so, but dreams have qualities that cloud the vision and for a long time we couldn't see past imaginary sun-drenched palm trees to the monumental reality of preparing a boat, and ourselves, for ocean voyaging. It says a lot for the selectivity of the human mind that conventional dreams of sailing off into the sunset recur and recur, yet everyone who's tried it has had to confront the impracticality of it all. It seems few of us learn from the experience of others.

Be that as it may, though, our first cold dose of reality was discovering that we didn't know how to handle a cruiser. Our little boat on the dam had been a poor teacher as all you ever had to do was let go the bits of string and she stopped, quickly, and we developed appropriate habits; rushing up to almost where we wanted to be, stopping, then jumping over the side to push the last few feet. *Vespera* was very different.

After some dreadful, and highly embarrassing, attempts to teach ourselves we enrolled with a sailing school to learn at least the basics and, incidentally, made a good friend in doing so. Munro, the school's principal, managed, without shouting once, to get us moving on and off the mooring without damaging anything and familiar enough with harbour workings to get a pilot's exemption certificate. We really felt we were doing something towards the dream.

But the next thread of reality was *Vespera* sitting quietly on her mooring while we champed at the bit four hundred miles away in our highveld home. Weekends were never again the relaxing interludes between captivity in the office; they took on a sort of frenetic identity all of their own.

The journey was the hard part and we tried every combination of route and departure time before settling on a regular routine, eventually learning to tell the time by the road signs; somehow always more significant on the mind-numbing drive home. Warden – "We're four minutes early"; Heidelberg – "We've made another minute", and so forth, but there was always a red light somewhere to mess up the arithmetic.

Not long after getting into this stride, consecutive weekends proved both humorous and disastrous. It poured with rain all through the first Friday night, so driving down was like riding a fairground water-slide, then continued all day Saturday. Friends were joining us on board for dinner that evening and arrived, after rowing across the anchorage, drenched to the skin. Only funny because it was hardly drier inside, with pots and pans arrayed under newly found deck leaks. A hilarious evening worthy of a cartoonist's attention ensued, but it carried on raining all day Sunday too.

Next Saturday was not so funny. Gloomy faces greeted us at the yacht club with news that the heavy rains had dumped tons of sand in the channel linking the mooring basin to the harbour and *Vespera*, in common with scores of other boats, was landlocked. She was too heavy to haul out on the club slipway and there was no suitable hard standing for a crane to lift her out, so she was there until the sand was cleared – and no-one would even guess when that would be.

A serious set-back for the dream. Understandably, I suppose, clearing the channel for a bunch of yachts that, between them, didn't amount to the value of a single ship rated fairly low in the priorities and it was months before we felt even reasonably confident that we might get her out, and in the meantime life had to go on.

Unable to make any specific plans – it's difficult to sail away without a boat – I took advantage of the first interesting contract to come my way in years, but it meant signing up for a minimum of eighteen months. As it happened it took all of that time, and more, to make good the ravages of neglect *Vespera* had suffered in her sandy puddle. There wasn't exactly a lot of motivation to sit in a noisy car for hours just to sit in an inert boat for a weekend. And, in our naïvety, we reasoned that equipment not being used wouldn't come to any harm, so we didn't do much maintenance either. We were about to learn another lesson.

At the very first opportunity, when a channel had been

dredged just deep enough for her to float through at spring tide, we escaped. The channel was all of a mile long, barely the width of the boat, and meandered round some serious obstacles; and it was only deep enough for about an hour. Six boats ran this gauntlet and, with some interesting moments, made it without significant mishap. But even this short trip showed the error of our ways over the maintenance: sticking fittings, stiff controls, lights not working… ad nauseam. Everything had worked properly the last time we'd been aboard but somehow, when no-one was looking, things had changed.

But, ravaged and uncared for or not, *Vespera* was out and we now faced a hard decision. Do we sell the house or not? It was very obvious that we needed to live aboard if we ever intended to catch up on the maintenance, let alone get ready to go cruising. But our much loved home was a nail pinning my foot firmly to the ground. Tina is made of sterner stuff though and reminded me that setting sail was similar to emigrating, and we only made a go of that because we pulled out the nails once before.

So the house was sold, along with most of our other possessions. We set an arbitrary limit to the amount of stuff we could move onto the boat by stipulating that if it wouldn't fit it in the car it wouldn't fit it in the boat, and everything else had to go. We cheated a bit by loading our little car down to its axle stops, leaving just enough room for Jess, the cat, to squeeze in on Tina's lap, and set off like that to become 'live aboards'.

It was an emotional journey. Memories of the good times the old house had seen while the family grew up washed across our minds all the time, but between those images flashes of imagination lit up the future. We kicked off our shoes and drove barefoot. We took off our watches and ignored the time and we turned off the radio to avoid the news. Then gradually, as the familiar road signs ticked past, the heavier feelings gave way to the brightness of tomorrow and, by the time we crossed the Durban boundary, neither of us had felt so free since the last time we broke up from school.

Unlike school holidays though our new-found freedom was jolly hard work. There was hardly time to settle down after the move before we watched *Vespera* being swung through the air by a giant crane to take up residence in a shipyard, marking as she did so the beginning of a period of concentrated effort. One of the hardest, and most expensive, I remember.

We had it in mind to be ready to go as soon as possible, and I suppose it's a fair indication of our competence at the time that we didn't understand there were only two basic sailing seasons from the east coast of southern Africa. If you want to go west you need to round the Cape near to Christmas time, and if you wish to go east it's safer to go in May. But we had no truck for such trivialities. We wanted to sail now!

Fortunately Munro, our sailing instructor friend, caught up with us while *Vespera* was waiting nakedly for a coat of paint and put forward the proposal that I join him as a member of his crew to deliver a new boat from Europe to Cape Town. This was a learning opportunity much too good to miss and Tina willingly, or at least only under minimal duress, accepted the task of staying behind to look after things.

Knowing what I know now I can say that the delivery was a comfortable and uneventful trip, but when I phoned Tina from Cape Town three months later it was on the tip of my tongue to tell her that the ocean was no place to take loved ones. I had spent hours (and hours and hours) in a miserably wet and windy cockpit beating into the trade winds of the old clipper route wondering how to break the news that, for all my dreaming, I wasn't prepared to subject her to this. I didn't voice these thoughts to Munro so it wasn't until much later that I learned these troubling conditions were 'ordinary'.

But, as I said, Tina is made of sterner stuff and, sensing what I was going to say, pre-empted me with the statement "Whatever you feel about it, I'm not going to miss the experience for anything". End of discussion.

In spite of being slow on the uptake about sea conditions I had learned enough from the trip to realize that *Vespera* was far from ready to go oceaneering. She was equipped with all the gear the authorities deem necessary for an 'Offshore' clearance and up to now I had been foolish enough to think that was the end of it.

Now I stood back and had a good critical look, not so much at the equipment covered by the clearance certificate but at pretty much everything else, and tried to picture how it would all work in the 'ordinary' conditions. More important, I tried to picture what would happen if anything broke and how well would we be equipped to cope if it did.

The result was a long shopping list, and an even longer job list, of things to be acquired or done prior to leaving and we spent a somewhat uninspiring year changing and up-grading fixtures and fittings until we were satisfied. Needless to say that year didn't fit very cosily into the sailing seasons.

The boat was ready; we were ready, and all we needed to do was load up with provisions, but it was neither one season nor the other. We had missed leaving with everyone going west so circumstances sort of dictated that we provision ready to depart in May and head into the Indian Ocean. The calendar left us plenty of time.

One episode occurred to relieve the year from the tedium of continuous work. Munro had a tail-end-of-the-season yacht delivery to do from Durban, round Cape Agulhas, to Gordons Bay near Cape Town, and invited us both to accompany him. Tina was going to do her first offshore trip in one of the world's more notorious stretches of water.

As it happened we made a hurried departure to avoid swells from a cyclone reportedly blowing itself out over the south of Madagascar, motored all night looking for wind, sailed during the daylight hours of next day, then motored in flat water all the way to Cape Town, rounding the infamous 'Cape of Storms' in brilliant sunny weather. If only all sailing could be like that.

May eventually came around and *Vespera* was fuelled and watered, even washed and polished, ready for the off. Food and groceries for a full year were on order and we only had to arrange delivery when I broke a wrist! One of those really stupid accidents that take you completely unawares. We were helping friends clean the bottom of their boat ready to antifoul when I fell from an oil drum and landed awkwardly, breaking one wrist and spraining the other.

The closer we got to the dream the more elusive it

seemed to get.

Tina hid it well but was very disappointed at this turn of events. We had been living on the boat for almost two years already and didn't seem any closer to sailing than when we first arrived. But Munro stepped into the breach again and invited her to join a six-week cruise with a group of students while I recuperated.

By the time they got back my arms were fixed and all the provisions were aboard, but it was too late to tackle the Indian Ocean this season. This effectively put off our departure for another year as Tina was so taken with northern Madagascar that she particularly wanted to go that way, which was fine.

However, seeing as we were as ready as we would ever be, we thought we might as well take a 'shake-down' cruise to Mozambique before setting off in earnest. It would be a good idea to check that all the new gear and our modifications would work together properly anyway.

It was as well we did. Stan, a friend and cruiser with many years' experience, came with us and pointed out several improvements that would make the sailing easier, not the least of which was that the self-steering gear would be more effective with a shorter stem. Heeding that advice paid handsomely over the years and making the alterations kept us busy, or at least stopped us getting bored, until May came round again.

Five years had passed since the big decision to buy the boat and our dreams had progressed through wild evolutions during that time. The sun-drenched beaches and palm trees hadn't changed at all but, having learned something of the price the sea can exact from dreamers, our view of them had changed a lot. Either from experience or through osmosis we had gained a better understanding of how little we knew, and were more scared of the unknown now than we had been at the outset.

Consequently when we said our good-byes it was with a somewhat nebulous plan to drift around the western half of the Indian Ocean for a while, possibly even staying within the confines of the Mozambique channel, to see how much we enjoyed it rather than with any spectacular venture in mind.

The first step in this nebulous plan was to sail directly to Tulear in the south of Madagascar to meet up with friends, who had left a day or two earlier, for a beach barbecue. Murphy's Law dictated that the Mozambique current, which sometimes runs and sometimes doesn't, was running at full strength when we sailed out of Durban and we had our work cut out to make any progress at all in the right direction.

Four days later we'd only made a hundred miles and got caught in the strongest gale we ever experienced, before or since. I will not try to describe it beyond saying that when the wind-speed instrument needle hit its end stop, and stayed there, we simply turned the instruments off and cowered under minute sails till it eased to manageable proportions – two days later.

Dreadfully dispirited we slunk into Richards Bay rather than carry on towards Madagascar. With their couple of days head-start our friends had most likely missed all the nonsense and would be waiting for us to arrive, but we really didn't know if we wanted to continue sailing.

That is not true, we knew perfectly well. Our palm-fringed beaches had dissolved in a torment of towering waves and screaming winds and we were no longer interested. Shangri-la was a myth not worth chasing; the realities of the obstacles on the way were much too harsh.

For the several days it took to tidy up and dry everything the future was a topic neither of us was prepared to broach. The cost to get this far had been enormous; our standing in suburbia had been irretrievably discarded, along with the house, the car and my career, such as it was. And it had all been a colossal mistake.

When we eventually faced up to what to do next we decided to note our thoughts down individually and put them in a barrel, then shuffle them into order all in one go rather than squabble about trivia as each idea was generated – which is our usual way. Strangely the idea that we should give sailing one more try won by a short head, well, more by a whisker really, so we put the dry sails back on, took on more fuel and water, and prepared to start again.

This time the departure was more successful and our only disappointment was to get to Madagascar and find no news of the friends we were supposed to meet. We heard numerous terrible rumours of yachts going aground or sinking but none of the details seemed to match their circumstances and any communications other than the grapevine were non-existent, so we carried on.

The island of Mayotte, in the northern end of the Mozambique channel, proved something of a turning point. We had been obliged by a failed water pump to stop there on our way to the cruising ground on Madagascar's north coast and the stop extended to six weeks while we waited for parts. This gave plenty of time for discussion about the next move but we found ourselves at an impasse. I had recovered enough confidence to want to carry on to the palm-fringed beaches of Boddam, where the dream started, but Tina was less than enthusiastic about the ocean crossing.

Having come so far we were reluctant to simply turn back and our discussions petered out in vague indecision until a friend suggested a compromise. Mombassa was only six hundred miles of reasonably comfortable sailing away and the coast line south from there to Dar es Salaam offers plenty of interesting places to visit. By taking this option we could defer any decisions until the next season and have some fun at the same time.

So instead of going back to Madagascar we went to Kenya, and we had a lot of fun without even bothering to travel up and down the coast. Our daughter Vanessa arranged to spend her annual holiday with us to take advantage of the coral reefs and her newly acquired scuba diving qualification, and we thought it a good idea to learn to dive as well so we could share her experience.

Local enquiries turned up Roger, an ex-Royal Navy dive instructor, who had exactly the right temperament to suit our approach to things. Tina has a deep-rooted fear of the water and the first exercises in the swimming pool almost put her off for ever, but Roger had a great reserve of patience and a way with friendly encouragement that helped her overcome the phobia. It was a big day in her life when she raised enough courage to throw her gear into the deep end and dive down to put it all on without assistance.

Meanwhile the dream was performing somersaults.

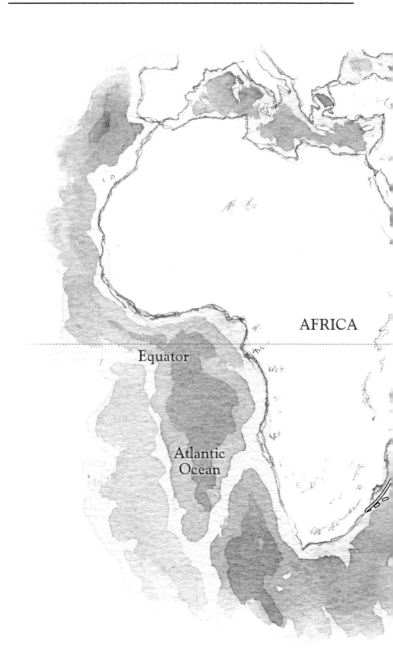

AFRICA

Equator

Atlantic
Ocean

INDIA

Salomon
atoll

Indian
Ocean

MADAGASCAR

⬭⬭⬭⬭⬭⬭⬭⬭ outward route
⬭ ⬤ ⬭ ⬤ homeward route
route after accident

There were a few boats anchored in the creek that had recently visited Boddam and the crews told stories of such delights that Tina was soon sold on the idea. At the same time I listened to reports of there being thirty or more yachts off the island at the height of the season and I certainly didn't want to go to the trouble and expense of an ocean crossing just to anchor with hordes of boats. I might as well go back to the mooring in Durban and spend the money on cold beer.

Adding to the mental turmoil was the news that our friends had indeed lost their yacht in Madagascar. The family were safe but the boat, with all their personal possessions, had been destroyed in a freak accident. Like us they were uninsured and the ramifications of the story led us to ponder deeply on what we had let ourselves in for.

However, there was another element about to enter into the equation. Susan, our eldest daughter, is an addicted traveller and, in spite of a flourishing career in London, chose to join us for a cruise. All the plans went back in the barrel for a reshuffle and Boddam came out as a definite winner – though somehow I think the draw was rigged – followed by a voyage to South East Asia, where we would think again. It felt quite odd to realize that at last we were set for a real go at finding our Shangri-la, and more strange still to be worrying that it might be overcrowded when we got there.

The timing of the trip was going to be a bit off as, to fit in with the plans of both daughters, we could only leave late in the season; so if there was a high-season crush we might just miss it. An unfortunate quirk of this timing prevented something of a family reunion though. The girls hadn't seen each other since their sister's wedding three years earlier and it was sad that the first flight Sue could get arrived a few days after Vanessa left for Johannesburg. What a pity.

Sue brought with her more advantages than just her company. In London she'd had access to stores selling all sorts of sophisticated equipment that simply wasn't available in Kenya at the time, and her hand luggage included an electronic autopilot and a GPS (Global Positioning System) receiver that was infinitely superior to our 'old fashioned' satellite navigator.

The sea was about to reinforce the lesson about choosing your sailing times properly. Boddam is two thousand nautical miles due east of Mombassa and the pilot charts show that light winds could be expected on a direct route at this time of year, though the currents would be advantageous. However, should we go a couple of hundred miles south the winds would be stronger, but not from a very good direction and the currents not so fair.

We chose the direct route, and in doing so subjected Sue to a fifty-day initiation into the pleasures of sailing. Light winds proved something of an under-statement and for twenty-seven of the fifty days we sat like Coleridge's 'painted ship upon a painted ocean' in the absolute stillness of a tropical calm.

Just before we finally ran out of patience *Vespera* ghosted into Peros Banhos, an atoll close to Salomon, and we quickly learned that Shangri-la is defended with sharp teeth. The depth sounder showed deep water, too deep to anchor in with our length of chain, carrying right to the edge of the coral, and we spent an anxious half-hour searching out a spot before dropping the anchor to the east of Ile Diamant.

It was not a comfortable place. A falling tide showed coral poking through the surface along the whole island and, although a bare hundred yards distant, the palm-fringed beach was as inaccessible as the moon. Our inflatable dinghy would be torn to shreds and it was impossible to swim over.

The chart did show a boat channel which should become visible as the level dropped, so we bided our time in patience. But a change in the weather foiled the attempted landing. Huge cumulus clouds boiled in the sky to the south east and wind from that direction would leave these coral teeth only a few yards to leeward, and the water depth was marginal for our anchor rode – so we left… and found out that corals are only the incisors. The real gnashers are the winds and we beat into them for three days to cover the thirty miles to Salomon, arriving there in pouring rain. This was nothing like the dream at all.

Unable to see the other side of the atoll clearly, let alone the coral bommies (bomboras, or shallow reefs) we radioed for information about the state of the tide and were delighted to hear friends Agnes and André, who had left Kenya the day before us but opted for the windier passage down south. They'd been much quicker and had been here long enough to learn the local lore and guided us in.

When the sun eventually got round to shining we could see that everything we'd read and heard about the place was true. It was spectacularly beautiful. Long white beaches and palm trees. Startlingly clear and blue water. Graceful birds swooping over the lagoon. Everything. Including lots of people.

The south easterly winds of the last few days had chased several boats from the over-crowded anchorage at Boddam and we joined the evacuees in the lee of Ile Takamaka, where we stayed for the whole three months of our visit.

My vaguely held notions of a 'Robinson Crusoe'-like existence couldn't have been further from the truth. You could wander off alone and escape to untrodden beaches, or lose yourself in the natural vegetation of the islands, but the essence of the experience was social.

To some extent the way such things work out depends on the luck of the draw. Along with tales of delight we'd also heard of individuals who'd upset the temporary community and spoiled the dreams of many. We were singularly fortunate in that we shared the whole three months with pleasant people. Of course the remoteness itself imparts a spirit of camaraderie and nowhere in the world could match the island barbecue sites, so we hoard our memories of Takamaka parties in the place we keep for special treasures.

It wasn't so much the get-togethers but a spin-off from them that was most significant to me. Someone erected a volley-ball net on the beach and in no time competitive teams emerged. Now I loathe team games. I can't stand to watch them and dislike playing them with a passion. So every afternoon, or as often as I could without being blatantly rude,

I made sure I was somewhere else at game time and those peaceful hours introduced me to beachcombing.

It soon became a family thing and we made regular trips round the nearer islands in search of shells. Some people take live shells to make sure they only collect prime specimens but we found that diligent searches of the tide-line turned up just as good shells without killing anything. And I can't think of a better excuse for a walk along a deserted beach as the afternoon sun slides away and palm-filtered breezes keep you cool.

We became fascinated by the hermit crabs that seem to inhabit every shell. Occasionally we would pick up a shell from an animal only recently dead, and these were usually empty. Everything else would have a crab in residence; even the most minute Cerith shell would have a tenant, often so small you needed a magnifier to see him properly.

Even tired old 'beachroller' shells became prized possessions as resident hermits could usually be persuaded to relinquish collectors specimens if offered alternative accommodation. We kept a 'home' box with as large a variety of sizes and shapes as we could find.

Time passed quickly, though I suppose it always does when life is good. Just a few weeks after we arrived the general westbound season came to a close and the number of boats thinned dramatically. Luckily we still had another month before our planned departure for Thailand.

Imperceptibly the island experience changed to something closer to my preconceptions, and before we left we gained some idea of what it would be like to live in Shangri-la rather than just visit it. Indeed had we had sufficient stores we might have stayed long enough to find out for certain.

However, other exciting prospects waited for us further along. Thailand and the east beckoned with all the allure of unknown places, so sailing away was easier than we expected.

A few days, or maybe a week, into the onward voyage Jess started acting strangely, sitting stock still and peering at the foul weather gear locker. At first we couldn't see any reason for this, then Sue noticed a pair of very small feelers waving about under one of the door louvres.

Thinking it was some kind of insect she opened the

locker to shoo it away and found the other ends of the feelers attached to a homeless hermit crab, clinging to the door for dear life with his body tucked between two slats as though they were a shell. We had no idea how he got there or when he'd come aboard but assumed he'd gone unnoticed sometime while sorting shells.

Not wanting to simply throw the little chap over the side into thousands of feet of water we selected a shell for him out of the 'home' box and put them both in a bowl to come to terms with each other, thinking we'd put him ashore with other hermits in Thailand.

Little did we know how this insignificant seeming act would change our lives, setting us on the road that led directly to being shipwrecked.

It started when we asked each other what hermit crabs ate so we could feed him. No-one knew. Then we talked about whether they drank fresh or salt water, but no-one knew that either. Question followed question. Can hermit crabs swim? Where do they breed? How do they find shells? How long do they live? – Don't know.

We thought it most unlikely that he wouldn't eat coconut so we broke him off a piece and left it in the bowl, together with a saucer each of salt and fresh water. Surely he would show us his preference when he needed to drink. The coconut was quite successful and he chipped away at it with his claws but he appeared to spend equal amounts of time in each water dish, resolutely refusing to answer our question.

Jess became totally absorbed with her new companion. She would sit beside the bowl for hours just watching, occasionally succumbing to curiosity and reaching out a tentative paw to roll him over. This creature with the ability to suddenly lose all its legs and then, after an interminable watch, grow them again was obviously beyond her reasoning power.

Thailand proved something of a disappointment for Hermie when we got there. We searched the beaches and foreshores for a habitat with a community of similar crabs but found nothing like him. In fact we found evidence that there were no hermit crabs at all as the tidelines were littered with empty shells. Maybe Malaysia would be more accommodating.

It was time now to think about the next move and

returning to the islands was the firm favourite, but that would be governed to a large extent by where and when we could get *Vespera* hauled out for some overdue maintenance. Her antifouling paint was eighteen months old and would need re-doing soon and the ocean crossing had left the topsides looking decidedly tacky.

Haul-out facilities in the Malacca Strait are limited and those we found were either extortionately expensive or very bad, in fact usually both. To make it more interesting the Thai authorities are adamant about the length of time they allow you to stay in their waters, and that period isn't long enough to organize things and do a proper maintenance job.

We finished up making a booking for the first available slot and having to leave the country while we waited, putting the whole nonsense down to some probably misunderstood difference between the oriental way of doing things and ours. On the positive side though our enforced trip to Malaysia was most rewarding.

On a sandy beach similar to the one Hermie must have come from we found a crowd of small hermit crabs. But they really were small, much smaller than our stowaway, and were different colours altogether from any we'd seen on the islands. Reluctantly we came to the conclusion that they were a different species and Hermie was no nearer to going back to his environment than he had been in Thailand.

We did learn one thing from the little chaps though. They obviously got a lot of their food by sifting through the beach sand for organisms and the like, so without further ado Hermie's bowl got upgraded to a redundant cat litter box with a layer of damp beach sand in the bottom. More questions arose though from just watching the local crabs. How, for example, could you tell whether they were male or female?

Once on Takamaka we had seen a hermit in 'berry', like a crayfish, so that had obviously been a female. We decided to look for another one so encumbered and, knowing that was definitely a 'her', see if we could detect a difference from any others. The idea might have worked but we never found another 'her'.

Meantime we were constrained to leave to meet our appointment with the boatyard in Thailand. I do not wish to dwell on this period but suffice it to say that following a series of head-on collisions with avaricious and inept yard managers we finished our maintenance too late for the option of sailing westwards that year.

Light winds to the east of Sumatra and lack of access to fuelling facilities in Jakarta without an expensive permit left us unenthusiastic about the option of crossing the equator and leaving SE Asia via the Sunda Strait, even though it would save six months, so we chose to wait it out in Malaysia. The silver lining to this was plenty of time to travel inland and we took full advantage of it.

Our travels didn't turn up a suitable place to rehabilitate Hermie though. This was where he influenced our whole future by imposing the decision on us that the only possible thing to do was take him back to Takamaka, and it became a challenge to keep him alive long enough to do so. He'd already given us a scare when he buried himself in the sand for several days without coming up for food or water.

Quite anxious about this, Sue dug him out and was most upset to find an apparently empty shell with a dried out skeleton beside it. Fortunately we checked the shell carefully before doing anything else and just visible round the first bend was what looked like a claw. I poked it gently with a toothpick and got a twitch of reaction and we concluded he must have moulted, if that's the word, his old skeleton ready for a bigger one. Strangely when he finally emerged he wasn't detectably larger.

A thing that surprised us was how difficult it is to find any information about hermit crabs. We joined a library in Malaysia but their entire reference section merely added the Latin name *coenobita scaevola* to what we had found out for ourselves. We wrote to all the people we could think of who might know anything about them and several responded with excerpts from encyclopaedias, but nothing that answered even the most basic questions, except one; we learned that they go to sea to breed. But where they hatch and how the hatchlings find their first shell, when still smaller than a match head, remains a mystery.

An avenue opened up when we read of a scientific expedition to Salomon and the other atolls that would take place the year after our pending visit. We wrote to the scientist putting the expedition together, who had been on a similar venture to the same place before, asking if he knew of any appropriate reference works on hermit crabs.

We also asked if we might help with some pre-expedition leg work as we would be in the islands while they were still making their preparations. In truth we were now so intrigued by the behaviour of hermit crabs we intended doing some 'un-scientific' research of our own anyway and the possibility that, while we had our feet wet so to speak, we might be able to contribute to something bigger was very exciting.

A branch of science swung back in our faces, though, as we made our way through life in Malaysia; that of the veterinary discipline. While we'd been lavishing our attention on Hermie's survival Jess had become very sick. For some reason her fur fell out in handfuls, far in excess of anything we'd seen before, and she spent most of each day grooming herself – which only made it worse.

She was subjected to the indignities of travelling in a crowded songthaw in Thailand, a noisy local bus in Malaysia, and once to a long and windswept trip by dinghy, to visit different vets while we tried to find out what was causing it, but the answer was elusive. Eventually we found a chap with a convincing story about deficiencies in locally produced cat foods and he persuaded us to change her diet to a 'scientifically enriched' dry food.

Things went well with the change and she wolfed the dry crumbles down as soon as we poured them into her bowl, so much so that we decided to stock up with them for our return to the islands. They were very expensive, and hard to find once we'd used the first bag, but more convenient than tins in that they took up less room, didn't weigh as much and were long lasting. Also, we hoped, they were good for Jess.

The vet assured us that within a month we would see a vast improvement in her coat, but it didn't happen. In fact by then, once the novelty had worn off, she was decidedly uninterested in the new-fangled food and we had to supplement it with tins she was used to. Of course we now had fifty pounds of the stuff taking up most of the cat food storage space so she was going to have to get used to it, at least as a meal extender, even if it didn't make her better.

Later we were bewailing the story with a fellow yachtie and he knew exactly what the trouble was – prawn poisoning. I can't think of anything less likely; any prawns that come our way I eat and the cat doesn't get a look in, but he was adamant. Apparently it's common in the Philippines among animals that scavenge around seafood restaurants and it comes from something in the prawn shells.

Sure enough, when we checked the labels on the cans, we discovered most of them were packed in prawn jelly, presumably made from shells, and when we stopped feeding her those particular brands her hair grew back like magic. Within a fortnight she started to look like a proper cat again and a month saw her back to normal. She wasn't going to be entirely happy though until the 'scientific' dry food was finished and neither space nor budget would allow us more than to feed her a half-and-half mix with the tins – a situation that would have serious consequences after the shipwreck.

Before we left for Salomon Jane, our other daughter living in South Africa, wanted to join us for a holiday. She had booked an air ticket when we first arrived in Thailand, but work and family pressures prevented her from confirming her arrival date until the last possible moment. This made for some interesting juggling of dates, places and needs in the months leading up to Christmas, the time she really wanted to come.

The short periods Thailand allow you to stay in their waters mean that to accommodate someone coming for a three week holiday you have to arrive within a day or so of your guest. As sailing doesn't lend itself very well to fixed appointments like this, dealings with customs and immigration sometimes have to be fudged, but even so you do need some idea of when to arrive.

At the critical planning stage we found ourselves two or three weeks unhurried sailing distance south of the Thai border and virtually unable to make the necessary plans. We had just re-launched from a highly successful haul-out on the Bernam river, in complete contrast to the Thai disaster, and were ready to go anywhere or do anything, but we'd fallen foul of public communications.

International calls from public phones work fine if you're

the caller, but the intricate timing dooms them to failure if you're on the receiving end. Faxes are the only viable alternative but even they were intensely frustrating. The Islamic weekends start at midday Thursday, local time, and the public facilities close down until Sunday. In South Africa of course the facilities are closed then and only open on Monday morning, again local time, leaving a communication gap of more than ninety hours. Extraordinary in an age when schoolchildren carry cell phones on their bicycles.

When the faxes finally caught up with us and the plans were made they were quite different from the original idea. Being a bit late for a choice of prime time flights Jane was stuck with flying in to Bangkok and travelling on to Phuket overland, then making her way to Penang in Malaysia to catch the plane home. Sue jumped at the opportunity of another trip to Bangkok to meet her and we reckoned to take advantage of the new situation by taking her to Malaysia by boat, thereby avoiding the need to abuse the immigration system.

About this time communications were significant in other ways too. In the first case a friend sold us a redundant HF radio transceiver which, once installed and working, gave us access to daily weather forecasts while on passage and regular contact with the cruising community. Secondly we received a letter from the leader of the upcoming expedition with some information about hermit crabs, and a most exciting proposition. Would we like to join the expedition to provide accommodation and transport for some of the scientists?

To do so would be hopelessly impractical. It would mean absorbing another full year into the sailing plan, which we couldn't afford, a round trip of some four thousand miles to reprovision and a whole host of smaller things that would be difficult to overcome; but we wrote right back with an enthusiastic 'Yes please'. The barrel was opened for renewed plan shuffling but until we had more information there were no plans to put in it, and now communication was going to be complicated further by our need to move between countries.

We had heard nothing by the time Jane arrived, and still nothing when we had to leave Phuket if we wanted to spend Christmas ashore on Langkawi, so we put it out of our minds and just enjoyed the cruise. Jane had such limited time that to spoil it fretting about tomorrow would have been criminal.

Then suddenly New Year's eve was upon us and the holiday was over. The two girls took the ferry to Penang for the last leg of Jane's journey – her flight left at some awful time on New Year's morning – and we settled for a quiet drink to celebrate the festival. Our extra time in south east Asia waiting on the seasons had been enormous fun but now we were ready for another go at Shangri-la.

We were anxious to get away as soon as Sue returned; shades of the fifty-day penalty for being late last time haunted us, and we had been checking the fax office every day but a combination of Christian and Islamic holidays made the weekend saga worse. Then, on the second day of the new year, we received a message confirming the expedition's interest and outlining some specific proposals.

Our instincts were to phone straight away to get everything settled, but in England it was half past one in the morning and we thought it a bit undiplomatic. All day we watched the clock creep round with as much patience as we could muster and the eventual conversation was more than satisfactory. Just about everything we hoped for was going to happen and the expedition sounded even more interesting than we first thought. The die was cast.

Sue got back the next morning, pretty tired from all the running around and inevitable shopping spree for the boat. She hardly had time for a night's sleep before we cleared customs and weighed anchor on our way back to Salomon. We dithered about whether to call in at Phuket for fresh vegetables, which were in short supply in Langkawi, and in the end opted to let the weather make the decision: if the wind took us northward we would stop; if it didn't, we wouldn't – it did.

A couple of blowy days later we crept into Phuket in the dark and anchored, as the sun rose, close to *Cairngorm* and good friends Kay and Clive from South Africa. Tina and Sue slipped off to visit their favourite vegetable seller, a meticulously honest lady who always had a friendly smile. A rare gem in these parts. She said if they came back at six in the morning she would select the best quality produce for us, and in the event she did us proud. The two of them returned laden with baskets full of mouthwatering fruit and vegetables.

The two extra days had been well worth it and, as soon as everything was hung up in nets in the better ventilated parts of the boat, we were ready to go. But the wind stopped, not a breath disturbed the casuarinas on the beach and there wasn't a sail to be seen; any boats on the move were doing so only under power.

Thinking it a bit silly, with our limited fuel, to start an ocean passage under engine we left the dinghy in the water ready to go visiting. If we were going to be delayed we might as well enjoy it. Luck had it that a big run of squid was in the bay and they were clearly visible in the glassy water. Clive introduced us to the intricacies of jigging for them and we caught enough for a delicious feast.

Next day came, and the next, but still no wind. The pilot charts came out again for me to worry over. Maybe the season, short at the best of times, had been early and we'd missed the window, but it didn't seem likely. Anyway, with the squid plentiful, good company and magnificent sunny days it would be churlish to complain and we made the best of it.

Another windless day started but a few clouds had formed and by mid morning we had a light breeze in the right direction. We stowed the dinghy, said more goodbyes, hoisted the sails and ghosted away. The wind increased a bit, then died completely. All afternoon we watched Phuket drift past as the tide took us north then, as darkness fell, the lights drift slowly back, but just after midnight the wind came and gave us a good, if belated, start.

To avoid a shipping concentration point north of Sumatra we aimed to pass as close to Great Nicobar as possible, or even to take the Sombrero channel further up if that was what the wind wanted, then carry on due west a couple of hundred miles before turning to cross the lanes as fast as we could. This way we hoped the different routes would have dispersed the ships a bit before we met them.

In practice this worked quite well. We had a fast, but very bouncy, trip out to where we started seeing ships and the wind stayed long enough for us to sail through them without anything untoward happening. We motored once for a few hours when a night-time rain squall blotted out the visibility but it was only a precautionary measure.

The next stretch would take us past the southern tip of the Maldives Islands then over the equator at a longitude of about seventy-four degrees east. The idea was to make the best of the north easterly winds then cut across the doldrums to Salomon making use of the currents.

This wasn't too successful but I suppose it worked as well as most sailing plans. The winds were not very consistent and, once past the shipping lanes, conditions changed to something more akin to tropical convergence zone weather; good days, bad days and lots of squalls. Fortunately the big seas of the last several days abated and we could get on with our regular passage routines.

Up to now cooking had been restricted to boiling the kettle and not much else. Right at the beginning we had a couple of saucepans leap out of the stove fiddles and strew food all over the galley, and clearing up called for plenty of agility. Once we realized our tempers were too valuable to waste on such nonsense we simply changed our diet until the sea quietened.

One habit we were glad to start again was the deck shower. Our usual practice was to take these harnessed to a lifeline inside the rigging. This gives you security and plenty to lean against while dipping for buckets of water, but with the large waves the deck was untenable without at least one hand free to hang on with. So the 'shower stall' had to be moved to the cockpit. Much safer but the contortions necessary were something of a trial for both patience and humour.

One day, while Tina was preparing lunch, she thought she heard an engine. A common enough occurrence on the boat with all its tight wires to resonate, but each time anyone reports it we have a look around then check to see what's vibrating. This time we all heard the noise but could find no reason for it. Eventually we saw a fishing boat hull down on the horizon. His engine must have been making a dreadful clatter for us to hear him so far away, but soon it got even louder.

As we watched we got the impression he changed course, though he was too distant to be sure, but he was definitely coming up behind us and the gap was closing. We were not happy about this at all; tales of piracy are commonplace and out here, several hundred miles west of Sumatra, you get to feel vulnerable.

Before he got too close we dug a couple of rocket flares out of the grab bag in case we needed to defend ourselves and watched his movements warily as he came nearer and nearer. Tina had the binoculars trained on him and could see a man standing by the wheelhouse, with binoculars trained on us. Situation comedy is written about such things but we didn't think it very funny, in fact we started the engine to give us mobility if we needed it. As he approached he manoeuvred to a position about fifty yards off our port side and slowed to our speed, the watcher still with binoculars clamped to his eyes and studying us intently.

This mutual observation seemed to go on for ever, with us keeping a careful eye and him peering into his binoculars. On the spur of the moment Tina waved, causing a moment's confusion on the other side, then the fellow lowered his glasses and gave a single wave back before ducking out of sight into the wheelhouse. Soon his head popped out again, hidden behind a camera, and he took a couple of photographs. With this he disappeared inside and the boat turned to motor away.

I think he was just curious, and it is a terrible indictment against the society we are handing on to our children that our reaction was fear and not friendship. It was also a great opportunity missed as we didn't have a single photograph of *Vespera* under sail.

In the days following this incident Sue saw two most unusual things. We were sailing quite briskly in beautiful sunshine when she shouted "Come and look at this", and we just got our heads out in time to see a turtle swimming close alongside. He was a little chap, about twenty inches long and, like the fisherman, just wanted to come and have a look. He swam alongside for maybe thirty seconds, giving us a good once-over as he did so, before submerging and swimming away. This was the only time we saw a turtle when out of sight of land.

The other thing wasn't nearly as nice but I suppose we should be grateful to be able to report it. The weather was quite normal with horrible black squalls all round and under one of them she saw a water spout forming. The phenomenon didn't last long and fortunately the thing collapsed before it fully developed but we paid a lot more attention to the appearance of the squalls after that.

On the home front it was about this time that Jess's diet problem showed its face. Her distaste for dry food had become an active dislike and she just stopped eating it. Given any other sort of food she ate as though starving so it had to be a problem with this particular stuff, and we couldn't tell if it was just one batch or the whole lot as it had all been mixed together in big storage jars. But the fact was she wouldn't eat it and it constituted most of our cat food stock. I would need to be a lot luckier with my fishing than I usually am.

Hermie, on the other hand, was having a great trip. We carried a couple of bags of fairly clean, damp beach sand so we could change his food supply now and then, but we didn't know if the organisms he ate from it would survive the modern-day packaging. We had collected it from the beach, bundled it up in plastic bags then sealed them straight away with packing tape. It wasn't a very scientific approach but we thought that, even if it all went wrong, at least it wouldn't smell.

He spent the first two weeks in his 'semi-hibernation' state changing his skeleton and we were more than half way before he re-emerged. At this point we treated him to a new bag of sand, which looked fine, and he attacked it voraciously. Although it can have no parallel in his life in the wild we found he often started his 'change' procedure at the start of a voyage, often enough for us to wonder if there was a correlation. We wrote the idea off as nonsense but if a mechanical event had been repeated with the same precision I wouldn't have been able to argue against it.

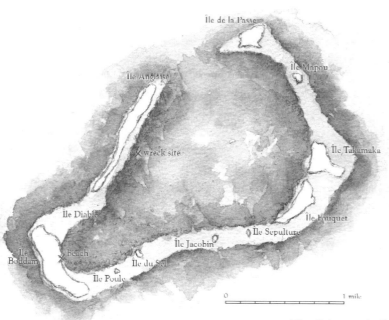

The Salomon Atoll

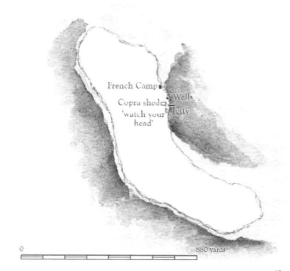

Ile Boddam

Twenty-one days out of Phuket we sailed through the channel between Addu Atoll and Fua Mulaku in the Maldives. We toyed with the idea of stopping to top up our fuel tank, but had only burned about five gallons and it didn't seem worth it. The wind was being kind and although the sea was a bit uncomfortable we were going well, in fact by our standards we were having a fast trip. With the turn south we were expecting the wind to swing northerly and then into the north west as we approached Salomon Atoll. The currents should do essentially the same and we predicted, based on our present performance, that we should arrive in three or four days.

This was, in itself, a bit disappointing. We had heard on one of the HF radio nets that the conservation consultant for the area was in Salomon at the time we were passing through the Maldives, and even if we met our most optimistic target we would not make it in time to meet him. As it happened we finished the trip with the most fickle winds and, among the customary squalls, we started getting days of flat calm. The next three hundred miles took us a week, much nearer to our usual performance.

About twenty miles from Salomon we began to see seabirds. They had been mysteriously absent coming across but first a few boobies arrived, followed by a squadron of gannets in formation, then a gaggle of noddies and terns lively enough to get Tina's binoculars twitching. We passed a huge shoal of tuna swimming with a school of dolphins and for the last few miles were escorted by several dorados. To counterbalance this beauty, though, it was a flat grey day with precious little wind and our projections showed we would make landfall after dark. Not a satisfactory state of affairs so on went the engine.

We arrived at the pass about four-thirty in the afternoon. Grey skies and the rapidly approaching dusk were going to make it difficult to see coral heads in the lagoon, but I wasn't happy about anchoring in the pass and certainly didn't want to spend the night outside, so decided to go in and see what it looked like. Once inside we found that the coral could just be made out and, as there were not too many heads on the direct line, we motored across to Ile Takamaka to drop anchor in the same place as two years before. An hour later it was dark. We hadn't had a lot of time to re-acclimatize but were back, and there weren't many people so it already felt more comfortable.

Morning couldn't come quickly enough and fortune smiled by blowing away the grey to make room for the sun. As quickly as possible we put the dinghy together and went ashore to renew our acquaintance with the picture-book beaches. We were astonished to see how the shape of the islands had changed and wondered if it was part of the evolutionary development or simply a seasonal movement of the sand, probably the latter. Anyway our shore trip wasn't just to look at the beaches, we wanted to re-introduce Hermie to his own kind.

His rehabilitation had been the subject of endless discussion over the last year but how to actually go about it was a long way from being decided. One thing we agreed about was that the first thing to do was get him used to other crabs again, and it would be both easier and more interesting to do it on the boat. Consequently we searched the waterfront for a similar crab and were confounded by choice. Were the grey ones the same species? Or the white ones? What about purple ones with big claws? And were the giant crabs in coconut shells just old guys who had outgrown their sea shells or different altogether? We didn't know.

The crab we eventually chose as the 'introductory package' was as near the same size and colour to Hermie as we could find. Before putting this 'friend' in the tray we dumped the old sand in favour of some native coral sand, added a bit of beach detritus and removed the plastic water bowls in an effort to make it as natural as possible.

When the two of them were put together the immediate

reaction was for both to retreat to neutral corners and bristle their feelers at each other. We can only imagine their mental or instinctive responses. One of them, I suppose, felt fear and confusion at his sudden change of surroundings, and the other surprise and curiosity.

Quite quickly they converged on common ground and, with a great waving and clashing of feelers, explored each other thoroughly. First Hermie climbed on top, then the other, and generally they chased each other round the box until the 'foreigner' excavated a hole in a corner to escape. Hermie didn't like this and continually harassed the newcomer until succeeding in digging him out. This procedure was repeated several times before a truce was called and the final event of the day was the pair of them burying in the same hole. All very interesting in an anthropomorphic sort of way but in truth it hadn't taught us much.

By mid-morning fortune realized it had made a mistake and the sun slunk out of sight behind towering clouds and the squalls came back. In this monsoon the sandspit anchorage wasn't particularly comfortable and the first squall hit at more than thirty knots from the north west, putting us against a lee shore. Larger waves came with the wind and, coming at us through the open pass, had the full fetch of the sea behind them. Nevertheless the anchor was well dug in so we stayed put.

Two days later we had to reconsider. The squalls were trying hard to spoil our enjoyment and were becoming a real nuisance. One particularly heavy blast put so much strain on the anchor that it pulled the chain through the snubber to come up hard against the windlass, bending the pawl like a banana. The waves were so unpleasant that Sue and I donned harnesses before venturing onto the foredeck to sort it out. Not the sort of thing you expect at anchor in a lagoon.

We found there was nothing to be done while *Vespera* was lurching about like a wild thing; we certainly couldn't handle the chain to refit the snubber. To make things more interesting it was low tide and we only had about four feet of water under the keel. When we dropped down the waves I was concerned that we might hit the bottom. Our only option was to go and anchor somewhere else.

Hauling up the anchor in forty-something knots of wind was not part of the curriculum when I learned about sailing but with Tina at the controls, motoring forward at almost full power, and Joe Muggins pumping fit to burst on the windlass handle the chain slowly came up. Sue was busy stowing the chain into the locker as it came aboard when a solid wave came over the bow and bowled her along the deck. Thank goodness for the harness.

We had a fair idea where the local coral heads were, which was just as well as they were not visible, and motored round looking for a better spot. The best compromise we could find was to anchor in seventy feet of water over broken coral, too deep for our length of anchor chain but I didn't trust the longer rope in sharp coral, so it was far from ideal. I don't like anchoring in coral at the best of times, not only because of the damage it does but the plough can entangle itself, necessitating the use of scuba equipment to retrieve it, and we don't have any.

Anyway the anchor set and held well for the time being, and the bottom was far enough away not to worry us. We decided though that on the first occasion that we could see the coral clearly we would move to the more protected side of the atoll. Over there the proliferation of coral heads oblige you to anchor further from the beach, which means either using a lot more dinghy fuel or doing plenty of paddling, but it's a fair exchange for protection from the prevailing wind and waves.

We made the trans-atoll journey under ideal conditions, with the tide just starting to flood and the underwater dangers shining out like road signs. When we reached Ile Anglaise we pottered back and forth, trying to relate the coral we could see to that shown on the chart, but could make no sense of it. We were trying, without much success, to find a particular spot that was shown to have sufficient depth and enough room to swing and eventually decided to anchor wherever we could and continue the search from the dinghy. Once stationary and able to take a more leisurely look we discovered we were, in fact, only a couple of hundred yards from the chosen spot so took *Vespera* there directly and set the anchor in a shade less than thirty feet of water.

The water was crystal clear and half an hour with snorkel and fins assured us we had plenty of room to swing without hitting anything, but also confirmed that the coral had changed since the chart was drawn. We thought it would be interesting to look into this further, but before we could do anything we had to locate ourselves exactly on the chart. The GPS didn't help much – in fact it caused the original confusion – so, using the sextant for accuracy, we took angles from a variety of places in the same way the original hydrographers must have done, and got a good fix verified by several sets of readings.

To make further observations easier we altered the coordinate system on our GPS receiver to correspond with this fix. Two years before we had found the survey mark erected by HMS *Sealark* in 1905, an engraved stone about eighteen inches square with its top surface set, as near as we could tell, on the tidal datum, at a point on the northern shore of Ile Fouquet. We had an idea to take the mean GPS position of the mark relative to known co-ordinates and establish the chart grid for good, but we couldn't find the stone as it seemed to be under five feet of sand this time.

Now *Vespera* was settled in gentler waters it was time for the next stage in Hermie's home coming: going ashore. So far he had been introduced to three or four of his fellows on his home turf but today was the big day. We didn't want him to be overwhelmed by the competition until he had at least found his feet so we went to a section of beach that had no crabs on to put him ashore for a spell. It may be, of course, that there were no other crabs around because of some undetected threat but we set him down on the sand at the extreme reach of the wavelets, making sure beforehand that he had a variety of leaves, seaweed and other foodstuff nearby to choose from, which might give us a clue to his regular diet. He scrabbled away from the water as fast as his legs would carry him and, three feet up the beach, retracted into his shell and stayed there. Information about crab behaviour was flooding in.

Our second morning off Anglaise opened with a flat, mirror-like calm. The water was as clear as can be and we went 'bommie watching' in the dinghy. If the surface is completely flat and you keep very still you can drift over the coral and see everything as clearly as you can when snorkelling, but you have the advantage of being able to speak to each other. We paddled gently towards a large 'bommie' and stopped in plenty of time for the ripples to die away before we got there, and for the better part of an hour watched the rainbow colours of parrot fish chewing on the coral with their strange rounded beaks, and the blue and yellow flashes of painted surgeons darting among the staghorns.

As we drifted back over deeper water a big shape edged towards us – a spotted eagle ray with two white remoras keeping station. He was very curious about this strange being trespassing on his domain and swam right up to look at us. The span of his wings was probably six feet, a little wider than the dinghy, so he appeared quite formidable and, unlike a lot of fish, he has forward facing eyes so we were very aware of him watching us. Sue had her camera poised and we kept as still as possible while he circled around, brushing against the dinghy with his wings, until the best possible shots presented themselves. We enjoyed a wonderful rapport with this creature for several minutes.

We had to start giving serious thought to how we were going to honour our commitment to the expedition. The nearest place to re-provision was Sri Lanka, with Kenya or Malaysia pretty much equidistant second choices. Although Sri Lanka seemed the obvious choice a number of factors militated against it. The best time to go there weatherwise would be June or July, which meant Sue would have to forfeit some of her island time and we would have to stock for an exceptionally long trip if we were to stay in the islands until the best season to carry on to Durban.

We also had information about the high cost of air fares in and out of Colombo which put the final damper on the idea. The least expensive place for Sue to go home from would be Kenya but the better place to provision was probably Malaysia, and Malaysia promised an easier trip.

If we left Salomon in August we could sail straight to Kampong Baru, do our shopping in supermarkets we already knew and make arrangements to haul out in Hutan Melingtan again. A direct return passage over Christmas would mean a slight risk of meeting a cyclone, but now we had the HF radio we were confident we could get timely storm warnings, and we would be back in time. A safer course would be to leave after Christmas but that would risk leaving the scientists stranded if we were delayed by even a day or two, and that was not acceptable.

With this plan pretty well settled we had a full six months in front of us to enjoy the islands. The extra interests transformed what had been, for me, somewhat disappointing on our first visit into something that fulfilled the dream completely. Hermie had taught us to question rather than just observe, and this corner of paradise brimmed over with thought-provoking images and happenings. The only thing missing was access to a decent library to answer the questions.

One of the great pleasures was fresh fish. Not being a natural hunter I have average to poor skill when it comes to fishing. In truth I don't enjoy catching them, but I have to confess that few meals can compare with a nice coral trout or red snapper straight from the sea. For a while at least the fishing was so good that a line dropped over the stern, with a lump of last night's fish as bait, would guarantee supper in half an hour.

During the days we would keep a watchful eye on the noddies and terns, and if we saw them gathering over the lagoon it usually signified a shoal of small tuna. The tuna would work themselves into a frenzy feeding on the fry and the birds would home in to swoop on the little ones that tried to escape. A pass or two with a lure was usually sufficient to replenish the biltong drying on deck, and tuna makes excellent biltong.

A regular task that wasn't so much fun was catching water. *Vespera* had a large awning equipped to catch rain but it didn't work well in the squally weather. At first we just opened the filler plugs and let water run straight into the tanks off the deck, but we found the rain was quite dirty. We then adopted the technique of damming the side decks with towels and scooping water from the puddles into bowls and jerry cans. These we left to settle then poured into the tanks through filters. The water was then much cleaner but sighting a rain cloud brought a universal groan from the crew, even if it did mean a nice freshwater shower.

It was during one such catching session that customs and immigration caught us by surprise. The weather had been horrible for two or three days and the surface of the lagoon was covered in white caps, so the seas outside must have been dreadful. One squall had already gone over that morning and the cockpit was filled with bowls of water waiting for the sediment to settle. Another squall was building and Sue was busy lining up jerry cans ready for the next rain, when she spied what she thought was a fast dinghy approaching. At first no-one else could see it, it was so well disguised by the white caps, and we were a bit sceptical as we couldn't think of anyone crazy enough to be fishing in this weather, then realized it had to be the Brits.

We usually make a bit of an effort to have everything shipshape when expecting officials on board; we'd even taken the trouble to make a British Indian Ocean Territories courtesy flag, but were caught completely unawares. They can only have been a mile away when Sue spotted them and at the speed they were coming we had four or five minutes at most before they arrived. Rain catching had taken priority over the breakfast washing up so the galley was a mess, the cabin was hung with wet foul weather gear and everywhere topsides was booby-trapped with containers of water. Frantic activity followed as we tried to clear up in time, but we didn't make it.

I don't think the boarding party minded the muddle though. All of them were soaked to the skin and just glad to have arrived on the protected side of the lagoon. The motion of their small boat had upset a couple of them and cups of hot tea with anti-seasickness pills were the order of the day. But there was plenty of humour in the situation and good-natured laughter soon took over. Whey-faced and dripping officials conducting the formalities with a bunch of bedraggled yachties are rich pickings for a perceptive cartoonist.

While this was going on we heard our friends Jim and Joy calling on the radio to say they were close to the atoll and coming in as quickly as the weather would allow. The boarding party had mail for them so settled down for more tea while they waited. Jim's report of the conditions outside was pretty grim and we certainly didn't envy the Brits going back to the ship; getting back on board and retrieving their boat was going to be extremely difficult.

Hermie was now going ashore every day. Although he was sporting a distinctly 'foreign' shell it was quite nondescript in appearance and a couple of times we thought we'd lost him. Tina painted a large red spot on the roof of his home to make him stand out on the beach but it was still quite a job to keep track of him. I really don't think our observations were going to make much impression on the advance of science, or add much to the breadth of human knowledge, but each day was different and we started to see similarities between his antics and those of other hermits.

One day we put him down at the water's edge and he set off in his usual knuckle-dragging gait towards an inviting clump of rotting vegetation. Suddenly he stopped dead in his tracks and waved his feelers about in alarm; a ghost crab had popped out of a hole right in his path. A nervous stand-off ensued which ended with a powerful attack by the ghost who just rushed across the beach, grabbed Hermie in his claws, and whisked him off towards his hole. Hermie's only defence was to retract into his shell.

If we had even an ounce of proper scientific detachment we would have watched this event to its natural conclusion and simply added the appropriate notes to the file, but this was not our way. Tina grabbed a big stick and leapt across the intervening space, yelling at the top of her voice and brandishing the stick like a dervish. Several hefty swipes did nothing more than leave divots in the sand behind the rapidly retreating marauder, until a better aimed blow frightened him into dropping Hermie and bolting for his hole. Sue fielded Hermie on the run and within moments he was back in a safe haven and the rehabilitation programme went back to the drawing board.

The atoll was filling rapidly with yachts as the season got under way. Several of the friends we'd made in Malaysia had arrived, some having sailed directly, as we had, and others having come via Sri Lanka or the Maldives. Ile Boddam, the traditional centre, was starting to hum with activity as the floating community grew. Beach barbecues and extended sundowners became the norm and the remote tranquillity had to yield a bit to the high spirits and laughter of the wanderers.

While the prospect of joining the fun was attractive we were enjoying our isolated Anglaise anchorage and decided to stay a few more weeks. This would see Hermie fully restored to the wild, in our eyes anyway, and by then we would definitely be in party mood. In the meantime we had the best of both worlds: our spot gave us the impression of being remote but a half-hour fishing trip in the dinghy put us in touch with our friends. A bit like suburbia really.

Sue and I went to Boddam with a bit of a mission one shining day. Armed with saws, files and other paraphernalia we were going to make a new pawl for the windlass, having given up trying to straighten the original one. Boddam has a few helpful facilities hiding among the trees, one of which is a large steel tub with very strong sides on which you can clamp a vice, an ideal work bench when you have heavy work to do.

On the way we stopped to snorkel over a superb coral formation that we found by chance in the middle of the lagoon. It was a bit deeper than others we'd explored, and quite different, and held our interest rather longer than the plan for the day allowed. By the time the pawl was finished it was a bit of a scramble to get back to *Vespera* before dark. None of us like the idea of motoring around the lagoon in the dark so the outboard engine worked hard this trip and the extra speed worked wonders for the fishing. In fifteen minutes we had a fine tuna for supper and another for the biltong rack.

Next day was pleasant inside the lagoon but it didn't look very nice outside. More of our friends arrived and all went directly to Boddam, with a couple just making it to anchor before the light failed. I had put the new pawl on the windlass and was pleased to find it fitted properly and worked well. Quite satisfied with the day we had a lazy evening and turned in early with our books. Later though, when the wind increased, Sue went up on deck to drop the windscoop over her hatch and called for assistance to take the sun awning down before an imminent squall struck.

By the time we had everything down the night was very black and when the first gust came it was an enormous blow that seemed to last for ages; and it only eased for a few moments before coming back even stronger. It came from behind, directly opposite to the prevailing direction, and swirled and buffeted us like mad. Out of curiosity we switched the wind instruments on and, as they showed we were getting forty-five knots and more, started the engine to relieve the load on the anchor.

But before we could do that we had to know which direction to pull in, and in the blackness it was impossible to see which way the chain was lying without going to the bow. There I found that the wind was blowing us right over our anchor and we needed to go astern to give the chain some slack. I engaged gear and ran the engine up to about one-third power, but there was no visible reference to indicate whether it was doing any good.

I could see Sue mouthing words at me from inside the cabin but, with the engine noise adding to the tumult from the wind, communication was very difficult. Only when she yelled at the top of her voice could I make out that she was telling me the anchor was dragging. She could hear and feel it through the hull though it was undetectable from the cockpit. I immediately increased to full power to try and stop her but, in the howling blackness, only the wind on the back of my head and the dimly lit compass gave any indication of which way to steer.

Then, after what seemed only moments, the engine quit, suddenly, but there was so much noise and violence that I didn't feel it, only realizing it had happened when the warning lights came on. This coincided with the first of three heavy collisions and both Tina and Sue shouted that we'd hit the reef. We quickly lifted the floor over the engine compartment and found water pouring into the bilge, though we couldn't see where from. There was a large bulge in the hull beside the transmission, but it appeared to be dry and at a quick glance we couldn't see anything else.

Something had to be done, and while the electric bilge pump looked after itself one of us worked the manual pump as hard as possible and the other two baled with buckets, but it didn't even slow the rising water.

Outside it was teeming with rain and the wind was driving larger and larger waves. Visibility was nil and the scream in the rigging blotted out any other sound. With all our senses overwhelmed like this it was impossible to tell whether we were still floating or if we were aground. We were obviously not going to win against the water – we couldn't even find where it was coming in, so we decided to take to the dinghy and stand by.

While I dragged the dinghy alongside we heard over the radio that another boat was on the reef near Boddam and all sorts of panic was going on down there too. We broadcast a mayday telling the others that *Vespera* was sinking which, on reflection, was a stupid and irresponsible thing to do as help was impossible, and we knew it, and abandoned ship.

BOOK TWO

VESPERA WAS DOOMED. The water level had already risen above the lower drawers in the galley and every wave was lifting the boat and smashing her against the coral. The hull made dreadful grinding and crunching sounds every time she landed and we had no way of telling whether she was hitting the edge of the reef or if she was being driven into shallow water. The continuous movement suggested she was still floating, and if she was against the side of a reef she could well sink in thirty feet of water, or even drift away, so boarding the dinghy took absolute priority.

With the painter still tied astern I managed to get the dinghy to lay in the lee of the coachroof and Sue scrambled in while Tina struggled with a very frightened Jess. Between them they managed to get her across and under enough control to keep her claws away from the air tubes. Tina scrambled over next and I went to get the grab bag and torch. While inside I thought to take a hand compass to help us find Ile Anglaise. This sounds ridiculous now, considering we'd been anchored less than quarter of a mile from shore, but it was so dark we could see nothing at all.

Sue had another thought while I was doing this and got back on board *Vespera* to collect the big awning she'd just taken down. By the time these things were done the water was over the floor in the main cabin and lapping at the galley work surfaces. In the dinghy we wrapped the awning round Tina and Jess, who were already shivering with cold as all of us had been caught in just our underwear. We were kept pretty busy then fending off to prevent the dinghy being damaged as the waves dashed us against *Vespera*'s side.

Amazingly, the cabin lights were still working, even with all the batteries under water, and we could see from the relative levels of boat and dinghy that *Vespera* was still sinking and several important thoughts started to nag. There was a possibility of being swept out of the atoll in the dinghy if we misjudged the direction or if anything happened to the motor, and we had no drinking water. I really didn't want to go back on board as the water was now almost up to the side decks and I was afraid she might go down with me inside, but I was more scared at the thought of no water.

As quickly as I could I went back on board and down the companion stairs to where a two-gallon jerry can of water was kept and grabbed it, together with a machete that was stowed alongside it, then rushed out to pass them over. I made one more hurried trip below to fetch the GPS which, fortunately, was clipped high on the cabin side. Now the water was up to my waist in the cabin and I didn't linger.

The dinghy was getting much more difficult to control. The coachroof still gave us a good lee against the wind but the waves were considerably larger. Hanging on while at the same time keeping us away from the stanchions, which threatened to impale us every time we came down, became a very vigorous exercise. Some of the waves were coming right over the boat and crashing down on us. Suddenly *Vespera* started to heel over towards us so, for the moment at least, we knew she was resting on the bottom and I decided to go inside again to get some clothes and the portable antenna for the GPS, which I had forgotten.

Most important was to get our foul-weather jackets, which were in a locker under the inside helmsman's seat. The locker is low and quite deep and I had to duck under the water to reach in and unhook the heavy clothing, an experience I didn't like one bit. Once these were passed into the dinghy I went forwards to the drawers containing our other clothing. Wading through the galley the water was up to my armpits but seemed worse because of the list to starboard.

All sorts of things were floating around to confuse things further; cushions and locker lids were sloshing about with food containers and bottles that had drifted out from the cupboards. My heart screamed at the enormity of it all when I shouldered aside the waterlogged case with my photographic equipment in to make room to dive for the clothes drawer.

Last thing to come out was the antenna, which was kept in a comparatively waterproof locker under the chart table. The water was just level with the table top and by being quick I was able to grab the antenna before the inrush of water filled the space and soaked it. At this point two particularly heavy waves landed in quick succession on the roof, tipping everything a bit further over to starboard, and it all felt very unstable.

The VHF radio was mounted at eye level under a shelf still above the water and was, like the lights, miraculously still working. I called to let the world know we were heading for the beach and went straight to the dinghy. Tina pointed out that the clothing drawer I had chosen held only more underwear, but before I could go in again another big wave landed on us and *Vespera* gave a big shudder, so I decided against another attempt.

With all the movement it was quite impossible to untie the painter so I took the machete to cut us free but just then a light flashed at the stern, then again. In my confusion I took it to be someone in a dinghy and spoke rather emotionally, then realized that a wave had dislodged our man-overboard light from its clip and it was flashing at the end of its lanyard. It took two or three swipes to cut the painter and we tore off down-wind. Fortunately the engine started without trouble and, taking a compass course from where we assumed we were, we set off towards Anglaise.

We knew from our daily excursions that there were large areas of shallow coral between us and the beach, so shallow in fact that we always paddled ashore for fear of catching the propeller, but even with the brilliant quartz halogen beam of our torch all we could see was rain and breaking waves. After what seemed an eternity we saw a faint reflection through the wetness that showed us the beach. We had to trust to luck to get over the coral without puncturing the air tubes and just ran straight in.

Jess was in serious trouble; saturated in salt water and barely conscious, her little heart was pounding away and her breathing was very rapid. Tina held her close to try and get some warmth into her and we wrapped them both in the heaviest jacket we had while Sue and I tied the awning between two palm trees to make a shelter.

Once we had this to crawl behind things looked marginally better. There was a box of waterproof matches in the grab bag and a few minutes scratching under fallen palm fronds turned up enough dryish sticks to light a fire. By this time the rain had eased sufficiently for us to see *Vespera*'s lights, still burning in spite of everything, and to see the strobe of the man-overboard light as it floated away. Wave action had broken the lanyard holding it to its life ring. We tried to call the people at Boddam to tell them we were safely ashore and that the strobe adrift in the lagoon was just a wayward light and not someone in distress, but the portable radio wouldn't work through the trees. However, a yacht anchored out near the pass heard us and got the message through.

The little fire made our wet and soggy nest a lot more acceptable and a space-blanket from the grab bag made it better still, but it was to be an endless night. Time had lost all meaning but piecing things together later it was probably only ten minutes between Sue calling for help with the awning and all of us taking to the dinghy, then twenty or thirty more before we were on shore; and that left a lot of minutes until the sun came up. We had shelter from the wind and the rain soon stopped, but even the cheerful firelight didn't make the ground any more comfortable or make the ants go away. Suddenly *Vespera*'s lights blinked out and the world seemed very, very lonely.

Sometime in the night, we think possibly around midnight, the clouds lifted enough to let some moonlight through and we could make out *Vespera*'s rigging against the horizon. The wind and waves were back to quite ordinary proportions and we decided it was worth a try to see if we could rescue anything. We stoked up the fire, both to keep Tina and Jess warm and to make a beacon to guide us back, and Sue and I motored out to *Vespera*.

What we particularly wanted were the diaries, photographs and address books. Tina's diaries and albums were stowed on a shelf under the port side-deck and Sue's were on the starboard side of the forepeak. All manner of things were now floating about inside, making it difficult to move around. I could see that Tina's things were above the water level, just, but the forepeak was another matter. I had to push past doors that were wedged open and climb over drawers that were stuck half in and half out of their slides just to get in there.

Sue's albums were where I expected to find them but I couldn't find her diary. The albums were wet but I took them anyway and went back to fetch Tina's. As I passed all this to Sue she explained exactly where her diary was and next time in I found it with her film negatives, which prompted me to look for all the other negatives but with no success. We returned to the beach quite pleased that we had rescued at least some of the memories.

The rest of the night dragged past. There were plenty of sticks drying round the fire and its light gave us something to focus on, but the ground was hard, everything was sandy and we were wet, cold and a bit shocked. What had started as a perfectly ordinary evening had become disaster and plunged us into despair. With everything we owned perched precariously on the reef life looked very different from the delights we had been enjoying.

Being ashore and having friends not far away we were not afraid for our lives, which had to be considered as something positive, but all of us sunk into our private thoughts and fears. My mind, I know, was an endless tumbling stream of doom and despondency. When we got back to civilization where would we live? No prospects. How would I earn a living with no regular address? No prospect. Where, indeed, would we go?

Some of those thoughts had been plaguing me for a long time. I was going to have to go back to earning a living anyway, and starting a new career was a challenge I wasn't looking forward to, but while we had the boat at least we had somewhere to live while I tried, and a bit of mobility if necessary.

Now there was nothing, and in the discomfort of the night every train of thought led back to the same place, despair. A few sticks on the fire to chase away the gloom, but all the firelight showed was my lovely wife huddling in an oilskin trying to keep Jess alive, her only shelter a canvas strung between two trees and her only bed the ground; and I had nothing left to give. And I saw my daughter, who had walked away from a hard-won start to come sailing, wrapped in a space-blanket and hunched against the windbreak with her own awful thoughts churning away. What had I brought my family to, with my outlandish dreams and not enough sense to say no? Despair. And the night grew longer.

I don't remember when, but sometime in the dark Tina remembered Hermie. At first we couldn't think what had happened to him, then Sue recalled that 'the hermitage' had been moved to the galley floor when we had to lift the boards over the engine. It had become known as 'the hermitage' when we took to putting an elasticated net over the top of his tray to stop Jess digging him out. This precaution now meant he couldn't escape. The thought that we'd looked after him for so long and brought him back to his homeland, then killed him by neglect, added its own weight to the general depression.

Slowly, very slowly, the firelight on the trees faded to grey, and as soon as I could see clearly I went out to where *Vespera* was lying propped on one side on a big bommie. I motored round her once or twice and, after a careful look, decided she was there for good.

The sun didn't really come up that morning but, at the time it should have, a flotilla of dinghies arrived from Boddam. Alan and Philippa in one boat, Jim and John in another, all friends from Malaysia, were followed by Ian and Chrissy whom we had met only briefly. Alan and Philippa came directly ashore bringing breakfast and a flask of hot coffee. Jim and John went to *Vespera* to inspect the damage and were joined by Ian and Chrissy, who snorkelled around the wreck for a long time. When they all came ashore Ian voiced the general opinion most eloquently by simply shaking his head.

The only thing we could do now was salvage as much as possible, but before starting we had to have somewhere to sleep. We had a small tent perfectly suited to the island in that it had an inner skin of mosquito netting and a fly sheet of plasticised nylon for waterproofing. To get it from its storage space under the foredeck meant moving a lot of other things out of the way and a steady flow of possessions started making its way to shore. All the cushions, drawers and other things that were floating around went first, and once the tent was out everyone just started with the things nearest the companionway and worked forward.

I found a large enough space between the trees and put up the tent, having cleared the ground a bit to make it less uneven. It was too close to the tide line but it would do for a few days, at least until the next springs. Tina and Sue found the driest mattress and some other necessities and put together a home. The flysheet waterproofing wasn't too good after its long stay under a hot deck but the little camp looked quite inviting.

The weather was its usual uncooperative self and stayed grey and gloomy all morning but at least the rain held off till later. Our friends Liz and Russell arrived from the Maldives and managed to run the bommie gauntlet to Boddam without too much trouble, and Ted, a feisty old single-hander with a big heart, brought his boat over from Takamaka to Anglaise to offer assistance.

Tina had spread the awning out in a clearing and she and Sue were fully occupied trying to get some order into the stuff as it arrived ashore. All the irretrievably damaged things were left in a heap, while those that could be recovered were stacked away as carefully as possible. Those things that had a big 'if'' or 'maybe' hanging over them went into another pile, a bit less chaotic than the junk pile but looking pretty much the same. They were making a lot of hard decisions.

By lunch time the rising tide made access to the lockers difficult and the sky was getting blacker and blacker, so our helpers left to attend to their own boats. The anchorage at Boddam, with its tightly packed coral, had been an awful place in the night and all the boats had been under threat; John, I know, had spent the worst of the squall motoring up to his anchor and I'm sure he wasn't alone, yet these people had left at daybreak to come and help us. What is more, there was the other boat on a reef in the anchorage and others had gone to help them.

Ted got a message to us that he had a large tarpaulin we could use to protect our things and before the weather got too bad Sue and I went to collect it. Now Ted had been giving us some good-natured joshing about our hermit crab since we'd arrived, telling us that the only thing he was good for was bait, but his first question to Sue was whether Hermie was alright. This was the last straw for her and she dissolved into uncontrollable tears, which visibly upset Ted who'd only been trying to lighten the load. Eventually she got herself together again and gratefully took the tarpaulin, and a hurricane lamp to use until ours could be found. On our way back we called at *Wanago* to thank them for relaying our messages and they gave us a huge pot of hot, homemade, soup and a lovely banana bread.

At the camp we decided the best use for the tarpaulin was to keep us, rather than our things, dry and tied it in the trees over the tent. It covered the whole tent and extended far enough forwards to give shelter to a couple of deckchairs and a small clay brazier brought specially from Thailand for cooking on the beach. Things were looking better every minute. They looked better still when we saw Kay and Clive arrive from Peros Banhos and come safely to anchor in the pass before the weather broke.

After the squall we carried on ferrying stuff to the shore. By the time the lockers under the quarterberths and the upper level of the main cabin were emptied the beach looked like an eastern bazaar. Hundreds of tins in plastic bags were stacked on the sand and an extraordinary mixture of things were tucked away under the trees, wrapped in plastic sheeting if we thought it worth the effort but otherwise just in lopsided heaps. All the fuel except that in the tank had been taken ashore earlier in case anything worse happened: twenty-five gallons of petrol, fifty of diesel, a couple of paraffin and a hundred pounds of cooking gas, and a special place had been set aside for that. On reflection I think it looked more like a rubbish tip than an eastern bazaar.

Later in the afternoon we watched as *Cairngorm* left her rolly anchorage in the pass to make her way to Boddam and, not long afterwards, I don't remember how, we got the news that the other boat in trouble was safely off the reef and apparently not badly damaged. On this positive note we called it a day and heated the remains of the soup for supper before turning in. It didn't matter that our beds were of odd-shaped cushions and a bit wet; we slept like logs.

Our wake-up call in the morning was a strange rustling outside the tent. It came sometime in the twilight before sunrise so gave us a good early start to the day. However, good start or not, I failed in my first task which was to identify the rustler. The moment I put my head out to have a look the noise stopped. Never mind, it was bound to happen again.

A quick cup of tea set us up and we went out to *Vespera* to take advantage of the low tide. Tina, who hadn't been aboard again yet, braced herself and went inside to try and come to terms with it all, while Sue and I donned masks and fins to take another look at the hull.

Quite a lot of damage could be seen from inside but not enough to account for the speed that the water came in. Looking from outside, with *Vespera* still lying sideways, wasn't particularly helpful either but it did look as though an outcrop had punctured the hull behind the galley, which would explain a lot. There was plenty of broken coral lying around which gave an indication of how hard some of the impacts had been; indeed one piece about four feet in diameter had cracked completely in half.

While we were poking and prodding under the hull we heard an urgent call from Tina in the cockpit, "Hermie's alive! I've found him!" She had been aimlessly looking about at all the small things, turning the ramifications over in her mind, and had waded forward into the forepeak. A curtain that usually closes the area off had been tucked behind a shelf fiddle to keep it out of the way, but it fell down as she brushed past and when she grasped it to tuck it back she saw Hermie clinging to the very top of the fabric.

We never found out how he got there. His tray was lying on its side in the galley, still under water, and the sand had mixed with all the sand that had washed in. The net was nowhere to be seen. Whatever, Hermie had escaped. Without wasting any more time we put him in a bucket in the dinghy and took him ashore. Then, while we were getting him organized with temporary accommodation, the forerunners of an army of helpers arrived, bringing news of lengthy discussions amongst themselves the previous night.

I can only imagine these discussions. Several of the people involved were friends and, knowing them well, I can picture them gathered round the beach table, but there were many there who were strangers to us. With a couple of oil lamps to light the scene and a jug of homemade wine to loosen the tongues it must have been a stimulating evening. The consensus of their thoughts was that *Vespera* could, and should, be got off the reef and floated to somewhere where a proper assessment of her prospects could be made.

It was with this news fresh in our minds that we watched everybody else arriving. There was so much enthusiasm, so many cheerful faces, and so much goodwill that I'm sure my vision of that evening is inadequate. My emotions were in a terrible spin. With all this support and generosity of spirit how could I possibly be sad, but when I thought of all the material things either damaged or destroyed how could I be anything but?

Anyway, given the enthusiasm on everyone's part to give it a try, the idea was a good one. There was even a flicker of hope in it, though I was sure in my heart that *Vespera* was finished, and whatever came from the recovery attempt would make the decisions easier.

The only beach in the atoll that had a sandy shelf suitable for the purpose was at Boddam, a mile and a half away, and getting her there was a monumental challenge. First, of course, everything that could be moved had to come off to make the boat as light as possible. This cast a different light on yesterday's effort which was aimed solely at salvaging what we could.

The distribution of people between the wreck, the beach and the ferrying dinghies changed continuously during the day as everyone just set to to get it done. A chain gang was soon in action and the stream of wet clothes, more tins, sails, soggy books and toilet rolls started moving ashore again. When Sue realized how confused things were going to get, with everything being dumped on the beach for triage then manhandled above the tide line or round to the camp, she had visions of Hermie being lost again. Taking Heidi from *Sumurun* with her to hold him, she took the dinghy across to ask Ted to look after him for the day, which he did with a smile and without once threatening to use him for bait.

On their return they were joined by Joy, from *Avon Grace*, who helped them for the rest of the day with the demoralizing job of sorting. Another group of ladies organized for a dinghy to be filled with our salty clothes and bed linen and taken across to Boddam for washing in fresh water. The wreck itself was a hive of activity with people on deck taking off loose equipment, the liferaft and safety gear, spare anchors, even the boom and mainsail. Others were inside emptying the contents of lockers into waiting hands to pass out to the dinghies.

Getting access to the damage was quite a problem. *Vespera*'s builders hadn't allowed for this sort of eventuality and all the furnishings had been solidly built on permanent frames. Quite obviously all the galley fittings and equipment had to be removed and, once the lockers and cupboards were empty and the drawers taken out, the stove was disconnected and passed to the 'removals' people. The rest of it was like one of those dreadful Chinese puzzles where you have to work out the exact order of doing things before they go together, only here we wanted to get it apart.

I knew how to get the cupboards above the sink apart as I'd done it once before and with plenty of hands to help the panels and shelves came out fairly easily. The only difficulty was that the wood had swollen, making the joints tight. Through the resulting gap we took out the starboard water tank, hoping that this would be enough dismantling, but it wasn't. The sink unit also had to come out, and it was one of those clever pieces of kit with no obvious mounting points. In the end it yielded to brute force and under it we found the supporting structure to be very strong. In fact, it showed evidence of having been built as the workbench on which most of the original boat building had been done.

Removing this proved a bit trickier. Even after taking out all the screws we could find, nothing would move it, at least not readily. Part of the structure had been splintered, obscuring some of the bolts securing it to the hull, but finding them didn't help as they were all bent and wouldn't come out. So, after much deliberation, it came down to brute force again.

By the time the largest part of it was loose the tide had risen enough to stop any more work inside. Everything had been taken off the deck and there were only odds and ends left inside so I went ashore with the others.

Tina and I got to the beach and were more than a little over-awed. We thought we had been busy out at the wreck but even more work had been done here. It didn't seem possible that so much stuff could have come from the boat. Above the tide line the beach was covered with cushions, books and papers spread out to dry, and the camp area was looking quite sophisticated with all our kitchen utensils and the like back in service, but the most amazing sight was the array of piles that had been sorted. They were all comparatively neat and tidy, and looked huge.

Given that *Vespera* is roughly forty feet long by eleven wide I expected the piles to be of similar proportions, especially as most of the inside volume is taken up by living space, but I was very wrong. The heap of 'irretrievables' seemed as big as the boat on its own and those things we considered worth protecting made another pile the same size. What I didn't realize then was that yet another load of things had been taken off to Boddam for immediate attention, among them my power tools and cameras and Tina's sewing machine. These were all going to be washed in fresh water and most of them found their way onto either *Bob* or *Cruise*, where they received tender loving care over a long period.

Anyway, back on the beach it was good to catch up with Kay and Clive again. They had had, shall we say, an interesting trip across but all was safe and well. I'm afraid we took advantage of their friendship and asked them to take responsibility for our grab-bag, with our passports, ship's papers, cash and all sorts of other important documents.

Then it was time to go home and a lot of tired and weary

people made their way to the dinghies. Jim and Joy took several of our favourite books back to their boat to dry them out carefully, and an enormous task that proved to be. Many of the pages had glossy pictures and the saltwater had gummed them together. Joy soaked them apart in fresh water and dried the pages individually, a process that went on for days.

When all was quiet we moved our attention to the animals. Sue went off to collect Hermie and we organized a freshwater bath for Jess. We'd put this off as long as we could as she hadn't looked well enough to take the trauma. She had spent all the time laying completely still in the tent, not eating, drinking or making any move to clean herself, but when we went to get her she raised her head in recognition. A first promising sign.

The bath was probably the best thing we could have done as not only did it get most of the salt out of her fur but it made her fight back a bit – she objects strongly to being bathed. Sue came back with Hermie and told us that Ted had caught us a nice coral trout for dinner – on a lure – and it was hanging in some shade along the beach. Then, while we were towelling Jess dry, Derek and Hilary arrived having come from Boddam specially to bring us a freshly baked cake. Morale was pretty good.

With our dawn cup of tea, after another good night's sleep, we set Hermie free. Obviously there would be no further opportunities to let him acclimatize slowly and we certainly wouldn't have time to observe the process, so he was just going to have to take his chances. He was, in all honesty, going to be safer among his natural enemies than he had been in 'the hermitage' when *Vespera* sank.

A strange mixture of emotions took hold of us as we watched him go. We thought it best to arrange things in such a way that he could escape of his own volition rather than just put him down in a strange place. Sue took the bucket that had been his overnight home, tilted it enough to let him scramble up the side, and made sure he would be able to clamber out when he got there.

It didn't take him long to realize freedom was at hand. Before our tea had cooled he was over the side and into a clump of fallen palm fronds. Since the episode with the ghost

crab we had several times seen him, in common with other
hermits, climb bushes or sticks to get clear of the ground and
assumed it to be a standard crab safety precaution. Now we
watched as he selected an old brown frond that stuck up at an
angle and slowly made his way to the highest point. With this
evidence of a revitalized instinct, and the simple fact that he
was still alive, we declared him to be a natural survivor and our
self-imposed task to be complete.

Long before any other activity started Kay and Clive
arrived bringing us a nice hot breakfast. This was a welcome
visit in many ways. It had been assumed by all and sundry that
Vespera would be salvaged and there was a general air that the
Australians describe well with the phrase 'She'll be right mate'.
It was quite beneficial to be able to voice our fears without the
risk of offending anybody, and to listeners who understood
our circumstances completely. I was far from convinced that
Vespera would float at all, let alone be salvageable. As yet the full
extent of the damage could not be seen, which was the
primary purpose of taking her to Boddam, but what we
already knew was pretty daunting and I couldn't imagine how
any kind of acceptable repair could be done. Like us they had
learned their sailing in South African conditions and
understood my refusal to even contemplate going back there
with a makeshift patch.

Anyway this little chat helped clarify in my mind the
concept of taking everything one step at a time. Right now we
didn't know the limits of the problem and any plans we might
devise were mere conjecture, so for the present anything
beyond getting *Vespera* careened on the beach could be safely
ignored. Nevertheless plots and schemes are, by their very
nature, positive things and the thoughts don't go away just
because you don't need to act on them; and by restricting all
the action to single, achievable, steps the outlook could be kept
positive. So started the day.

A swarm of dinghies could be seen approaching, like a
miniature multi-national armada, and I went out to the wreck
leaving Tina and Sue on the shore. There wasn't much galley
woodwork left in place and quite quickly it joined the results
of yesterday's labour on deck. The target for today was to get
temporary patches over all the holes and bulges, and to do this

we were going to use combinations of wooden panels and cushions, the wood to provide stiffness and the cushions to match the patches to the shape of the hull. Timber props would be used to drive them home and hold them in place.

All the visible holes were on the starboard side and the first to be tackled was underneath where the water tank had been. This proved a good choice. There a large bulge where the hull had failed but it was reasonably accessible and had plenty of working room all round it. It also offered comparatively easy positioning for the props so it was a good one to learn on.

We found one of the foam mattresses to be the most suitable cushion and the lid from a saloon seat locker just fitted between the ribs. So far, so good, but the fun part was making the props fit. Alan was doing sterling work collecting suitable poles and a stockpile was already on board to chose from, but each one had to be trimmed to the right length and the ends cut to the correct angles.

This particular patch needed three props to make it secure. The first one was hammered home with a satisfying thump and the second one carefully measured. Then, with such instructions as 'Can you whip this off here?', with a pointed finger and 'At about this angle', with a tilted hand, the 'riggers' sent the pole to the 'carpenters' for finishing. On its return it was offered up and hammered into position, where it fitted perfectly; but it changed the compression of the mattress causing the first prop to fall out. Some quick sleight of hand got them both driven home together but adding the third prop was a repeat performance, only more so.

We learned a lot from this. Smaller patches with single props were much easier and we used them wherever possible, and props cut roughly to length and fitted using wedges made the carpentry less demanding. From there the work went at a furious pace. Up until now the tide had been falling so conditions inside were as good as they could be and a fine good humour prevailed.

The smaller patches meant that the materials had to be cut to suit and it was hard to watch the cushions Tina had so painstakingly covered being hacked to pieces, or the carefully finished boards being roughly sawn to size. I had to keep reminding myself that it wasn't our home being destroyed but a wreck in the process of salvage.

There was a lot of activity in the water as well; Ian and Russell were busy preparing for the next stage. They began by hauling all the anchor chain out of the locker and laying it out on the bottom, after buoying it for recovery later. Next they took the two spare anchors and dropped them in position to provide leverage points to haul *Vespera* upright and to give some means of control when she floated.

The plough anchor, with a few yards of chain and a nylon warp, was dropped far out in the lagoon. The warp was extended with a spare headsail sheet and led through a block already taken to the masthead on a halyard. My home-made seventy-five-pound 'hurricane' anchor was dropped inshore at the edge of the bommie and another sheet led to the top of the mast in the same way.

An awful lot of pulling and heaving went into setting these anchors properly, but they didn't want to cooperate and in the end both men dived to set them by hand. Finding places where the anchors could hook and at the same time leave the nylon warps clear of sharp edges on the coral proved impossible, at least within the limitations of diving without scuba equipment, and the exercise was temporarily abandoned.

Back on board, the shoring up and patching had reached the more difficult areas. Some of the crushed and broken places had skin fittings in, where pipes that run through the hull are attached, and the panels had to be shaped to fit around them as closely as possible. With the limited materials available the design of them called for considerable ingenuity. Odds and ends of plywood and the like were contributed by everyone who had them, which made it easier, in fact possible, but it still took a lot of thinking.

Just about the time that the more intricate panel shapes were called for, the tide started to interfere. Up to now the places we were working on were only covered by water up to our wrists, or maybe elbows, and you could take however long you needed to measure up and fit; but once you had to duck your face under to reach where you were working you lost that advantage. Snorkels solved the problem for a while but either time changed gear or the tide came up very quickly.

Two of the men, Frank and Heinz, had prodigious breath-holding abilities so had the misfortune to draw underwater duty. There was a particularly difficult spot, with two skin fittings close together in the middle of a large bulge, that kept Frank submerged for ages. Every now and then his head would pop up for a quick gasp then disappear back down into the swirling water.

His task was made more problematic by the props already in place. *Vespera*'s galley and saloon looked more like an adit into a coal mine than the inside of a boat. With all the surfaces tilted to one side it was hard to resist the temptation to lean against them to help balance and it must have been harder still not to push on them when working underwater.

Heinz had found a spot at the other end of the boat which offered a similar challenge. There were several flaky places along the bilge adjacent to the engine compartment and underneath the chart table. These could be seen quite easily but even if you stretched out on the floor – the usual way to work on the engine – they were out of reach. Heinz discovered that by standing inside the keel and ducking under a floor beam, already under a foot of water, he could just get to them.

Over and over again he tried to measure up for the patches but kept floating to the surface, and he couldn't do it from there. He solved the problem by recruiting somebody, me, to stand on his back to keep him down. This was a most alarming business. I tried to time how long I could hold him down without drowning him by holding my own breath while I did it. I thought I had it right the first time but his cheerful face emerged to say 'longer, longer'. Next time I held him down till my eyes were popping out of my head but 'No, No. Must be longer'. In the end I held him down until he wriggled free and each time I mentally rehearsed the appropriate first aid procedures.

I don't know where the idea originated but the concept of making a fast-setting mortar to seal the patches by mixing ordinary cement with sugar became the topic of lively discussion. It was all entirely academic when it started as we didn't have either commodity on board but, sure enough, before the day finished someone had spirited some out of the air. Then we faced the knotty problem of what ratio to mix them in and whether to use it wet or dry. We tried everything and the outcome was one of those spectacular failures: all we succeeded in doing was dirtying up the water, but it had been worth the try.

At last all the known holes had patches over them with props driven in hard to compress the cushions and it was time to see if it worked. Three portable generators had been brought over from the boats at Boddam and positioned on top of the coachroof, and five electric bilge pumps, plus *Vespera's* own, were connected to them via a set of batteries. All the generators were started and the pumps switched on and we watched the water level carefully, but the movement of the tide confused things a bit until we made a gauge with a piece of hose on a skin fitting.

Ted had obviously been waiting for a visible clue that the shoring up was finished because, as soon as the first watchers sat down in the lopsided cockpit for a break, we heard the 'putt, putt' of his dinghy coming to join us. As he tied his painter to the pushpit he handed up a large bag of ice-cold beers. Brewery advertising executives couldn't have orchestrated a more spontaneous cheer, however much talent they bought, and we settled back to watch for the water to go down, greatly refreshed.

The pumps poured steady jets of water over the side and the level crept down the outside of the gauge pipe, infinitely slowly, until it showed an inch of difference; then didn't go any further. This was very disappointing. We had a good look at all the patches but couldn't see any tell-tale swirls of water coming in. The job was going to have to go back to the drawing board or, to be more accurate, the beach table at Boddam.

Work on the shore had been progressing just as quickly but more successfully. The ladies had been every bit as ingenious and drying-racks made of driftwood were covered with photographs and papers. Sue had established a recovery procedure that was working well with the log book and some of the important manuals but it meant turning a page of each one about every thirty minutes and it kept her pretty well occupied.

This was not all, though. Making sure everything in the 'retrievable' pile got retrieved, or at least ensuring they didn't get any worse, kept a veritable horde of people busy and continuous re-examination of the 'maybe' pile to see if anything could be upgraded was a demanding job.

Anyway it was time to cover things up for the night, as this evening we were going to Boddam for a drink with our friends and to discuss what could be done the following day. We put down a bowl of fresh food for Jess, though she still hadn't recovered enough to start eating, hung Ted's lamp in a tree so we could find our way home in the dark, and left with Alan and Philippa.

Boddam was an extraordinary sight. We went ashore at the head of the path to the well and, as we emerged from the screen of palms, were confronted by rows of washing lines covered in familiar clothes. Lines had been strung between some old pillars by the well and the palm trees by the water tank, from the papaya tree to the old shed, festooned among the rafters of the shed itself and from tree to tree in the clearing known as 'the paddock', and every inch of them was draped with something of ours.

There were bedsheets and blankets and shirts and shorts, jackets and trousers and skirts spread in a great confusion of colours. Even the rag-bag of clothes beyond redemption had been washed and hung out to air and the ladies responsible were well pleased with themselves, especially young Bar and Netta from '*Summerwind*'.

Wash bowls and buckets of fresh water had been set down around the well with all sorts of things that needed 'de-salting' in them to soak; the toolboxes, spare fuel and oil filters and the HF radio to name a few. Quite obviously not one person who had come to Salomon to enjoy its charms had spent a single minute of the last few days indulging themselves. Every waking moment had been given to us and we were overwhelmed.

As dusk fell we adjourned to the beach table, or 'French camp' as it was generally known, for sundowners, and the conversation soon came back to *Vespera*'s plight. I listened to ideas from several schools of thought, the most persistent being that the authorities in Diego Garcia should be asked for help. They would probably have flotation collars and all manner of interesting toys to make it easy but I said no, as emphatically as I could. If they did come who was going to pay? I couldn't, and under the circumstances wouldn't have been able to justify it even if I could.

Most of the other thoughts were of the 'how to' rather than 'we should' variety and lots of good ideas got tucked away for future consideration. For the immediate future the plan boiled down to wrapping the wreck in plastic or canvas sheeting to waterproof the patches from the pressure side and hopefully cover any holes we had missed. It was quite late when Alan gave us a lift home and we crashed into bed.

Patrick and Nicole were among the first people we saw in the morning. They were both enthusiastic scuba divers and had brought their equipment along to have another go at setting the anchors. Between them they managed to manhandle both into good spots where they couldn't move and, with all the slack in the lines taken up, everything was clear of cutting edges.

When the regular flotilla arrived they brought with them a wide assortment of tarpaulins, groundsheets and rain-catchers, I should think just about every piece of waterproof material owned by the community. This was very worrying. Whatever came from *Vespera* was one thing, all of that being fair game for salvage material, but here I could see expensive, and wholly irreplaceable, equipment being put at risk for the sake of a wreck that would probably never float again, and that wreck was mine. I could see other much more valuable things, like friendship and trust, being put to the test as well if things went seriously wrong. However, my concerns were brushed aside and these people kept giving.

On board it was immediately apparent that there was

some damage that hadn't been found yet. Without the pumps to distort the picture the tide was ebbing and flooding at the same rate inside the boat as out, and was doing so without any visible turbulence. Obviously there was an unplugged hole somewhere. Patrick and Nicole were still busy with the anchors so at this stage nothing could be done about standing the boat upright ready for its wrapping but the awnings and tarpaulins were spread out so we could judge the best way to apply them. All the props and patches were checked and found to be alright; everything was still in place and jammed as tight as could be.

The moment everything was ready 'operation stand-up' got underway. The strongest men in the party were nominated for winch duty and the sheet from the 'up' side warp was taken to a halyard winch. Unfortunately the blocks that could have led it to a more efficient two-speed winch were already in use at the masthead, so they just had to pull harder. However, the block at the masthead gave us a lever almost fifty feet long and the anchor was positioned for the best possible line of pull.

For the first few turns of the winch nothing happened except the nylon warp stretched, squeezing water out of the rope like the sweat from the foreheads on deck. Nothing moved. A bit more slack was given on the 'down' side and another pair of hands went to the mast but still nothing happened. Then those of us not at the winch went to stand on the 'up' side deck, like the weather-rail crew on a racing yacht, and slowly she came up. Getting her to stand square with both sides equally tensioned called for deft rope handling but it didn't take much longer to do than it takes to tell, and *Vespera* had taken her first step.

Straight away the work of placing and lashing covers started. Several pieces were already tied at deck level and only had to be dropped over the side and have securing ropes knotted round them. Half the people were in the water ready to position the ropes and the others were getting spare lines and sail-ties, even the tow-rope, ready for use.

Through all the bustle Philippa approached me carrying a couple of face masks and told me there was something I ought to see. We got in the water and she led me round to a

place a little aft of where I knew *Vespera* had been punctured.
I ducked down to have a look and, clearly visible now, behind
a rock that had hidden it when the boat was tilted over, was
another jagged puncture. The cement had cracked and crazed
around a gouge about four feet long that was roughly in line
with the cabin floor supports.

This place was not visible at all from inside the boat but
from where I stood I could see plenty of torn mesh and
broken stringers. Large chunks of cement had broken away
from the reinforcing matrix leaving only a crumbling skin of
pebbles. I can only think that the rock was partially plugging
the hole when we gained that inch with the bilge pumps –
they certainly wouldn't manage it now.

Knowing where the extra hole was I climbed back on
board for another look from the inside but, no matter how
much I squirmed and contorted, I could neither see nor feel
anything. To gain access to it from here would mean removing
the chart table, helmsman's seat, steering console and a large
part of the floor. As the floor and its structure supported all
the cabin woodwork it really meant stripping everything out
and, eventually, rebuilding most of the interior from a bare
hull, and that was assuming the hull could be repaired. There
was no future in this.

As soon as I made up my mind to this I blurted out that
I was quitting. Then, cravenly, left Philippa to tell those who
hadn't heard while I went to break the news to Tina. I could
feel the disappointment radiating from the boat as all those
people chewed on the thought that their efforts had been in
vain and my heart burned a hole in my chest, but to do
anything else would be dishonest to my family.

Clive gave me a lift ashore and it was a silent and
mournful trip until this great friend clapped me on the knee
and said 'Pete, that was a good decision. A clean break that
you won't regret.' I was having a lot of trouble with my eyes
at that moment and couldn't respond but those words have
engraved themselves on my soul. I knew he was right; but it
wouldn't make it any easier to tell Tina that we were back at
the end of the road. When I found her on the beach I
stumbled over the words I needed and she gave me a tight
hug and told me she already knew from the look on my face.

Together we went to tell Sue.

The rest of the morning was a sad and disjointed affair. To be truthful I don't remember what I did or what went on around me. Even my thoughts wouldn't form properly as I grappled with the new set of parameters. To be sure they were not so different from those of a few days ago but now they were overlaid with guilt. I couldn't help feeling that not only had everything been lost but I had let my friends down as well, and this in response to their boundless generosity. But all I could see ahead was disaster.

Trying to think back I can't imagine what I expected to happen; certainly everyone would gather up their generators, pumps and tarpaulins etc., but I don't think I even considered what they would do then. My ill-mannered gracelessness in simply walking away is something that flushes my face with shame whenever I think of it. But whatever I thought, and however rude I was, the people at the wreck just carried on trying.

Some time later John, Philippa and Russell came ashore for a chat. They were still convinced that *Vespera* could be floated; all it needed was a little more ingenuity. I was not very receptive to their proposals but they were determined I should hear them out. After their dissertation, which I listened to with the half of my mind that wasn't staring bleakly into the future, I tried to explain the reasoning behind my decision. Even if the wreck could be spirited back to Durban, where all the necessary repair facilities were available, I could neither afford nor justify the sort of expenditure I could foresee. I had more responsible things to do with my money.

In turn they explained, correctly, that the damage had not yet been fully assessed; they also thought that any decision taken at this stage was premature. I disagreed. They continued in the vein that there were plenty of willing hands available to give things another go and that everyone wanted to see the boat on the beach. The argument that they wanted to satisfy themselves, one way or the other, about the prospects for repair was an emotional, but powerful, one.

In the end I grudgingly, and ungraciously, acquiesced to yet more effort on the understanding that the exercise was really now one of curiosity and should only be undertaken while it provided some entertainment. That comment upset a lot of well-meaning people but I meant it. The only value I could see in the whole business was that it would be a challenge, even fun in its way, to try.

Immediately all three left to join the others at the wreck and within minutes a party was off to Boddam to collect some old hardboard sheets from the abandoned settlement. These had been left there by someone who had moved on and were now put to use as bracing under the spider's web of ropes. Fenders and buoys were wedged under them to hold the tarpaulins against the reverse curves of the garboards. It was not entirely successful.

The next inventive idea was to deflate some dinghies, feed them between the ropes and tarpaulins then pump them up to make the seal. That this should even be considered made me very angry. Putting an expensive generator at risk, or even a spare piece of canvas, is serious enough but dinghies fall in a different category entirely. A dinghy is as basic a necessity in Salomon as drinking water. If, for any reason, you lose yours you have no real alternative but to leave.

During the ensuing argument I was informed 'they are our dinghies and we'll do with them as we wish'. This was pretty far from the spirit of what I had acquiesced to and I became very depressed. I couldn't bear to watch so stayed at the beach.

Nothing would hold my attention there either; I wandered rather aimlessly from one pile of junk to another, picking at this and prodding at that, but my mind couldn't escape from the wreck. Gary and Derek came ashore while I was so engaged and called me aside for a quiet word. They were concerned that I was being driven into a place where I didn't want to be and, if that was the case, wanted to help me sort it out. I can't express how much I appreciated this gesture.

I described the situation to them in much the same way as I had to the others. I believed there was no future in a serious salvage attempt but could see no harm in taking *Vespera* to Boddam, as long as it was treated as a light-hearted venture. I probably whinged because I was in that sort of mood but eventually persuaded them, and myself, that things were okay.

I felt decidedly better a little later when I learned that the evolution with the dinghies had been concluded without loss. It hadn't worked but at least all the boats had survived and were back in service taking people home.

A few die-hards were still on board long after the main body had left and Tina and I went to show our faces and see how things were going. Jim was standing in the cockpit with a most awkward looking stance, trying to relieve some dreadful mischief that had befallen his back, while John and Russell perched in the companionway. They were completely absorbed in more verbal design work but broke off to greet us with some cheerful words. It's hard to stay angry with friends who still smile when you are behaving badly.

Anyway they told us the saga as seen from the wreck and it didn't sound very hopeful at all. The others had left to go home under a general air of despondency. It seemed that at this stage only these three had any faith left, but even for them the solution was being elusive. John and Russell went back into the water for another unhurried look at the problem and Tina went with them. They checked the edges of each tarpaulin for loose spots and trimmed and retied the securing lines wherever they looked sloppy.

While they were doing this I made an awful discovery. The tail end of one of the anchor warps, a brand new three-quarter inch nylon rope, had been wrapped round the hull lengthwise and used as the main lashing point for most of the securing lines. The other end was the line between the shoreside anchor and the masthead. The general reaction was that it wasn't really a problem, it would be simple enough to cut it when the boat floated. I objected noisily as it was several hundred dollars' worth of string and, at this point, much more valuable than the boat. In the end another rope was tied in the same place, all the lateral lines transferred to it and the warp undone and coiled on deck.

While transferring the lines several 'iffy' places showed up under the tarpaulins and something had to be done about them. The only ammunition left was a large sack of regular plastic shopping bags, the sort supermarkets pack your groceries in. No-one could think of a way to hold them in place until the idea was mooted to simply poke them into the bad spots with a stick.

With Jim unravelling the tangle of bags, Tina squashing the air out of them and Russell placing them and ramming them home with a sail batten it didn't take too long and, before they could escape, we started all the pumps to suck them into place. Once again the level fell against the gauge; about as quickly as grass grows, but fall it did and it was a happy boat-load of men who set off for Boddam later.

The phantom rustler was back in the morning, in fact two of them, and Jess didn't know what to make of it. She was beginning to show a bit of interest in the goings on around her and a scrabbling noise from the back of the tent, followed immediately by one from the front, actually got her to perk her ears up. I sneaked a look through the end screen and saw a nice big coconut crab, about eighteen inches across his claws, shuffling though the leaves. I found another one about the same size dragging a small pot from the camp kitchen when I unzipped the door.

The spark of curiosity from Jess was a welcome sight. Sue put down some food for her and she took a good meal, the first for several days. She seemed to draw some solace from endlessly cleaning the same part of her coat and had licked a patch on her chest completely raw. There wasn't a trace of fur left and her skin was cracked and bleeding. We were at a loss to how to stop it getting worse.

However, she was going to have to look after herself today as, if it was ever going to happen, this was the day *Vespera* was going to Boddam. The weather didn't look too bad, there was little wind and the dawn sky was overcast without being threatening. An early morning inspection showed that the water inside was still moving with the tide but nothing appeared to have come adrift overnight. Low tide was due at about half past seven and it was midway between neaps and springs so proceedings would begin with the water just above the old galley floor.

A pervasive air of optimism seemed to precede the larger than ever swarm of boats coming across. Lowell, Gary, Yoav and Patrick brought their dinghies with big outboard engines to provide motive power and so many people brought baling buckets we only needed some plastic spades to turn it into a bank-holiday outing. With all the cheerful faces and bubbling humour it was impossible not to be swept up in the flood of enthusiasm, in spite of my deeper feelings.

The plan was this: when she started to float she would be controlled using the masthead lines then, as soon as there was enough clearance underneath, the driving dinghies would nudge her off the reef along the path she had cleared on the way in. She would then follow a route close to shallow water or other reefs in case she went down again. By the time she got to Boddam there should be enough water in the tide to ease her round a bommie by the jetty then push her sideways onto the shelf. Philippa was going to take the helm and Alan direct operations from the base of the mast.

Right on time, as the tide bottomed out, the pumps started and a baling programme was worked out. With things as they were two 'bucketeers' could use the companionway to discharge water and another use a hatch in front of the coachroof. This was not very efficient – much of the water going through the companionway would finish up in the cockpit and, as part of the cockpit floor had been used to make a patch, would just come back in.

The situation was improved a hundred-fold by taking out one of the large polycarbonate windows from each side of the cabin. Now seven people could bale at the same time and most of the water would go out directly. An eighth person manning the manual bilge pump would complete the team. I was so inured to it all by now that I hardly flinched when the crowbar bit into the varnished wood and rope trims to break the windows away from their seals.

A last minute thought was to remove the self-steering gear before leaving the reef. It wasn't so much that it was heavy but it was pretty badly bent and might make it difficult to steer, and it was certainly an unnecessary hazard to the dinghies. The job didn't call for a lot of finesse. The bent securing bolts were persuaded out of the mountings with a crowbar and the whole thing pushed backwards into the coral. Once it was there we manhandled it out of harm's way should *Vespera* move backwards and a buoy was tied to it so we could find it again.

Baling was now the order of the day. The water was creeping slowly up towards the main cabin floor and was already deep enough for easy (easy?) bucketing from the spaces above the transmission and the locker beside it. After a bit of a shaky start a rhythm developed and the water began to fly. On the starboard side a person could stand with one foot on the engine rocker cover and the other on a floor beam and throw right-handed through the window. A second could position his feet on two beams and throw left-handed through the same window, while a third could stand in the quarter-berth locker to throw through the companionway. The port side was similar but opposite handed.

To get this to work at all called for choreography rather than organization. Several times in the early stages the 'left-handed bucketeer' would lean forward to fill his bucket just in time to catch an upcoming bucketful from the right-hander full in the face. The task developed a vocabulary all of its own. Watching the ladies come to terms with it was more entertaining but the gentlemen had the edge on language.

John and Ian had been in the water since they arrived, checking and adjusting ropes and tarpaulins and making sure none of the plastic bags escaped. I think they were the first to notice *Vespera* wobble on her keel. Alan went to the mast ready to take control of the lines while Patrick and Nicole took station by the anchors to make sure they stayed put. Most of the people had been on the go now for three or four hours and Tina thought to grab this last opportunity to go ashore and fill some flasks with hot coffee before the real action started.

Bucketing went on with renewed vigour and Sue and Kay came from the shore to assist. A replacement routine had established among the 'bucketeers' and as soon as anyone tired a rested person took over. Russell had his hands full keeping the electric pumps running. Hundreds of gallons of water being hurled about played havoc with the wiring and he often burnt his fingers pulling hot wires apart when they short-circuited.

Before Tina could get back with the coffee *Vespera* floated free of the bottom. Alan juggled the lines to keep her as still as he could and called for power from the big dinghies.

With those pushing like well-rehearsed harbour tugs she moved off slowly, then swung wildly off the chosen path and someone discovered that the buoy marking the main anchor had become entangled in the lashings. There was a great deal of noise and confusion at this point and communication was all but impossible – familiar ground, but this time luck played a friendlier card.

Alan was trying to make some sense of the swing but it didn't correspond with his fixed reference points and the way the dinghies were pushing. With all the generators and outboards running and the continuous splashing of water he hadn't heard the cry about the tangle and until the buoy line was cut *Vespera's* behaviour was unfathomable. However, it finished well and in a few moments she cleared the bommie. The masthead lines were run out through the blocks and left for the divers to recover.

Tina could see the activity from the beach but could do nothing about getting back to the boat. Sue was supposed to fetch her as soon as the coffee had had time to boil but had been swallowed up by the baling monster the minute she stepped aboard. As it happened the stranding made Tina the only person with time to experience the full rush of emotions. She has tried several times to describe her feelings but the note she made in her diary probably says it best, "When I saw her turn away and start to move I got to my knees to thank God and pray that no-one would get hurt, and all I could do was cry."

The tussle with the anchor buoy had disturbed some of the ropes and either John or Ian, or both, swam round to tidy it all up. It must have taken considerable strength to do this while swimming at boat speed, but even after finishing that they swam alongside all the time *Vespera* was afloat. Although we were only moving slowly the water sometimes got under the leading edges of the sheets, lifting them away from the hull, and their quick reactions were needed to tuck them back down before any plastic bags came adrift. The propeller wash from the dinghies was also apt to upset things and could have wrought havoc without their constant attention.

Mid-morning is probably the best time to cross to Boddam from the point of view of seeing the reefs but the light this morning wasn't particularly good for it and a couple of dinghies went in front as pathfinders. We wanted to miss the reefs, of course, but at the same time didn't want to be too far away from them. The pathfinders took station over the seaward edges of adjacent bommies then, as *Vespera* passed the first one, it would leapfrog to the next unmarked point and so forth.

Passing the first marker raised a cheer but some of the balers were getting pretty weary. Fortunately there were people still arriving so fresh muscles were introduced into the team and each newcomer meant the resting periods became a bit longer.

Conditions were quite stable now and the water level had steadied an inch or so below the cabin floor. However it was all very dynamic and that level was a good indicator if the baling slowed or a pump stopped. Although it was a hard task-master it was also good for morale that a couple of fresh hands at the buckets could halt the rise and drop the level noticeably in a few minutes.

The way the route developed, with the pathfinders ranging ahead to find the safest way, *Vespera* and her out-riders stayed quite close to the shore and disappeared from Tina's view somewhere near the half-way mark. To keep herself occupied while waiting for them to re-appear she worked at preparing the camp to move. For the time being our piles of 'work in progress' would have to stay where they were but the living quarters had to go now. There was plenty for her to do.

The next milestone was passing the southern end of Anglaise. This raised another a good cheer even though spirits were flagging a bit. Lifting a couple of gallons and throwing it out the window every three or four seconds isn't very hard at first but it stretches the sense of humour after an hour. Franco and Alessandro applied their Latin temperament to the problem and started a water hurling competition. They also put some rhythm back into things with a very loud rendition of some sea-shanties – well, I think they were sea-shanties but they may have been Italian rugby songs because there was a lot of laughing.

Once the first baler complained of it being hot work

and got a bucketful of cold water over her head for her troubles the routine degenerated with people subsiding into fits of giggles, but still the water flew. All of a sudden, it seemed, we passed the first boat in the Boddam anchorage. Now we were nearly there it was too easy to be complacent about the baling and I think if it hadn't been for Russell's endless reminders that the pumps couldn't cope on their own things might not have ended so well.

Then we passed a second boat, and a third, and soon we approached the bommie near the jetty. Alan returned to his station at the mast to coordinate the dinghies and the rest of us kept baling. As we rounded the bommie the driving dinghies reversed power to stop the boat then pushed and pulled to turn her port side to the beach before manoeuvring into position to push her sideways onto the shelf. It was still an hour to high tide but, as she was going to have to be pulled further up the shelf on the spring tide anyway, it was considered a waste of energy to keep her floating any longer. A great sigh of relief from the bucket brigade.

So, as *Vespera* drifted into line with the chosen spot all the outboards went to high power to push her on as firmly as possible. The contingent who had been getting things prepared on the island rushed out to take mooring lines. These were taken to palm trees at the water's edge, one forward and one aft, and hauled up as tight as muscle could make them to prevent the tide from washing her off the shelf.

There was a tremendous atmosphere about the place. The impossible had been done and every head was held high, every face had a shine. The air was filled with that indefinable charge that goes with spectacular achievement. I had thought the venture over-optimistic at best, and I know I wasn't alone in that view, but the faithful had proved their point. Some of the details will fade from memory, are already fading, but the vibrancy of that moment will remain.

I was glad the tarpaulins and patches had to stay on until the spring tide, four days later, as I didn't want to spoil this day with the realities of an objective inspection. The thought that Tina was on her own on Anglaise, with no-one to relieve the tension, was sitting heavily and as soon as it was reasonable to escape I set off with Heidi, who drove their faster dinghy, to

fetch her. Before we had crossed the gap between the islands
we met Lowell coming the other way with Tina, Jess and the
tent, so we just turned tail and followed them back.

Up to the time we actually stood on the beach we hadn't
given so much as a thought to where on Boddam we should
set up our temporary home. Heidi solved the problem
immediately by inviting us to share the week-end retreat she
had made with Bar and Netta. The girls had a small tent they
used as a playroom and had pitched it in a clearing close to
the French camp. The place had been cleaned and tidied up
neat as a new pin. There was plenty of room for our tent if we
used the space behind theirs and we gratefully took advantage
of their offer.

Tina and I began to organize ourselves while Sue went
back to Anglaise with Gary to collect the rest of the camp. I
put up the tent and Tina re-commissioned our little brazier to
make a cup of tea; a slightly more time-consuming business
than it sounds as the water tank was a couple of hundred yards
away. However, it brought home to us how lucky we were to
find ourselves on an island with water and firewood.

The spacing of the trees didn't lend itself so well to tying
up Ted's tarpaulin as the camp on Anglaise but we managed to
get the tent itself covered. A sheltered area to cook in was not
important anyway as only a few yards away was a nice covered
barbecue spot with its own makeshift oven and a woodpile
with a roof. Once the tent was up we put Jess inside as a
couple of dogs that lived on the boats had the run of the island
during the day. Jess had lived on board for five years now
without any exposure to dogs and we didn't think this was the
best of times to get her re-acquainted.

Once things settled down we went to join the others and
found several of the euphoric smiles changing character

somewhat as the back pains and sore arms lost the benefit of flowing adrenalin. Jim in particular had aggravated his back further and was walking with some difficulty. It was fortunate for everyone that Sue from *Kekeni* was a trained nurse and I think it illustrates the level of effort everyone had put in that she could be seen rowing round the anchorage, morning and evening, for several days on her 'back repair' rounds.

One way or another it had been a momentous day, the sort that would traditionally finish off with hours of revelry and lubricated celebration, but the sore backs and general weariness would have put a damper on things. We also had our own highly personal reason for wanting to defer such a party; the next day was our thirty-first wedding anniversary. A word or two was sufficient persuasion to put things off and we spent a quiet evening on *Cairngorm*.

Our anniversary dawned gentle and non-descript but the tides, and *Vespera*'s position on the shelf didn't allow any work to be done. About the only thing we could do without disturbing the props was remove the generator we used for powering the power tools. It is a small unit, driven by its own petrol engine, and is mounted behind the companionway steps.

This fairly simple task presented its own challenge under the circumstances. The normal procedure calls for hinging the steps out of the way then kneeling on the cabin floor with your head and shoulders through a rather tight aperture. In this stance you can just reach the furthest fitting.

As it was now you couldn't kneel down as the floor wasn't there any more and new bracing points had to be located. It didn't seem to matter where I put my feet, or what I leant on, I couldn't get it right and a couple of exhaust clamp bolts were tantalizingly beyond my reach. In the end I made a basic mistake. Having undone the mountings I lifted the unit and pulled it forwards a little to let me work my arm up behind it to loosen them, but I hadn't reckoned on the whole thing sliding down the listing crossbeams when I let go and in a few seconds it resolved my need to get at the clamps. It tore the exhaust off completely, crumpling the flexible stainless steel pipe like so much foil. Not a good start to a festive day.

The next part made up for it though. At the camp Sue

had taken time out to make us a special anniversary lunch. She'd made a table in the clearing outside the tent, decorated it with wild flowers and served up a feast. In this she had been helped by the youngsters who had sorted out all the food tins. Every single tin had been taken from its plastic bag, rinsed in fresh water to remove the salt then carefully dried and stored away in the shed.

Looking at the neat rows of tins, all sorted into groups by their contents, the hours we'd spent with a marker pen labelling the lids suddenly seemed less of a chore. None of the paper labels had survived and without the cryptic 'B.Beans' or 'PK.Lunch' we would have been stuck. Even so we had a couple of dozen unmarked tins, obviously bought at a different time and missed in the marking exercise. It was very much a pot-luck affair finding out what was in them and gave us a good idea of how life might have been.

Fortunately there were two distinct can types in the unmarked group. The numbers on the lids meant nothing without the code so one lunch time, to satisfy our curiosity, we opened one of each – pork in spicy sauce and evaporated milk… However, the combination prompted some memories and we became reasonably sure that all the unknowns were the same two commodities. The marking pen was put to use again, just a little late.

Anyway this trial was still in the future and such concerns had no place during this evening's celebrations. The beach table staggered under an array of delicious and unusual salads, freshly caught fish were cooking over hot coals and, again, wild flowers provided decoration around the oil lamps. All the sore muscles were, if not cured, at least well enough rested to allow the smiles back and it was a magnificent party.

As the evening matured, with everyone in talkative and exuberant moods, it was fascinating to hear the individual stories of what happened the day before. It was only now, as we listened to what others had seen and done, that a real understanding of the magnitude of the achievement emerged. Fittingly, two Thai ceremonial fireworks, with the gunpowder packed in clay pots and sealed with wax, had survived and Sue let them off under the palm trees to mark the occasion.

Tina and I were moved beyond words that amongst the

other good reasons to be celebrating everyone considered the importance of our anniversary to us and we received all manner of good wishes and thoughtfully produced cards, especially touching as you can't just go and buy such things on the islands. For a while we were able to imagine the shipwreck conversations around us were merely academic and hide ourselves in our own pleasant thoughts. To improve things further the *Kekenis* had loaned us an enormous airbed, one that filled the tent from edge to edge, and invited Sue to stay onboard with them.

Next day was still two short of spring tides so *Vespera* was left to look after herself and attention was focused on getting more of our things from Anglaise. Ian volunteered to use *Cruise* as a tug to pull a string of dinghies which could be used as barges to ferry stuff across. This was a fine gesture as it saved a lot of outboard fuel, a singularly precious island commodity, and turned a heavy chore into a much more convivial affair.

In common with most, Ian had moored *Cruise* to a chain shackled round a large rock rather than relying on an anchor in the coral. Taking this up and resetting it later would be a protracted business so in preference to all that rigmarole he simply buoyed his chain and left it on site. I don't recall how many dinghies he towed or how many people he had on board but it was a significant proportion of the population.

Top priority was to bring all those things already successfully dried; the log-book, manuals and that sort of thing. Then there were all the surviving groceries, the dish-washing liquid, bleach, wash-cloths etc., and all the toiletries. It's astonishing to see a year's supply of such things stacked in one place… but I digress. Next, from the 'retrievables' pile, came such sundries as my drawing board and guitar. The list went on and on and before long the dinghies were full and tethered behind *Cruise* for the return journey. There was still a mound of stuff left, the boom and mainsail and all the fuel, in fact most of the heavy and awkward things, but there was simply nowhere to put it all.

As luck would have it the wind increased a bit and the dinghies had a pretty rough ride back with plenty of water slopping over the bows and a lot of the stuff got wet again before *Cruise* was safely back on her mooring. Now, in addition to finding somewhere to store it all, we had to find a suitable place to dry it again and the shed seemed the best bet.

Given that it's an uninhabited island the shed is a first class facility, but it really wouldn't count for much at home. It's a building about a hundred and twenty feet by thirty with coral block walls and a corrugated iron roof on huge rafters; well, half of it still has a roof. Under the least leaky part of the roof is a raised floor of coconut palm planks, which is great for storing things clear of the ground even though it's in the same state of repair as the roof.

The tins and all the washed and aired clothes, now neatly folded and packed away in bags, were squashed up to make room for the new arrivals which were stacked around them as tidily as possible. The wet things were laid out in a place of their own where they could dry without disturbance but the exercise suffered a few casualties, one of which was Sue's meticulously revived log-book that was now just a mush.

We got involved in some back-to-front planning during the day. The radio enthusiasts had been in contact with *Stepping Stone* and *Brumby*, both currently in the Maldives and coming on to Salomon, and these folks would be pleased to collect any materials we needed and deliver them to us; but of course they needed some information. We couldn't move *Vespera* up the beach to take off the patches until the day after tomorrow, so any decision about whether it was worth trying to repair her was some days in the future.

Several of us gathered round the beach table to talk over some possibilities. Ferro-cement is a pretty basic composite of ordinary cement plastered over a wire mesh armature and if we could even guess at some quantities of cement and reinforcing rods and, more importantly, define any specialized items like curing additives or underwater epoxies, then they could at least keep a watchful eye out for them on their travels.

A lot of expertise with ferro-cement sat around this table. One man had built his own similar boat, another had personal experience of major repairs in the material and a professional civil engineer added a touch of class to the gathering. Before even trying to make up a material list a number of topics had to be addressed, and one which would greatly influence the choice of materials was the estimated 'shortest dry time' we would have to work with. This 'shortest dry time' is the time that would elapse between the falling tide uncovering the lowest point to be repaired and the rising tide covering it again.

One of the yachts had a set of local tide tables but that still left us with two unknowns, how far could we get *Vespera* up the beach and how low would the lowest hole be once the damage was chipped away. Of course there was no way of knowing.

It seemed more advantageous to develop a way of keeping the water away from the cement until it had taken its initial set and a few ingenious ideas were discussed. The engineer had prepared a substantial proposal of how to tackle the job and all sorts of ideas were grist to the design mill. It's in the nature of creative meetings like this that subjects clash and shoot off at tangents, and suddenly we were talking about epoxy-based fillers or glass reinforced epoxy sheathing.

I recall holding forth at length about difficulties encountered in the past with *Vespera*'s antipathy to epoxies. I also recall that the engineer's proposal didn't get much of an airing due to the dynamics of the discussion, but I don't recall what it was specifically that caused a most distressing upset. One chap interjected and put forward the argument, very forcefully, that all this dithering wouldn't get anything done; one person should be put in charge to make all the decisions and everyone else should work under his supervision.

Had this been a commercial discussion he could well have been right but the concept was out of place here and set everyone back in dismay, particularly me. Unfortunately the interjection was worded in such a way that it came across as the stuff of a trade union confrontation, not of people generously giving their time and knowledge to help me out of a jam. Worse still, rejecting the idea caused tempers to flare and it was as well that Tina chose this moment to come and warn of an approaching squall, thereby creating a reasonable opportunity to duck and run.

I slept very badly that night. Even before our first trip to Salomon we had heard of 'island politics' and it all but put us off coming. It's a phenomenon that thrives in small communities and seems particularly virulent among the diverse people who become yachties. However, during the first visit we had survived without a single attack and had been confident we could do so again, but here we were on the threshold of a major outbreak and our misfortune was the underlying cause.

The restless hours just wouldn't go past as I racked my brain for a solution. The diplomatic ability to defuse such a situation is a gift given to few, and those few don't include me. What made it even harder was it was all so well meant. The chap who felt so strongly, a valued friend, is as generous as the day is long and was only concerned that every thing should be done to my best advantage, but those who disagreed with him felt the same way. It was a night every bit as long as the night of the accident.

Tina caught the full brunt of it in the morning. We were sitting in the 'kitchen' having a quiet cup of tea when she was approached for a bit of woman–to–woman pressure to get this chap put in charge of the hull repairs. It was all quite ridiculous as we didn't yet know if we wanted to try, but no matter how much tact she used the pressure became louder and more demanding until she could contain herself no longer and swore dreadfully, burst into tears and, in her own words, 'ran away to hide'.

This was a far more serious tragedy than losing the boat. Up until now Tina had borne all the heartache and despair with uncharacteristic stoicism but this put an end to it. When she eventually came back, shivering in distress, she found me murderously angry at the turn of events and it took some time for the pair of us to calm down enough to consider what to do. I've already said it was well-intentioned and we felt we were being ungrateful at not giving in to it, but it would have been a mistake and other valued friendships were at stake.

We had to try and smooth things over. If nothing else, Tina wanted to apologize for her outburst so we gathered ourselves together and motored out to our friends' boat. Thank goodness tempers had cooled and things were brought back to a more acceptable state of affairs. It took considerable effort on all parts to achieve this and we are truly grateful.

Other pressures were brought to bear as the day

progressed. The notion of asking for assistance from Diego Garcia had taken hold throughout the community and I received countless offers from people willing to let me use their radios. Not only was I regaled with imaginative stories of ways they might help but I was given serious advice on the best way to approach them.

Here was another trap just waiting for me to fall in and I couldn't see how to avoid it. I had already disappointed one pair of friends and now I was faced with the disapproval of others if I evaded the issue. Things had come a long way from the original idea of bringing *Vespera* here to see if it was worth trying to save her.

I had to give in in the end and arrangements were made for me to use a radio in the afternoon. I mentally rehearsed all the pitfalls I could think of and tried to think of some answers. What would happen if I asked for help and they sent a salvage team? – I would be bankrupt. What would I say if they asked what assistance was needed? – I still hadn't had a look so I had no answer. More immediate still was the question of whether we would be allowed any option but to abandon everything and fly out; the authorities would be quite within their rights to insist on it. I didn't know what to do. Contact time came round and I steeled myself for the unknown – but we couldn't get through.

A couple of other boats tried to establish contact using different transmitters but no-one was listening, or at least no-one was answering. We would try again later, which gave me more time to worry about what could go wrong. Fortunately it also gave me time to think of a compromise that might get me off the hook. I had been told that news of our sinking had already been sent to the authorities so decided to give them a simple situation report. This could cause no offence on Diego Garcia, wouldn't commit me to anything I didn't want and would, I hoped, satisfy those who considered the contact necessary.

When I eventually got through it was after office hours and I got the impression the poor man had been called away from a private function, but it went off fairly easily. He couldn't quite fathom out why I was calling but was courteous and friendly and offered to help with information about specialized materials and so forth, but said it would be easier if I called in office hours. As the transmitter clicked off for the last time I heaved a great mental sigh; it was done and nothing dreadful had happened, and now I could concentrate on caring for my family. Tina was at her lowest state ever.

The high tide we had been waiting for was in the early afternoon, which was most convenient for the moving exercise. While I had been neglecting things here some of the men had taken advantage of the way *Vespera* was lying to improve the patches. All the fothering sheets had been hauled up tighter and some had extra padding wedged underneath to make a better seal. This time she wasn't going to make a journey, she just had to float for an hour or so to the top of the tide, so bulk was more important than tidiness. One hole had been fitted with a semi-permanent cover of flexible plywood, screwed down using wooden plugs in holes drilled in the cement and bedded down on a self-curing sealant, to see if that would be a viable means of patching her for an ocean voyage.

Their work was not in vain. Almost as soon as the pumps started, within minutes of the lowest tide, they sucked out enough water to create a pressure gradient across the re-vitalized patches and were able to maintain sufficient head for her to float without having to call for balers. Time is difficult to measure under these circumstances but I should imagine, looking at the end result, that the keel floated free of the sand about four hours later.

Once again everyone turned up for the occasion and there were plenty of line handlers to pull and heave. Every time she lifted an inch the call went out to haul in the slack and slowly, slowly, she crept further onto the shelf.

With everything working out so well and the relief of not having to bale, much of the gloom from the day before was dispelled and good humour prevailed. Finally, with half an hour to spare, the keel moved over the lip and a few minutes of vigorous linework had her solidly on the sloping part of the beach. All the ropes were put under tension and the block on the halyard put back in action to run a line from the masthead to the base of a palm tree, to make sure she fell the right way as the water went down.

Now we could make a start on checking the damage, and the props in the main cabin were knocked out to let us get at the engine, which had to come out to gain access. The weight of the beast posed some interesting problems. Even with the lumpier parts taken off, the heat exchanger and starter for example, the assembly with the gearbox weighed a quarter of a ton. It had to be lifted until the top of it almost touched the coachroof, some eight feet, then moved backwards about the same distance and squeezed out through the companionway. That wasn't the end of the story either – from there it had to be lifted over the side and transported ashore.

First we needed a beam to attach a lifting tackle to and a search party set off to see what was available on the island. In the meantime John and I began undoing the mountings and taking off the removable bits. Before we finished, the shore party returned with a huge log, fifteen feet long and eight inches or so in diameter, which they poked through the front hatch of the coachroof and out through the companionway. The mainsheet was suspended from it as a lifting tackle and the initial load taken up.

With all the detachable bits off, the rest was lifted as far as it would go on the mainsheet. The sump was well clear of the floor but still a few feet short of the companionway sill; it was also several feet too far forward. All we could think of was to make a ramp and slide the whole thing up it but this, of course, needed a support for another tackle.

Gary left in his fast dinghy to bring the boom from Anglaise. When fitted this would give us a two-fold advantage: it would give us a hard spot to mount the slide tackle and provide the means to lift the assembly over the side once we got it to the cockpit. While he was away the shore party went foraging again for a suitable slide.

They found two fairly smooth planks and laid them against the sill with their other ends wedged under a floor beam. Jim loaned his mainsheet to use as the slide tackle and this was hooked between the boom and the transmission casing. Then, with two or three people on each side to keep things steady, the tackles were manipulated until the unit sat on the ramp. An oily board had been laid on the planks first to help it slide.

Now both tackles were hauled on until the lifting one came to the end of its stroke. The slide tackle was locked and the log supporting the lifting gear repositioned to give more scope. The process was repeated, and repeated again, and the engine assembly gradually moved up the slide. The companionway caused a lot of consternation. With the engine hanging in the middle of the gap, the lifting beam and tackle above and the slide rails below there was simply no room for guiding hands, and for an exciting moment the effort degenerated to brute force, again, and suddenly the beast was resting on a cockpit seat.

Now we had to get it ashore. The dinghy was lashed alongside and some logs laid across the airtubes to make a reasonably strong floor. We doubled up the topping lift with the main halyard to make the boom arrangement as strong as we could and, with some trepidation, took the engine weight on the tackle. Everything seemed okay so we swung it out and lowered it into the dinghy.

We were able to walk alongside in the shallow water to hold it steady as the little barge was pushed to the shore and only one hurdle was left, getting it from the dinghy to dry land. There were no convenient strong points or lifting gantries here so Alan went back to retrieve his giant log. Slings were tied round it and under the engine then, with three men to a side, lots of martial arts–style shouting and a great welter of splashing, the whole caboodle was run ashore and deposited under a takamaka tree.

Altogether it had been an encouraging day. The general mood inspired Alan to treat the anchorage to a few tunes from his bagpipes as the sun set and we joined them later to broach a fresh batch of home-made banana liqueur. The world was looking better and better.

Low tide next morning was an excellent opportunity to untangle the ropes and tarpaulins. I expected this to go quickly; after all, the difficulty keeping them in place so far suggested they would fall off by themselves if left alone, but several of the lines were trapped under the keel and we wasted a lot of time trying to get them out. A couple of them seemed to be stuck in the sand for good so the ends were just coiled up and hung over the lifelines.

Inside, the other props and patches came out easily, allowing us to concentrate on getting the electrical storage batteries out. Alterations made to the boat when some new ones had been fitted in Malaysia made their removal a bit awkward, but nature had done some of the preliminary work already. Because the lights had been on at the time of the sinking the cables had been immersed in salt water while carrying current and electrolytic action had destroyed the end fittings; in fact on the heavier cables there was little evidence that end fittings had ever existed. Anyway, we got them out and sent ashore before the rising tide stopped play.

Someone must have taken charge of those batteries straight away as I didn't see them again until a couple of days later, when I found them in the shed with all the contaminated acid drained off and the plates flushed clean. I don't think anyone knew whether they would survive this treatment but it was surely worth a try. I had half a jerrycan of fresh acid and Ted had the same, or a bit more, and this was enough to replace the electrolyte in three of them. As soon as those were filled they were taken to various boats and hooked up to windchargers or solar panels to see what happened.

After lunch John came to the beach and started working on the generator's petrol engine. This was a forlorn looking thing now as all the cover plates were rusting and the aluminium castings were pitted with white oxide from their dunking. It didn't look at all promising when he pulled apart some wire connectors in the ignition system to let water drain out, and unscrewing the oil drain produced a stream of slimy grey muck.

But John was quietly confident and persisted with his tests and adjustments until, eventually, he pronounced the victim ready for resuscitation. There was spark at the spark plug, fuel at the carburettor and compression when he turned it over. A sharp tug on the starting cord, accompanied by mild vocal encouragement, and away she went, running as sweetly as ever.

While on a winning streak he set to work on the main engine. It would be some days before it could be run as Russell had stripped the starter motor down to dry it, so the plan was to make use of discarded sump oil and fill the engine right to the top in an attempt to keep corrosion at bay. Here we were quite lucky; some previous visitors had been a bit naughty and left a few gallons by the rubbish bin instead of burning it.

As with the small engine, when the drain plug was unscrewed a rush of watery grey goo poured out, quickly followed by oily black goo. We turned the engine over by hand to pump oil through the galleries and everything seemed reasonably well. Even the pre-heater plugs, which had been taken out to make turning over easier, were not too rusty. A good squirt of penetrating oil was pumped into each cylinder through the heater apertures to keep everything free in there and, as evening was coming, the whole thing closed up to wait for another day.

Back at the camp another surprise was in store. The youngsters had taken down their week-end tent to move to another spot (I can't help feeling we had driven them from their retreat) and in its place Philippa and Heidi had erected their lovely five-man tent. They had loaned it to us for as long as we needed it and had gone to a lot of trouble siting it to the best advantage. It was completely protected from wind and rain and the mosquito net window looked out through the palm trees onto the lagoon, with its string of small islands across the horizon. Each morning the dawn lined these islands with silver and gold before the richer colours came and we could lie abed and watch it.

With two tents available Sue moved back ashore and took over the smaller one. Jess lived in there with her, in fact stayed in there all the time and was becoming frustrated with her lack of freedom. While on the boat she was quite content to stay inside and an excursion into the cockpit was unusual enough to cause comment, but the last week or so had been traumatic and had changed her outlook a lot. She still had that great open sore on her chest but returning vitality was making her more alert and inquisitive, though at the same time more nervous.

Next day we made the first real attempt to define the hull damage. Jim and Joy armed themselves with hammers and joined Clive and I to start breaking out the crushed cement. At first it was easy, as a sharp tap would dislodge any loose pieces and they simply fell out of the mesh, but as time went on there were no more loose pieces. Most of the pebbles were firmly attached to the armature and the only way to get them out was for one person to hold a dolly, or heavy hammer, hard up against one side and for another person to crush it by striking from the other. Rather like putting a nut in a nutcracker and hitting it with a hammer.

This caused a lot of interest and before long there was a line of willing helpers waiting to have a go. Good thing, too, as it was a tiring job. We found from experience that it was best for the person on the outside to hold the dolly while the one on the inside used the hammer. When we started it seemed more logical to do it the other way round and it worked quite well while the pebbles were large, but as the lumps under attack got smaller communicating where the dolly was needed became more and more difficult.

The essence of the problem was that looking from the outside in was like looking from the sunshine into a coalbin, so the hammer man couldn't see where the dolly was. Once we learned that the inside person could easily spy out the remaining particles and call directions to the dolly holder things speeded up considerably. Even so communication between pairs of helpers was, at the risk of a pun, a hit-and-miss affair.

In the cacophony of smashes and bangs that rang through the boat it was hard to tell who was speaking, let alone what was being said:-'Forward about an inch'; 'Up a bit'; 'A bit more'; whack. 'Forwards again'; 'No forwards'; …'Who am I talking to now?'; …'I'm sorry, who's holding the square hammer then? …you'll have to move around a bit until I can see you'.

The tides controlled both when and how much work could be done in a day. Wielding a hammer underwater is an exercise that not even the most ardent keep-fit enthusiast would recommend, and the work windows when the holes were out of the water changed with the moon. To make the most of the time available it was quite usual for a hammer or dolly to be passed to a fresh pair of hands in the same way the baling had been done. A good thing about the time restraint, though, was that the enforced knocking-off time coincided with sundowner time, at least for the first few days.

Sundowners also re-opened the discussions about repair materials and methods. It was still academic as clearing out the damage was far from complete and the holes were proving bigger than first thought. I had been pondering vaguely on the use of epoxies, in spite of the known problems, as some years before a friend had successfully repaired a hole in his ferro-cement boat using a mix of epoxy resin and sand plastered over the original armature, but the process was entirely dependent on the repair site being dry. No-one knew if an underwater-curing epoxy could be used in this way, whether it could be worked into the right consistency, or if it would take a strong enough initial set to withstand the wavelets as the tide came up.

There were plenty of opinions on the subject, almost as many as there were people, but the only thing known for certain was that epoxies were expensive. It was also highly probable that any specialized form of resin would be difficult to find. Especially in Salomon. More important, though, I was still of the opinion that any expenditure at this stage would be a mistake and continued talk of these exotic materials made me nervous, particularly as we couldn't hear what was being negotiated over the radio.

I had been spending wakeful hours, when I should have been sleeping, mentally listing those things which I felt, honestly, were worth taking back to civilization. It wasn't a very long list. Several people made generous offers to transport us, and such belongings as we could rescue, to Africa and this seemed the most responsible course of action. The diminutive list of things we would take with us made it more so.

That circumstance changed a little as the list grew. Ian had revived my electric drill and angle grinder and Russell had got the VHF radio working, but the principle was still sound. The safest way home was with our friends.

However, developments had established a momentum of their own and a tentative list of materials was radioed through to the boats in the Maldives. Chipping away the damage carried on, while the tides were appropriate, for several days. One of these saw us dismantle the lower part of the hanging locker and drawer unit to chase a crack and the hole we found there forced us to cut away part of a bulkhead. Another had me busy with a borrowed power saw removing part of the main structure under the inside steering console. This was the area that worried me most and I was anxious to gain access with the least amount of hacking.

With no traffic load on the cabin floor it was alright to take its support away as it could be built back later anyway, but the floor itself was more problematic. It was made of thick plywood on two-by-three-inch bearers and formed an integral part of the cabin woodwork. Assessing what could be cut without weakening anything was a time-consuming business, though it became easier after I sacrificed the lower part of another bulkhead because that made it possible to crawl in underneath, and from there I could see which of the bearers carried additional loads.

Working conditions for the 'inside' man when it came to breaking away the cement here were about as unpleasant as any I can imagine. You could approach the site in two different ways, by going headfirst under the cut-away bulkhead and worming your way forwards face down, or by creeping in sideways from the engine compartment. Entry from the engine compartment had the advantage that you could chose which shoulder to lie on, but it gave no support to your hips and after a few minutes your knees felt ready to explode.

Whichever way you went you couldn't escape the rough edges of broken cement and torn mesh that always seemed to stick out where you needed to lean, or the fact that once in place you couldn't move your head as it was sandwiched between hull and floor. Panels were cut out of the plywood between the bearers to let in a bit of light and possibly allow access for a helping hand, but it didn't do much to alleviate the claustrophobia of the unfortunate fellow down there.

To compound it our usual working method of hammering from the inside wouldn't work here. It was all the inside man could do to get a dolly to the work site and anything else was unthinkable. This left the man on the outside to control a task that he couldn't see, while flying grit and cement particles falling around the inside man meant he had to do his part with his eyes shut.

Although this was difficult and unpleasant it was the reason behind the whole exercise. Cutting away the bulkhead had revealed that one of the ribs had crumbled and as we chipped at the edges, looking for sound material, the holes got bigger and bigger. As far as we could tell the limits of the more accessible holes had been defined. All the edges rang cleanly when tapped with a hammer and all that remained before repairs could start was to poke out the small debris trapped in the mesh.

The cheerful atmosphere that surrounded the helpers as they prodded and stabbed at those irritating little particles did much to sustain those busy with 'that' hole. This had increased in its level of difficulty by extending upwards and backwards until the floor bearers prevented the dolly from going into place. It looked as though the fracture might 'top out' before the chart table/icebox assembly would have to be destroyed, so there was a hint of optimism, but without the dolly the pebbles refused to break.

The same ingenuity that floated *Vespera* off the reef was called on to resolve the impasse and before long a couple of substantial, if very rusty, levers found their way onto the boat. These were brought into play in conjunction with a chunk of angle iron, maybe four by four by half an inch and a foot long, and a Heath Robinson arrangement dreamed up to wedge the angle behind the pebbles.

Where the dolly simply wouldn't fit one flange of the angle could be eased up against the bearers and held in place with the levers. This entailed two 'inside' men working at the same time but, as they couldn't both get into the work space, it had to be done at arm's length. I have no idea how long it took. Logic tells me it was done within a tide but my memory tells me it took a month. However, that day saw the final definition of the holes, and we hadn't had to destroy the entire cabin. The overall cheerfulness increased and overflowed into sundowner time, and then into meal time. Ian had caught a couple of beautiful coral trout which were cooked over hot coals and the evening turned into one of general feasting.

Spontaneous evenings like this did more to raise our spirits than anything else. While we were always aware of the special goodwill towards us the company of friends simply enjoying Salomon was, of itself, a tonic. We were surrounded by all the good things that go with cruising and it was enough to remind us that the accident had only altered our perspective of it, and not the reality. It was extremely hard, no, impossible, to stay depressed when everything else looked so good.

That night I had to come to terms with the next step. I still favoured the option of travelling back to Africa with our friends but, so far, hadn't accepted any of the kind offers. It felt dishonest, somehow, even to talk about it when so many people were working on the boat. But I was chewing hard on whether I was right or wrong, whether I was being unfair to my family to be nice to our friends, or even if it wasn't just plain immoral to let anybody waste more of their prime time working on *Vespera*. There was a lot of gristle in this mouthful.

Tina and I had a long chat in the morning and decided, firstly, that if we stopped them trying now we would upset everyone anyway and, secondly, that as long as we didn't spend too much money it wouldn't hurt to see what could be done. We would think about the next move if she floated again and would decide then, with the benefit of hindsight, if the repairs were good enough to risk an ocean voyage.

With this clear in my head I made it a priority to ensure that whatever materials were bought fitted in with this plan. Not having a radio any more meant we were dependent on second-hand information of the discussions with *Brumby* and what we heard was often unclear. We'd had a lot of experience of trying to unravel the truth from once- or twice-interpreted stories off the radio nets, which helped us ignore the wilder inconsistencies, and Jim finally solved the problem by inviting me to sit in on one of the conversations.

A tentative repair programme had been sorted out. We would use ordinary cement mortar, such as was used in the original construction, with a curing membrane to protect and harden it. I had a roll of plastic drawing film that could be used as the membrane but everything else had to be found. There is an awful lot of sand on Boddam but it is all from coral and apparently of little value for mortar so good sharp sand, fresh cement, reinforcing bars and tying wire were the most important needs. Chicken wire mesh could be foraged for among the abandoned gardens on the island.

We could see now that the area of the holes totalled about thirty-five square feet so estimating the quantities we needed was easy, but deciding how much extra to get for experimentation, wastage and so on was much harder. The simple answer was as much as possible, but bags of sand and cement are not the easiest things to find room for on a passage-making yacht, especially as they have to be kept dry. Anyway, we settled on some quantities and Jim passed the request on in the morning. We also asked for some acid for the other batteries and a small amount of epoxy if it could be found.

Now, with that settled, work could start on the actual repair. We couldn't do anything about replacing the torn mesh until the reinforcing bars arrived but all the hole edges could be dressed to make good joints. Ideally they would have rough surfaces, to make a key, and be chamfered on both faces, but even if this standard couldn't be attained they had to be clean and free of loose particles.

Wherever it was possible, that is neither too close to the water nor anywhere that a slip could damage the mesh, we used an angle grinder to make the chamfers. While quick it wasn't ideal as it left a smooth surface that had to be roughened afterwards. In the end it all came down to manual labour and a hammer and sharp chisel were the best tools. Altogether a fiddly business that called for patience and persistence.

Tina and Sue got stuck into the piles in the shed. Some of the 'retrievables' that had been washed and dried were showing signs of short life expectancy. The tins of food were our major concern as rust was showing around the seams on most of them and had taken quite a hold on several. One particular batch was uniformly rusted over their entire surfaces and, piecing together the evidence, we deduced that these were ones that had received special attention when we stowed them. It was our habit to store a few days' supply of tins in a plastic bag and label each bag with the time it would last rather than a list of its contents and, thinking to give a bit more protection to those that would have to last longest we had squirted some commercial corrosion inhibitor into the bags that would be stored at the bottom. The manufacturers claimed the spray would dispel any moisture and leave an anti-corrosive film on the surfaces. It certainly distributed the film well but something in it wasn't very good for the metal and all the affected cans were marked down to a 'use first' grade.

Discussions at the beach table produced the idea that dunking them, even those already rusting, in waste sump oil would inhibit their exposure to oxygen and slow the deterioration. Sue undertook this project and whenever the tide kept her away from the boat she could be found at the back of the shed up to her armpits in oil. Dunking was the easy part, draining them off to leave a film that was, we hoped, tacky enough to do its job yet dry enough not to ooze black gunk over everything took ages.

She spread a cloth over a plastic sheet on the ground then, as each tin came out of the oil bath, placed it on there to drip. Some hours later the sides and bottoms would be about right but the ribs around the lids still held slippery puddles, so she would turn them over and leave them a few more hours. When they reached the right stage of gooiness she packed them away in the original plastic bags, to stop sand or dust sticking to them, and stacked them in the dry part of the shed.

Tina was doing the same with the hand tools. Like the tins, they'd been washed in fresh water but instead of being dried had been left immersed. I think the stagnant, oxygen depleted, water had some beneficial effect but even so they were now in a sorry state. All those with moving parts, the hand drill, pliers, shifting spanners and such, were frozen into rusty facsimiles of themselves.

Here the approach was to tap around the locked up

joints with a hammer to dislodge the larger particles, then soak them in a bath of the ubiquitous sump oil. Afterwards she would mop them off and attack the joints again until they came free, work them until free became easy, then redunk them and leave them on a cloth to drip. Later we were very glad of the time she spent on this as most of the tools survived and became vital as time passed.

While they were busy evolving the technique to make gunky oil stick to things, others tried to find the means to get it off. A lot of equipment that had been loaned to get *Vespera* this far had been stained with oil or diesel and no amount of washing seemed to remove it. Ropes were the biggest problem as even small drops of oil seeped in and spread along the fibres to make large stains. Soaps and detergents were tried in both hot and cold water but the best we could achieve was to fade the marks from black to oily brown, roughly on the same scale as the marks on our consciences when we returned them.

Our consciences were also under siege from the strain all this was putting on our volunteer helpers' health. *Vespera* was causing plenty of cuts and scrapes from brushing against torn mesh and stiff muscles were endemic. Jim's back was the most serious victim and every hour he spent crouched over a patch, and there were many, must have cost him dearly. Eventually it became bad enough to stop him for a couple of days and we were even more grateful for 'nurse Sue's' ability and medication.

There was, however, another medical problem quite separate from *Vespera*'s victims that had a profound effect on the community. Ted found himself in a lot of trouble, which he attributed to ulcers, and the distress he was suffering didn't respond to any available treatment. He was not a young man, except in spirit, and being sick while alone on his boat must have been very worrying. In spite of this he decided to leave for Gan, in the Maldives, to seek help and we all breathed a sigh of relief when we heard he'd arrived safely.

The calendar showed April 8th, bringing a welcome break in the daily work as it was Ian's birthday. A full-scale island celebration was planned and everyone stretched their imaginations to produce new and exciting dishes. Top on the list was the main course of reef fish cooked in a Maori style 'Hungi'. Several of the fishing enthusiasts left in the morning to try their luck and returned with a magnificent coral trout, a nice bass of some sort and another intriguing fish that no-one could identify.

Alan and Philippa dug a large pit, filled it with logs and lit a good fire under them, then stoked and tended it until a rich bed of coals covered the bottom. When the time was judged to be right a layer of green palm fronds was spread over the coals and the fish, wrapped first in cloth then layers of wet sacking, were laid on top. The whole thing was then piled over with sand and left.

While it was cooking the beach table was loaded with mouth-watering salads and several varieties of 'Salomon pudding', a trifle-like concoction with a flexible recipe based more on the contents of the cupboard than any culinary considerations. Interest quickened as the time to remove the sand approached. Experienced eyes had judged the weight of the fish and the condition of the coals and a very exact cooking time decreed.

At the precise moment, the sand was shovelled aside, the sacking carefully unwrapped and the cloth-covered fish reverently lifted out and transferred to where they would be served. Perfection. Three different flavours, three different textures and every scrap tender and juicy.

After we'd all eaten our fill, which hardly dented the mountain of food, we settled down to a lazy afternoon of swapping stories, quick repartee and laughter. Two or three hammocks had been put up round the clearing and several beach chairs added to the comfort, while the sun shone from a clear blue sky. Liz entertained with some evocative and sentimental songs, beautifully sung and accompanied by her own guitar, and Russell followed suit with some not quite so sentimental songs to set the tone for the evening's revelries.

Several people had dinghied across the atoll from other islands to join in the festivities but had to leave early to navigate back through the coral in daylight. Before departing, one of these couples gave us an envelope with strict instructions not to say a word. We later found it to contain a number of high denomination currency notes, more than enough to cover the cost of the materials being brought to Salomon. Extraordinary generosity, even by the standards set by these extraordinary people.

Then, as darkness came and oil lamps flickered into life, the feasting began in earnest and continued well into the night. By the time the last people went back to their boats there wasn't a scrap of food left, and a prodigious amount of liquid refreshment had gone the same way. On evenings like this we were glad to only have a few yards to walk back to the tent.

Sometimes, though, living beside the communal gathering place and doing our daily cooking in the barbecue fireplace on the beach was a bit double-edged. The company was great but often we couldn't cook our evening meal till everyone else went to bed. We made it a rule not to eat or prepare food by the tent to discourage, or at least not encourage, rats, so the French camp was effectively our kitchen and dining room.

The better aspect was that it was extremely pleasant in the mornings, when the rays of the early sun were broken up by the palms to make sitting round the table comfortable. Jess would come with us and soon found a place that became 'her' spot, but as soon as the dogs came ashore, usually just after breakfast, we had to put her back in the tent. We did try a confrontation to see if they could share the island, and it would probably have worked out if we'd had time to supervise the first few days, but we didn't.

I think it was while the 'Hungi' preparations were in hand that Jeff arrived on his beautifully built little catamaran *Betong*. He had an old school friend, Juan, along with him, taking a short break from his office, so time was particularly precious, but in spite of this the very next day they went over to Anglaise to pick up the last, and most difficult, of the things left there.

Betong had the advantage of only needing a few inches of water to float and had large, comparatively open, spaces on deck. They retrieved the self-steering gear from the bommie and all the heavy gear and fuel drums from the beach, then landed them on Boddam at high tide. In these conditions they could take the boat right up on the sand near the path to the shed and simply pass the stuff down to waiting hands.

A day later I walked into the shed and found Jeff quietly repairing the steering gear. He had stripped the bent parts off and laid them out for inspection and was obviously deep in thought about how to make a workable unit out of it all. It is an auxiliary rudder device with a trim tab servo to operate it and the main stem, which carries both the rudder and the wind vane, had a distinct bow in it. This meant that the bearings were no longer properly aligned and the transfer shaft down the middle was a bit tight.

The rudder and trim tab, originally made by filling steel frames with polyurethane foam and covering them with glass-reinforced plastic, had both been damaged to the extent that the frames, which also carried bearings and operating levers, were bent out of square and the surrounding foam and glass crushed. Two of the three brackets that mounted the whole contraption to the transom had cracked welds as well.

A boat builder by profession, Jeff carried a small stock of glass fibre cloth on *Betong* and, with some resin that survived the sinking and blocks of polyurethane foam cut from a stray fishing float, he did a superb job of patching both the rudder and the tab. How he managed to straighten the frames with the facilities on the island is completely beyond me but, when he finished, everything looked and worked just fine. The stem still had a slight bow in it but the bearings had been eased and were perfectly free. I might also say that his glassfibre work on top of mine was a good illustration of the professional edge.

The only things he couldn't fix were the cracked welds. Not many yachts carry sufficient power generating equipment for welding machines so the options were somewhat limited. I could ask the marines to take the brackets to Diego Garcia next time they came or, probably better, ask the ship that brought them to do it while they were here. However, this decision could safely be left until we knew if the hull repair would be good enough.

When work on the hull reached the stage that little more could be done until the materials arrived, Alan and Clive mounted a great food-gathering expedition. The idea was to catch lots of fish and preserve them by smoking. Sometime in the island's history a smoker had been built in the corner of the shed, from materials obviously garnered from the fallen buildings, and they were anxious to give it a try.

They equipped themselves with heavy hand lines and, as the tide came high enough to let them cross the reef, slipped out to fish the coral drop-off. On their return several hours later beaming faces showed eloquently how successful the first part of the venture had been. They had a dozen fish and a very large head. This giant fish had been fought to the surface but before it could be gaffed a shark had bitten it off cleanly just behind the gills. The body section at the cut was about the same size as a large man's thigh, food for thought for those who like snorkelling outside the reef.

However, that was simply evidence of one that got away and the real task of the day was just starting. All the fish had to be cleaned, cut into suitable strips and mounted on wire hooks for hanging. The smoker was basically a corrugated iron chimney, about a yard square and ten feet high, with a grill set in the top to hang the fish from and an adjustable flap over the top to vary the amount of smoke. The fire box was a forty gallon drum set into the side at ground level and had its own damper for controlling the fire.

One chap had used the device regularly and advised that good hardwood logs gave the best results, but fallen hardwoods are a scarce resource on Boddam and better utilized for grilling. Sprouting coconuts provide equally good smoke and are plentiful, but more difficult to burn, so a combination of the two seemed best. By nightfall all the fish had been turned into neat fillets and hooked up in the smoking zone, and the fire had settled down to a good smoky smoulder.

The trick now was to keep the maximum amount of smoke around the fish, by opening or closing the top flap, and stopping the fire from either going out or flaring up too much by adjusting the damper. There was a sharp learning curve involved here and for a while conditions fluctuated between a roaring fire with no smoke and a spluttering fire with so much smoke you couldn't see across the shed, but once the balance was found it worked a treat. The only thing left to learn was how long to leave it. Six or seven hours was the advice from the veteran, 'But you just have to keep checking it'.

Before turning in Tina and I walked along to see how they were doing and found them in fine spirits. The process was working well and they had a huge pile of coconuts split and ready, and enough logs to keep the fire going. A jug of pineapple wine was ready to hand to ensure that the smoke dried only the fish and not the fishermen, and all was well.

There was still a haze of smoke around in the morning and we were surprised to see Alan's dinghy still at the shore, so we went to see what was happening. The pair of them were not so chirpy now; the fish had taken much longer to cure than they expected and the wine had long since run out. However, all was successfully concluded and they were busy removing the fish from the chimney when we arrived. After a full day fishing in the sun and a full night in the singularly uncomfortable shed they were ready for bed.

Another stroke of good fortune came our way that morning. All the contaminated fuel from *Vespera*'s diesel tank had been transferred into jerry cans and taken ashore as soon as we got to Boddam, and Mark, from *Paquita*, had a simple filter that could remove the water just by pouring it through. He spent most of the day pouring fuel from one drum to another and by the time he had finished very little fuel had been lost. Even the waste came in useful as, after settling for a while in a drum, it was a particularly effective fire lighter. A God-send on rainy days.

Stepping Stone also arrived that day with the first load of material from the Maldives. They had big bags of sand and cement and, of more immediate importance, the reinforcing rods and rolls of tying wire. As soon as these were unloaded work on the hull started again. The parts of the armature exposed in the holes had been pushed, pulled or otherwise forced back into place and the shape was reasonably fair. With this done it was easy to see where new reinforcing was needed but first we had to get some stiffness into it. The primary need here was to build up the broken rib. Most of the steel in the smaller holes would hold its own shape but in the large ones it could be moved by pressing with your fingers, so the rib was vital.

The original was a welded framework of heavy bars and still roughly in place, but several of the bars were broken and the bend could not be straightened. We decided to make up small elements that had the required shape on the outside but fitted snug against the distorted shape on the inside, then wire them into place. A broken door hinge from the island made an excellent bending tool and once we got the hang of things it went quickly.

Doubling the broken stringers was much simpler. A suitable length of reinforcing was cut and wiggled in through the mesh until it lay alongside the broken rod, then loops of tying wire were used to fix the two together. As the job progressed the structure became stiffer and stiffer, but even when everything was done a couple of panels were still a bit wobbly. Here we introduced some extra bars that ran diagonally across the stringers and they took out the last bit of floppiness.

While this was happening some experiments were being done on shore with the cement. Alan was going to do the plastering and needed to find out how dry a mix could be worked into the mesh, how well and when it could be finished, and so on. Humphrey had performed miracles in Gan when he found a construction site whose chief engineer had steered him to a source of cement that would cure in sea water without the need for a membrane and we were all interested to see how this would work.

Clive took some pieces of mesh and folded them back and forth to make good facsimiles of the armature while Alan and Philippa prepared a number of carefully measured cement batches. The first couple of samples were plastered but found to be too wet, so the mesh was cleaned out and drier batches tried until the workability was right.

The next concern was to see if the samples would

harden in the time between tides. The tide tables we'd been studying actually referred to Diego Garcia, a hundred and twenty miles away, but the local tides seemed to be within half an hour of them so they gave us a reasonable indication of what to expect, and when. But the configuration of the atoll appeared to effect the range quite a lot. I had done some measuring, fumbled at some arithmetic and reckoned we would have two hours and forty minutes 'least dry time'.

Two hours and thirty minutes after plastering the samples could be pressed with the fingers without leaving a dent. So far so good, and ten minutes later they were carefully eased off the board they were made on and hung in the water. In fact we hung them from *Vespera*'s life lines to make the test as close to reality as we could. It was not a towering success. One of them dissolved like icing sugar as soon as it touched the water and the other started shedding lumps after a few minutes. Obviously more experimentation was needed.

Foraging on the island produced plenty of clean wire mesh so there were no problems replacing all the damaged stuff. Where the wire was missing altogether we simply tied four layers on each side of the stringers. In other places where some strands had been broken but the general mass was still there we tied a layer or two over both sides to tidy it up, judging how much to add by the extent of the damage.

This meshing was another great communal effort. Sorting out the reinforcing and stringers had been easier with just a few people working at a time, but for this there was a bit more elbow room. In fact, it was a labour-intensive job: one person could cut and trim the mesh to the right shape but he needed an assistant to help him tie it into place.

The ties were short lengths of wire bent in the middle, like oversize hairclips, and you poked them through the mesh, points first, with one point either side of the elements you wanted to tie together, then someone on the other side would twist the ends together with a pair of pliers.

We found it best for several pairs of people to cut and place the mesh, using just a few ties to hold the pieces in position, and to have other pairs following behind to put in the balance of the ties. The final touch, and by far the most painful on the knuckles and fingers, was to cut off the loose ends and poke the sharp twists that were left down inside the armature, using some special tools Jim made from reinforcing rod.

With the benefit of hindsight I think we might have made a mistake here that cost a lot of extra work. *Vespera*'s designer called for the mesh to be tied to the stringers at four-inch spacing, that is at every second rod. Other designers, who specify a different type of mesh, call for ties at two-inch spacing. We decided to go along with the 'two-inch' school of thought, thinking it might add some extra rigidity, and eventually found that, not only did it mean a lot more ties but, combined with the extra layers of mesh, it made forcing the cement through the armature very difficult. However, the structure did feel more rigid before the plastering was done so it was probably worthwhile.

Trial mixes with the cement were continuing. *Brumby* had arrived with the rest of the material and Humphrey was able to contribute a lot to the experiments as a result of his discussions in Gan. Another positive addition was that the tides seemed to be giving us more time than predicted. Anyway a few more samples were made and twenty minutes added to the 'pre-dunking' period and the final formula for the mix emerged.

The ratio of sand to cement, one and a half to one, was easy enough and we earmarked a couple of measuring tins for this purpose. The amount of water was critical and we finished up trimming an empty beer can with a pair of scissors until it held the exact amount. Samples made and hung in the sea after three hours showed no sign of deterioration and twenty-four hours later were very hard.

Bea and Lowell on *Wanago* had a strict schedule that required them to be in Tanzania by a particular date, and one day they came over from their anchorage near the pass specially to offer Sue a lift. Sue knew that whatever happened she wouldn't be leaving Salomon on *Vespera* – even if she floated again and the patches looked sound I was not prepared to put three of my family at risk for the sake of a damaged boat, and this was a tempting offer. It was by far the easiest way for Sue to go as, from Tanzania, she could choose either England or South Africa as her destination. However, she had similar offers from boats leaving later and I think she wanted to stay and see what happened to *Vespera*, so she declined.

In another act of generosity Bea brought over some strong baskets which she gave us to store things in. Spiders and scorpions found their way into anything stored either directly on the ground or on the elevated floor, and were not very pleasant. Far more serious though were the rats. These guys were plentiful and supremely agile, and could wriggle in through the most amazingly small holes. Although the Boddam rats are clean and, as far as we know, free from disease they are voracious eaters and anything not positively defended will be destroyed in no time. These baskets, with heavy lids over them, were a pretty substantial defence.

In fact keeping rats out of our food supply was fundamental to living on Boddam. Any container left improperly sealed overnight would guarantee a visitation by the furry marauders before morning. Even a dusting of flour or sugar round a closed lid invited their attention and it didn't take them long to learn to chew through plastic covers. Consequently we transferred as much of our remaining edibles to glass jars or bottles as we could. Used jam jars and empty gin bottles acquired a previously unimagined status.

Those dry goods that survived had mostly been stored in small plastic bottles and we hadn't carried enough gin to solve the immediate problem. Fortunately all the boats that had even minimal available space took as many of those plastic bottles as possible and stowed them out of harm's way for us. That we had any stores to do this with handsomely repaid all Tina's and Sue's earlier fiddling with funnel and chopsticks filling the small bottles, as the goods kept in bulk hadn't fared nearly as well.

Our flour, for example, had been stored in either large screw-topped barrels, holding about fifty pounds each, or in the sacks it came from the mill in. Water had got into everything to a greater or lesser extent and the sacks were just great gooey globs that got no further than the beach on Anglaise. The barrels were a bit better. On opening them we found a sticky paste, about the same consistency as the stuff we used for gluing pictures into scrap books as kids, but by probing carefully we learned it was confined to the tops. Sue exercised great patience and lifted out all the paste with a spoon, managing to retrieve nearly half a barrel of good flour.

This led to some experimental bread-making. The galley stove was in the shed along with all the gas bottles, but salt water had gummed up the controls and none of the burners worked, so baking had to be done in the 'Boddam bakery'. Here again we were lucky. Several of the ladies had already tackled this brute and learned most of its less desirable tricks, and how to cope with them, and gladly passed on their knowledge. We knew that, used properly, it could produce superb bread as we'd been grateful recipients of many earlier efforts.

The oven is supremely simple. Built of ordinary bricks, it consists of a tunnel about two feet wide by the same high and three feet long. One end is closed off by more bricks and the other is open. There is no chimney. On each side of the tunnel there's a row of bricks laid on the floor to make ledges on which the baking trays sit. The finishing touch is a sheet of corrugated iron that can be propped over the open end. To use the oven, you light a fire inside, let it burn to coals, put your bread in and close it up until it is done.

Sue mastered the art quite quickly but Tina took longer. It called for a fine balance between the time the bread started rising, the time the fire was lit and how much wood was used. Every time they thought they had it right something would change; the temperature would slow the dough rising or the wood would be too damp to burn properly, but between them they devised some recipes forgiving enough to make the most of what we had.

One day, while a trial bake was under way, I walked up to see how it was working out and bumped into Franco on the way. He was returning from the 'yacht club' but asked me to accompany him there as he had something to show me. The 'yacht club' is the best preserved of all the abandoned buildings and is basically weatherproof, having a good roof and solid floor.

When I walked in I found all our charts neatly spread out to dry. The crew of *La Bamba* had been tending them carefully, turning them over if they started to curl and packing them away when they were dry enough. The last time I'd seen them they had been in soggy wet piles and just teasing them apart was a 'tour de force'. Now here they all were almost entirely restored.

Closer to the boat, things were not going so smoothly. The consensus was that the basic technical problem of repairing the hull was solved and the job now just had to be done. Consensus is, sadly, the correct term to use as 'getting the job done' had become top of the agenda for the Salomon politicians and the whole scenario had degenerated into an ineffective multi-party democracy.

As soon as I realized that politics were inevitable I tried every trick I could think of to avoid getting involved; as beneficiary of the goodwill that was the subject under debate I was in an impossible position, but none of my tricks worked. Of course the nature of a democratic anything is that some people with carefully considered views get overridden, which is hard enough to accept when the topic is self-serving but becomes extremely difficult when it concerns a life-or-death arrangement for others. And an ocean passage in an unsound boat is very much a life-or-death affair. Consequently, to use the same terminology, we found ourselves being lobbied on all fronts.

We were at our most vulnerable when any of us found ourselves alone. Well-wishers would choose such times to advance their views as it was then that it caused the least offence to others, and quite rightly so, but I was made sharply aware of my lack of diplomatic skill as I tried to deflect those opinions I actively disagreed with while acknowledging the spirit in which they were meant.

One thing it did do, though, through the family discussions it generated, was confirm our decision: if *Vespera* floated again that was fine; if she didn't, that was also fine as it would have proved the point. Best of all would be if the repairs eventually proved sound, but that was in the lap of the Gods. As things stood she certainly wasn't worth losing friends over.

With this in mind all I could contribute was mediation, and keeping the peace rather than any other consideration was the major criterion. Fortunately most of the views were reasonably close to my own, the only serious difference being that I prefer to do things in their own good time and think them through carefully on the way, whereas the general feeling was 'the more the merrier and let's get it done now'. As it happened, tides and the change in monsoon bringing onshore winds enforced the latter, so my view came to nought anyway.

The differences of opinion led to a certain amount of polarization, made more intense by the diversity of characters, and was at its most hurtful when it flared between old friends. It became obvious that people were choosing their times to come and help, when those with differing views were not there.

On reflection this was the hardest part of the whole episode. Boddam had become as constricting as the smallest prison on earth with nowhere to escape to. Whatever happened I was going to end up hurting some of the people who were being so generous, and deep down I was convinced it was over a lost cause. Many times I wished for the means to blow *Vespera*'s remains to bits and solve the problem for good. I bitterly regretted changing my mind about leaving her on the reef.

If I look hard enough for a silver lining though I can see one in the continuous change-around of people coming to help. This made sure I was always busy and that repair work progressed. Certainly it was the moral pressure of willing helpers working on my problem that stopped me simply packing it all in. At the end of each day I was more grateful than ever to have old and trusted friends around.

Anyway, Easter was approaching and with it the spring tides that would allow access to the lower holes. The steelwork in the higher ones was complete and the edge preparations had worked out much better than I expected.

Essentially all that had to be done was repeat the process lower down as soon as the water would let us. I don't know whose sense of humour guides such things but the water receded so early on Easter Saturday that by five o'clock in the morning there was a full team at work. By lunchtime the water was back but the preparations were finished and plastering could begin.

A master plan had been drawn up to enable this to be

done in the minimum amount of time so as to give the plaster the longest possible set before being submerged. Each individual task had been broken down to its smallest parts and those parts allocated to individual people. My afternoon was spent scratching around making sure that all the things we needed would be ready: measuring cups and sieves for the sand and cement, buckets and stirring sticks for the mixers, flat boards to carry the mortar, pots and brushes for the epoxy, gas and matches for the heating torch, etc. It seemed a very long list for such a simple job.

By early evening, when the water was down again, the weather was being so kind we decided to plaster a couple of the smaller and easier holes and take the opportunity to go through the procedure to make sure it was viable before committing ourselves to the bigger patches.

First we cleaned the mesh with acid to remove any surface rust and washed it down with fresh water. Then we dried the cement edges by brushing methylated spirits on them to absorb the water, then heating with a small flame to evaporate it all. Epoxy resin was then brushed onto the dry edges and, before that cured, the mortar worked into the mesh from inside and finished off by the plasterer outside.

These first holes went very easily. Philippa organized the mixing and Clive the cleaning and drying, then I worked the mortar into the mesh and Alan finished them off. It was completely dark before we finished and Alan put the final touches to his work by the light of an oil lamp, but altogether it was a most encouraging start and boded well for the morning.

During the night I discovered the real meaning of the civil engineer's expression 'keep the plaster damp until fully cured'. The curing time is twenty-eight days, so for four weeks, or until she floated, the patches had to be sloshed over with buckets of water; every half-hour in the heat of the day but mercifully only at two- or three-hour intervals at night.

Easter Sunday was another big day. The early morning tide was one of the best available, though an onshore breeze delayed it somewhat, and first light saw everybody standing by their respective tools. The little waves brought in by the breeze tried everyone's patience as we waited for the first hole to clear and enthusiasm was bubbling by the time we could start.

Very soon it became obvious we'd fallen into another trap. What had been easy with a few people the night before was almost impossible with so many hands today. In our quest to make the best of the available time we had hopelessly over-organized things. Interested onlookers, who also wanted to help, exacerbated the problem and chaos reigned. In the end the fact that anything got done at all is testament to each individual's good sense.

Quite apart from the milling throng we encountered a couple of problems that had to be sorted out against the clock. Jim discovered a patch in the mesh that hadn't been finished as well as it should, fortunately before it was plastered over, and an emergency team had to make it good quickly. Much harder to resolve was the previously mentioned difficulty of forcing the mortar through the extra steelwork.

Two conflicting requirements met head on here. We'd learned by experiment that the mortar mix had to be very dry, but at the appropriate dryness you had to push so hard to work it into the tightly clamped mesh that the larger panels flexed as you worked on them. Alan had developed a technique of plastering round the edges first, to ensure a good joint, then working steadily across the panel to complete it, but the flexing put a distinct limit to the size of hole that could be patched this way.

While we were busy with the limiting patch we discussed what to do about the remaining two holes. One was roughly the same size but lower down, and it was already too late to attempt it during this tide. The other was almost twice the size and consequently less rigid. We decided to tackle the large one in two parts: today we would start at the top and work downwards until we felt we couldn't go any further, then we would finish it off with the other outstanding patch on another day.

This was far from ideal, but then repairing a boat on the beach of a remote atoll was not exactly ideal in the first place and it was the best we could do. Before we gathered up the tools for cleaning we had half the large hole plastered and the remaining area was no larger than ones already done, so things looked good.

However this view was not unanimous. Some people thought the day's achievement first class, most considered it a pretty good shot given the circumstances and that it had been successful, while the chap who had originally wanted to control the operation was so disappointed he disassociated himself from it all. I thought it had gone quite well.

The weather wasn't going to let us get away with things so easily. The monsoon change-over was well underway and the winds were variable and unpredictable. The onshore breeze of the morning had died away to nothing while we were working but as the tide started to flood it came back, not with any strength but enough to bring back the wavelets that hassled us earlier. Now instead of the patches being gently submerged they were subjected to the breaking of sloppy little ripples, only three or four inches high but enough to wash away some mortar.

There was nothing that could be done about it now. We could only carry on wetting down the unaffected plaster and wait for next morning. When we could next inspect things properly we found that a small patch had also failed from water seeping into the mortar from the ballast encasement inside. There was no ready solution to this as the encasement couldn't be drained, at least not until the hull was sound when it could be pumped out.

Our first attempt at making good the failures was simply to dry the affected spots, paint them with a slurry of neat cement and plaster over them again. This was the first job tackled on Easter Monday and while Alan and I were busy with it Clive acid-washed and rinsed the edges of the last holes. He found some evidence that the weeping problem could arise there as well so we decided to call a halt while we watched to see if the slurry would hold up. This was a major decision as that day's tide was the last usable one for a fortnight and the monsoon winds would only increase. However, it seemed pointless to waste valuable material if it looked as though the job would fail.

It was something of a relief to see that the slurry and mortar fix worked perfectly well on the patch that had simply washed away, but the failure caused by weeping was more troublesome. Commercial remedies are available to cure this problem but on Boddam all we had was sand and cement and it took plenty of trial and error before we found out how to do it. Then, as soon as the tides allowed, the first of these failures was repaired and we'd learned how to tackle the others.

But I'm getting ahead of myself. Easter, and the days immediately after, was an action packed time on many fronts. There is a large cross by the jetty, erected by missionaries in nineteen hundred and thirteen, and it's traditional for visiting yachts to paint it each Easter Sunday. Sue 'volunteered' the younger folk to help and they trimmed away the undergrowth around it and painted it with the help of a makeshift ladder.

When they finished she rewarded them with homemade Easter eggs. She'd taken some clean coconut shells, painted bright patterns on them and filled them with chocolate sweets that had survived. This gesture backfired a little as Heidi was the only one of the group who celebrated Easter. Two of the others were Jewish and a third came from an atheist family. However, they all enjoyed the chocolates.

Russell had been busy all this time and, in addition to fixing the body of my favourite camera, had already stripped another, made a tape cleaning device out of Sue's ruined cassette player and got the main engine's starter motor working. John soon had that mounted on the engine and, as *Vespera*'s batteries were still being charged, brought along the batteries from *Kekeni* to try it.

Everything else was ready to go. The manifolds and exhaust pipe were on, a cooling system had been rigged up with a hose drawing water from a bucket and a plastic bottle served as a fuel tank. I was most impressed when, once the electrical connections were good, the engine started almost immediately. As soon as she'd blown the gunk out of her cylinders she settled down to a good healthy burble.

We let her run for twenty minutes to warm up and dry out the last vestiges of moisture, then stopped her to change the oil. We did this three times, using previously discarded oil, to flush out any salt that might have been left inside, but not long after the third change she kicked a couple of times, puffed out a spurt of white smoke and stopped. Long, blank faces all round as we tried to find out what had happened.

After a fairly thorough examination during which we found nothing – everything turned freely and there was plenty of fuel, water and oil – we fired her up and she started without hesitation. A minute or so later though she stopped again, this time as though she really meant it. At his stage it was quite late in the day and an 'internal' examination was deferred until tomorrow.

A sorry sight greeted us when we took the crankcase off next morning. In spite of all the oil changes the sump was full of spongy metallic waste and the oil pump's delivery tube was missing. In the time before the sea water was drained out and the engine filled up with oil an aluminium alloy casting had corroded away to nothing, possibly, or probably, aggravated by the fact that the batteries were still connected when she sank.

Further investigation showed that the big end bearing for the first cylinder had been destroyed and the main bearings either side of it had over-heated, but that seemed to be the extent of it. John spent a long time cleaning the crankshaft journals before declaring them fit for further service. The main bearing shells were not too badly damaged and could be used for a single voyage, but the number one big end bearing had melted. Fortunately for morale this discovery coincided with finding the solution to the failing cement so we had something to ease the disappointment.

I think it was the day after this that we suffered the worst confrontation of the political crisis. It began when the only couple really at odds with my way of thinking came ashore while we were having breakfast. My heart wanted to burst as even the simple morning pleasantries were forced, which was ridiculous given the situation, and the contention couldn't be put off for long.

It was basically still the same problem. The chap was convinced that the repair of the hull would be done better if he was in charge, and I was, …am, equally convinced that to put anyone 'in charge' was just plain wrong. It was a most acrimonious exchange, with the ladies taking the weight of it again, and in spite of a great deal of effort all round I feel I lost a friend that day. *Vespera* will never repay that cost.

Sue was particularly thoughtful now, even though she was hurting as much as we were. She gathered up our nicest clothes and some of Tina's toiletries and put them ready by the shower, packed a special picnic lunch and loaded it into the dinghy and, as soon as we returned from our last peace mission, bundled us off to the other end of the atoll. During our respite we seriously discussed the possibility of asking for a naval demolition party to remove the wreck.

We also discussed our other options and the only specific action common to them all was to make whatever arrangements we could to get our surviving possessions back to Durban. We would carry on from day to day taking what ever luck came our way, but getting our things away would be a positive move. So, with today's decision made, we enjoyed a friendly visit with *Cremona* off Ile Takamaka before heading over to Ile Du Sel for lunch.

The radios were busy at net time and once more we were on the receiving end of goodwill that defies description. David on the yacht *Waiari*, presently at anchor in Lumut, Malaysia, had already been to Sitiawan, located and bought a set of bearings and despatched them to us via Diego Garcia. How could we be so disloyal to these fine people as to even think of leaving without *Vespera*. Here was another person, who didn't know us from a bar of soap, putting down hard cash that he wouldn't see returned until Claire and Humphrey, who had agreed to take it back for us, arrived in Malaysia some months hence.

Less welcome tidings came from the Maldives. Ted had died shortly after returning to his boat from the hospital. Word spread around the anchorage quickly and all of us were saddened at the news, but memories of Ted's character brushed some of the sadness away. None of us had known him for long but his mannerisms and approach to life were distinctive and we felt a wake would be more in keeping than a mourning. He had an emotional farewell that night.

Soon the tide was right again for another go at the holes. We had learned a lot from the frantic activity of the previous effort and this time fewer people made things much easier. The sky was rather grey on the chosen morning but it started calm and gentle, which was a good sign. Plastering the largest hole in two goes paid off handsomely as with half of it already done the whole thing was more rigid and easier to work with.

And thank goodness too as this second part was in the spot under the chart table that caused so much discomfort during the preparations.

Round the boat the atmosphere was full of excitement. All the holes on the starboard side had been repaired and *Vespera* was looking like a boat again. She wasn't quite as fair as she was before but she presented a fine picture sitting there on the beach. The sun had driven away the grey and a blue sky added to the cheeriness, but it was the smiles on everyone's faces that made it.

Until the new mortar took its initial set, wetting down the surrounding patches called for some ingenuity. Any excess water that ran over the new surface put it at risk, but not wetting the adjacent areas put them equally at risk. Sue overcame this by wiping the hardened patches with a sponge and mopping up any run-off with a towel. In the heat of the sun this was a full time job, like painting the Forth bridge, and we left her to it while we cleaned up and went for lunch.

The southeasterly wind must have been waiting in the wings for the moment its entrance would have the most dramatic effect. On our return to the beach we found a brisk breeze stirring the water and a distinct swell visible under the ripples. Nothing much, just enough to give you an occasional splash if you motored a dinghy against it, but it was a singularly unwelcome sight as the water level approached the patches.

We tried a number of ploys to defeat this onslaught. Sheets of corrugated asbestos from the island were propped in strategic places as breakwaters and were quite effective at first as the waves would expend their energy breaking on the sheets, leaving a harmless swell to run along the plaster. However as the water got deeper the impacts increased in strength and, no matter what we did, kept knocking the breakwaters down.

The only thing for it was to hold each sheet in place by physical strength, but even with one end jammed in the sand and the other hard against the hull the surge would sometimes knock it from your hands. People took it in turns to crouch in the rising water and wrestle with the sheets but it was heavy work and the spray made it chilly. Sue performed a feat of endurance by hanging on until the waves were above the new plaster, finishing the day exhausted and blue with cold.

Now the 'wetting down' era started in earnest. The way the boat sat on the beach meant the patches caught the full strength of the sun until mid-day, and until then you could almost watch the surfaces drying. Tina and Sue hung blankets over the vital spots and each time they wet the boat they gave them a good splashing as well. Evaporation from the thick cloth tended to keep the temperature down and the air directly over the new concrete a bit more humid.

But waves and wind tore the blankets to shreds over the next few days, steadily reducing the washing line appearance to something more like a rag-and-bone man's cart. As they tore, the ladies lashed the pieces together again, or suspended them individually in the best places, until the bits were too small to be effective, but by then the back of the job had been broken.

The very best part of this period was that, having run their course, the politics went the way all politics ought to go and old friendships could be seen flowering again. The evening gatherings at the French camp took on their old cheerfulness and simple enjoyment of the unique environment was back in vogue. It was an enormous relief to see people drifting back to doing those things they came to Salomon for.

Arts and crafts came very much to the fore. In addition to the musicians, who'd been joined by a fine harmonica player, the little community boasted two artists who specialized in pen and ink drawings, a painter who performed magic with water colours and a couple of ladies who discovered their talent for creating cartoons. Another lady had the knack of weaving baskets and mats from palm fronds.

Cooking was another talent exercised to the full. The Boddam oven was, at best, a cantankerous ally when it came to the family bake but the fancy loaves and rolls, not to mention meat pies and fruit cakes, were proof enough that the pioneer spirit lives. Sue developed the 'Castaway cookie' to a high degree and could transform half a dozen coconuts, with a few spoonsful of flour and precious little else, into a tray of excellent biscuits that would provide us with snacks for a week. Well, sometimes, if they were particularly good, they only lasted a day.

We split the boat wetting duty in such a way that Tina and Sue did it during the days and I did it at night. The only snag we had to contend with was a group of sting rays that took a liking to the new concrete reef on their beach. They were not very big, certainly not more than a couple of feet across, but they could disguise themselves extremely well. To start with they were the same colour as the sand and, when they settled down to lie in wait for whatever it is they lie in wait for, they had a way of spreading sand over their backs to make them all but impossible to see. The only tell-tales, usually, were their long, straight tails which they either couldn't or wouldn't hide.

These rays became such a menace that, even though the water was shallow enough to wade out to *Vespera*, we took to going backwards and forwards in the dinghy. Then, to make life more interesting, the rays took to using the dinghy as extra camouflage and it was always worthwhile checking for tails before wading the couple of paces necessary to get in.

One moonless evening I took my regular stroll from the camp, shone a torch around the dinghy – no rays – and poled my way out to the boat. I threw a few buckets of water over the outside and stepped aboard to repeat the process inside. It was pretty dark but long familiarity made the job easy, then I poled back ashore, tied up to *Vespera*'s bow line and stepped into the shallow water; straight onto the back of a ray.

I wish I had a film of my leap back into the dinghy; I would use it to show off to my children. Even in the dinghy I was concerned as those tails are quite long enough to reach over the side. I found the torch and shone it around then, seeing nothing, stepped out – straight on it again. But this time I was looking where I put my feet and there were no tails to be seen. My ray was a piece of foam cushion from *Vespera* that had washed up the beach and been buried in the sand. My heart was still racing when I got back to the tent and all Tina could do was laugh.

To some extent I got my own back by taking a couple of fishing trips outside the atoll. It's always safer to take two dinghies when you venture out to sea and for the first trip Clive went in one while I went in another with Alan, and got a lesson from a master. We trailed a lure over the reef on the way out and picked up a small bait fish before making our way round to the lee of Boddam.

Within minutes Alan had a lovely snapper and I followed suit shortly after. Another one came, followed by a fine peacock cod, then Alan's bait attracted something that whipped his line away at great speed, burning through his glove before eventually breaking: strong indication that sharks had taken an interest and we both changed to heavier tackle.

The baits had scarcely hit the water when the first one struck and a couple of minutes of give and take with the line brought a small black-tip aboard. All this activity whetted Clive's curiosity and he abandoned his trolling for tuna to come and join the fun. Soon a second shark came, this time to my line, and I was glad of Alan's expertise at dealing with them. He has a way of quelling them that's both humane and quick, and retrieving your tackle from a shark that stays still is very different from doing so with one that actively doesn't want you to.

From there we let the boats drift along the reef, hoping to catch one of the big coral trout that lurk there. Clive prefers a more deliberate approach to his fishing and likes to seek out the most likely spot before setting a bait. Consequently he happened to be leaning far over the side of his dinghy, with a diving mask clamped to his face, when Alan hooked a beauty.

Now fishing is not usually a spectator sport. It's not often you get to witness an heroic battle and get a live commentary from the underwater world at the same time, but here I had a ringside seat and all the makings of a spectacle. Alan was working hard, heaving in line as the fish yielded and gradually giving it back when the big pulls came. Every now and then Clive would raise his face from the water, like a turtle coming up for air, and shout "Hold him, he's going for the coral", or "Look out he's snagged the line". Whether these exhortations had any real effect on the struggle I couldn't tell, but all too soon the cry came "Quick, quick, there's a big shark circling".

Well, big man as he is, Alan couldn't do much about the 'Quick, quick'. It was a very strong fish he was fighting and it was getting a lot of encouragement from Mister Shark. "Hurry now, it's closing in". Snap. All of a sudden the line was hanging lifeless over the side. A unanimous groan escaped and all that came up was another head. Never mind, a small chunk of that head used as bait caught a fine snapper that the sharks didn't get and it was a real pleasure to contribute a fish rather than accepting them all the time.

Even while I was off enjoying myself our friends continued working on our things. Ian stripped and cleaned Tina's sewing machine and, although some of the protective surfaces had suffered a bit, all the parts except the shuttle, which was too rusted, were in working order again. At the same time John manufactured a replacement delivery tube for the oil pump.

This was a work of art equal of any of the superb drawings and paintings being done. The only part of the original that still existed was a short pipe that fitted inside a bore in the block, which wasn't much but it provided a clue to what was missing and gave an idea of dimensions. We could see from the surrounding bits that the new part would have to support the pump as well as contain the oil, so the design was quite important.

I didn't see the work in any of its intermediate stages but the construction principle was borrowed from *Vespera*'s hull. An armature of heavy steel wires provided the basic support, a few layers of finer wires added some toughness and a moulding of epoxy putty gave it the required shape. It was a big event when I was handed a complete, working, pump with all the flanges and fittings in the right places and ready to be fitted.

Jess wasn't enjoying the extra activity round the camp that came with the relative freedom from working on the boat. She was still very nervous and didn't like being confined to the tent when she could hear so many interesting sounds, but then she seemed even more afraid in the big wide world outside. Her morning walk to sit with us at the French camp was always a mixture of enthusiastic escape and hesitant advance.

Nevertheless one evening it was all too much for her. Maybe a crab had scrabbled at the fly-sheet or a rat rustled some leaves nearby, but whatever happened had lifted curiosity above caution and she'd ripped a hole in the door flap and gone. Under more normal circumstances this would have meant little more than irritation at the damage to the tent, but we were anxious about our jumpy little friend.

By the time we discovered she was missing the dogs were back aboard the boats so we didn't have to worry about them and our only real fear was that she would get lost. We called a few times and rattled her food bowl without any response so started a more vigorous search. The tangle of fallen palm fronds made excellent camouflage and our chances of catching sight of her were thin, but we thought if we wandered round the more accessible places and called she would probably come back.

Darkness came suddenly, as it does in the tropics, and we still hadn't found her. We collected torches from the camp and continued looking but it was hopeless. Our evening meal was a hapless affair as we were too concerned to do it justice and I spent most of it arguing the case that her instinct would take over and she would appear for her food at breakfast time, just as she always used to.

I managed to persuade Tina that this idea was reasonable, but Sue wouldn't be convinced. As soon as she'd eaten she set off into the night, calling and calling, but there was no reaction. Tina and I packed up the kitchen things ready to return to the tent and could still hear Sue in the distance, crashing through the undergrowth and endlessly calling. When we'd finished we noticed a difference in the sounds and realized there was no more crashing. Sue was obviously on a clear path and her voice sounded nearer so she'd probably come to the same conclusion as us.

Then, 'Here she is, here she is'. Jubilant cries from the

darkness. Tina and I grabbed torches and set off towards the sound and found the pair of them barely fifty yards away. Sue had seen her in the torchlight, prowling along the path heavily traumatized. Her eyes were glazed and unseeing and she was panting with fear. At first she was unapproachable, like any frightened animal, but once she recognized the voices behind the lights Sue was able to pick her up and comfort her.

This escapade didn't do much to change her attitude to being kept in the tent and the hole she'd torn in the door made keeping her in trickier. We tried to plan the days such that one of us would be nearby at all times, and this was quite a burden for the ladies. Luckily for us, if we all needed to be away at the same time, as often happened, Heidi would come and cat-sit.

During this interlude, while we waited for the cement to harden, I had plenty of time to think about how to tackle a hole on the port side. The boat was lying right on it at the moment so the first task was to stand her up straight to let us get at it. We also needed drying time between the tides again so it would have to be done at springs. Alright so far, but how could we cure it? Hauling her upright could be done with anchors and ropes to the rigging, as before, but it didn't seem very safe to leave her like that for a month.

However, the first twenty-four hours is the most important curing period and at the end of it the cement should have attained seventy percent of its final strength. I was going to gamble on it being enough. If the boat could be flooded by the tide, so there was no pressure difference across the patch for a full day, then it should be strong enough to float. Furthermore, once the initial set had taken place we could give it some extra support from inside using a prop with a sandbag to spread the load.

The plan was to use *Vespera*'s own buoyancy to do the work of standing her up and, with all the other holes repaired, we only needed to wedge a decent temporary patch in place and pump out the last of the water at low tide, and she ought to come upright on her own. We put a good patch on, took one of the now reasonably charged batteries and the bilge pump aboard and, as the tide went down, closed the sea cocks and started to pump. *Vespera*'s bilge pump alone moves five tons or more of water in an hour and it didn't have to run too long.

Once she was dry she could be left to her own devices for an hour or two and we used that time to make sure the ropes to the rigging were properly secured. I watched with great interest while the tide came up as I'd never had the courage to careen *Vespera* before and was looking forward to seeing at what point she would start to float. It wouldn't be a real test, of course, as she would normally be a few tons heavier than now, but even so…

The water was just a few inches short of the deck when she bounced for the first time, so I still don't know if she could be safely beached with all her gear and a full cruising load, but it certainly worked fine here. Slowly she stood up and all we had to do was adjust the lines as she went, giving a bit here and taking a bit there until everything looked right. At this point we opened the sea cocks again and took off the patch to make sure she sat down hard on her keel.

We wanted – no, needed – to plaster at the first opportunity and that was due at five-thirty next morning. This meant that breaking out the hole, wiring in some mesh and preparing the edges had to be done today, and part of the same humorist's law that prescribes pre-dawn starts has its corollary in the evenings, so it wasn't until half an hour before dark that we could start to swing a hammer.

Alan took the inside job, and to reach the spot he had to kneel in the water under the saloon table with his head and shoulders in the locker where the hole was. I sat in the sand under the turn of the bilge with the water lapping at my chin and my face hard up against the hull to get at the other side. I don't know which of us was the more uncomfortable but I remember thinking that I'd been given jobs as an apprentice that I enjoyed more, and that's saying something.

Fortunately it turned out to be a smaller hole than we thought and the armature was still in good condition. An oil lamp and underwater torch gave enough light to see to finish the job and a couple of hours later we were drying out with a cup of tea round a fire in the 'watch your head' club (a ruined building with a partial 'split level' roof, one end of which had beams low enough to bump your head on every time you walked through it). The fire was particularly welcome as a fresh onshore breeze was blowing and it had started to rain. Not a promising omen.

But the next day started well. Wind and rain had both stopped and the water was calm, allowing us to plaster the patch with no difficulty, the job being done and the tools cleaned and put away before breakfast. High tide the following afternoon was the highest expected for a month and the last chance to get off the beach before the on-shore monsoon set, and it looked as if we might just meet its deadline.

We spent a good part of the day swimming in the lagoon looking for a good place to anchor *Vespera* if she floated. Better still would be to find a large coral head she could be chained to as, without an engine and with so many reefs around, she would be helpless if a similar squall occurred. It was a pretty hopeless quest. There is only really room for four or five boats to lie off Boddam in safety, and there were seventeen boats here already.

Ian was more than generous over this. *Cruise* was still chained to the same rock they had returned to after towing the dinghies to Anglaise, and this rock was not only the safest mooring in the lagoon, it was also closest to the beach, so it was a highly sought-after position. Anyway he said he'd been toying with the idea of taking *Cruise* to Peros Banhos for a couple of weeks and had decided to go now so we could use his spot.

The big day came and Tina took first wetting-down duty. She came back, with worry written all over her face, to tell me that *Vespera* was leaning over and all the weight was being held by the rope to the masthead. The tide still had three hours to fall and the load would increase all that time if we didn't do something about it.

When I got there I found the water level inside higher than the water outside. Obviously the skin fittings were not letting water out as fast as the tide was falling so I started the bilge pump straight away. As the level came down to the level of the sea cocks I closed them off and kept on pumping until the bilge was dry. It didn't cure the tilt but at least it minimized the load.

As the tide bottomed Clive and I walked round to check everything and were a bit concerned at the way the sand had built up on the shelf between *Vespera* and deeper water. It looked as if the keel would have to lift about six inches to clear the hump, and the tidal prediction made that eventuality doubtful. We decided that in any event she would have to be pulled off stern first so that the slope of the keel would allow her to turn, but that did little for the uncertainty about the depth.

Clive suggested we dig a trench along the path she would have to travel, which seemed an easy solution until we tried it. No matter how gently you eased the shovel out of the banked up sand the water washed half its load back into the hole. We took turns at this thankless task until I had to go and make arrangements for the afternoon, and he laboured away for several more hours.

Three o'clock in the afternoon was the best estimate for the time of high tide and we guessed that *Vespera* should float half an hour before that. We were hoping this margin would allow her to float through Clive's channel. We already had lines ashore from both bow and stern and a line out each side from the masthead. By letting fall the halyards the masthead lines could easily be transferred to points on deck so we were confident we could hold her in position until dinghies could tow her away.

Lunchtime was the prompt the weather was waiting for to turn sour and in no time it knocked up a sturdy onshore swell, with white caps showing all over the lagoon. We tried to rationalize the situation by pretending the waves would help break *Vespera* out of the sand, but I don't think anyone believed it.

By two o'clock there was a clutch of dinghies gathered round ready to help with pushing and pulling but, as luck would have it, two of those with bigger engines were out of commission for maintenance. However, there were plenty of smaller ones to take their places.

Ten minutes later the teeth of worry were gnawing at my stomach. *Vespera* should be bouncing by now if she was going to float, but she sat there solid as a rock. We tried alternately tightening and slackening the bow line to see if we could turn her a bit, but no go. Next we pulled as hard as possible on the seaward line to the masthead to try and tip her further over and lift the keel that way.

We winched the rope in until we simply couldn't winch any more but not a tremor. Twenty past two. We needed more pulling power to seaward and all we could think of was to set more anchors with ropes to other winches. *Vespera's* second anchor, with a few feet of chain and a nylon warp, was hurriedly lowered into a dinghy and taken out at a slight angle forward of the beam, where it was set under a solid coral. While this was being done Gary rushed to collect his spare anchor, which he set directly in line with Clive's channel. Half past two.

The forward anchor warp was led to the windlass and the stern one to a sheet winch. The only available rope long enough to reach this anchor was an elderly half-inch polypropylene line, but we didn't think we were strong enough to break it so that was okay. All the seaward lines were hauled up tight, including the one to the masthead, and we were rewarded with a slight rocking. Twenty five to three.

For the next big effort a whole row of dinghies pushed on Vespera's landward side while we took up the slack in the ropes. On the word 'ready' the people at the winches strained and all the outboards hummed at full throttle, but still she stuck. Frederick came zipping across in *Toti's* tender to join the fray and add another fifteen horsepower to the thrust. Twenty to three.

Everyone not needed at the winches got off *Vespera* to lighten the load while Gary and Frederick positioned their dinghies to give the maximum pull along Clive's channel. We locked the windlass with as much tension on the bow anchor as we dared and cleated off the masthead line halyard under the same condition, freeing Mike to help me double-hand the sheet winch. Quarter to three.

Again the cry went up and we sweated the winch round with all our strength. The old half-inch rope was visibly stretching and I was no longer so sure about not being able to break it. Gary and Frederick revved their engines to full power, pulling exactly the way we needed, and the swarm of smaller engines worked just as hard trying to budge the keel out of the sand. With this sustained push *Vespera* trembled and the ropes sang like violin strings, but she still refused to go. It was too late. The tide wouldn't give us so much as another quarter inch and the sand was just too high.

Some of the dinghy drivers backed off their engines in exasperation – all we were doing was wasting fuel. Then Brian from *Born Free* took it into his head to swing from the rope to the masthead to see if he could set *Vespera* rocking. As he climbed high enough for his feet to clear the water and all his weight came to bear we thought it might just work. With a great shout Yoav leapt up to join him on the rope.

Vespera teetered backwards and forwards like a tightrope walker who'd lost his balance and everybody sensed victory. The big engines roared and the smaller ones worried away like angry bees. Water boiled and frothed, brown from the sand churned off the bottom, and the deck shivered under our feet. We gained a quarter turn on the winch but couldn't tell whether it was the boat moving or the rope stretching.

Loud shouts of encouragement could be heard over the engines and *Vespera* shivered again. Another quarter turn on the winch, then another. There was a great burst of activity on the shore as people rushed to ease control lines but I didn't see it. All I could see were the turns of rope creeping in over the stern as we heaved on the winch. She wasn't exactly floating but she was definitely on the move. The big engines seemed to respond to the vocal encouragement and we slid steadily over the sand towards deeper water.

The moment the keel dropped off the shelf and *Vespera* could move freely a huge spontaneous cheer went up and the focus of our efforts changed. Dinghies scurried around changing position ready to tow us to the mooring. As the control lines to shore were let free they had to be gathered up before they could foul propellers. The halyards controlling the masthead lines had to be disengaged and all three anchor lines cast off and got under control. It was five to three.

The scramble to get this finished was every bit as frantic as the fight we'd just won against the clock. This time the enemy was a black squall marching across the lagoon to add its temper to the unpleasant conditions. It was only two hundred yards, maybe less, to the float Ian had left marking the

Île Mapo

Île F

Ja

Vespera on the reef

Vespera on the reef

Taking sailbags off Vespera

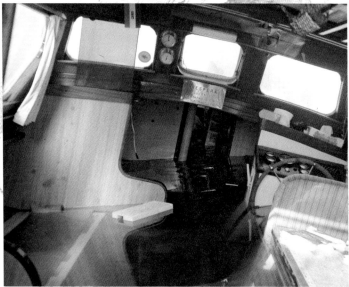

The accomodation awash

Île Map

Landing Vespera's *stores at Anglaise*

Preparing camp

The first camp on Anglaise

The beach from the 'Watch your Head Club'

Peter husking coconuts on Vespera's *anchor*

Tina with home-made baking trays at the Bakery oven

Stormy days

chain but that's a long way to push an unwieldy boat in a rain squall.

As if by magic everything was taken in hand and *Vespera* edged forward: round the shallow reef by the jetty, round the boat moored close by, and straight to the mooring. Fortunately the squall, which arrived as we picked up the chain, lacked the strength of its predecessors and we were able to get our own chain shackled round the coral as a back-up without difficulty.

Vespera was afloat again.

BOOK THREE

ONCE WE'D FINISHED on deck we had a good look around inside. Although refloating was a significant event it couldn't alter the stark realities we still had to face and the prospect was dreadfully depressing. Somehow the boat looked worse now she was back in her own element than she had lying on the beach. Over there she was just an inert reminder of better things, here she was very clearly a wreck.

What had been, an hour or two before, simply the means of gaining access to the hull were transformed back into gaping holes in the interior. The only bit of flooring left was a few square feet in the forepeak and saloon: there were no bunks, there was no galley, the remaining doors stuck out stiffly on broken hinges, the windows were missing, every nook and cranny was filled with smelly sand and, worst of all, the bilge was filling up with water. There was some merit in the argument that it might be wave movement draining puddles from the inside lockers and we could but hope this was the case.

When the current squall passed we made our way ashore to join the throng. Everyone was in high spirits at another huge achievement, one I have to confess that I hadn't thought feasible, and we forgot the sand and water for the time being. Lona had produced trays of delicious doughnuts, the sort of luxury you could kill for in Salomon, for an immediate celebration and before the party broke up we organized for a full scale 'Do' at the French camp that evening.

While Tina put together a bowl of punch for later I went back to the boat to rig up an anchor light so we could find our way when we came to check on things, and found the water in the bilge almost a foot deep. It was very muddy so there was still a case for it being water draining from hidden places, so I simply pumped it out.

At the camp the ladies were steeping canned fruit in rum as the basis for the punch and it augured well for the evening that they were doing it in a five-gallon pail. I asked them to cast a spell on the weather, which was degenerating into continuous rain, but it seemed they were fresh out of magic.

It takes determination to don oilskins and splash your way through a quarter of a mile of rainswept waves for a few hours of merrymaking, but there were some pretty determined partygoers out there. We stoked the fire to make it as inviting as possible and, as soon as the wet logs could be coaxed into burning, the flames lit up the first arrivals as they sloshed their way up from the beach. In spite of the weather the refloating was well and truly celebrated.

During the course of the evening Russell came with me to check how *Vespera* was doing and we found lots of water in the bilge again. Some, at least, was rainwater, which was pouring in through the cockpit where the boards were missing, but we had no way of telling if that could account for all of it. We inspected the patches, particularly the new one, and as far as we could see everything was fine. All the surfaces were damp from the endless wetting down and the supporting sandbag was dribbling a bit but no more than we would have expected from its soaking.

It was pointless delving any further while it was dark so, having pumped out again, we returned to the party. With a glass of punch in my hand it was easier to ignore the niggling worries, but when everyone went home Tina and I decided to stay on the boat so we could pump out when necessary. Sue would stay in the tent to look after Jess.

The rain was still coming down in torrents as we climbed aboard and the prospects for the next few hours were bleak. Tina wrapped her oilskins a bit tighter around herself and huddled in a corner of the cockpit with a coil of rope as a cushion. There was just enough panelling left of one of the forepeak bunks for me to sit on and I wedged myself in there, also with a coil of rope to lean against.

Judging by the amount of water that had come in and the amount of time since it was last pumped we thought it best to wake up every two hours to check and, on the understanding that she is the lighter sleeper, Tina took the alarm clock. This was silly really as both of us sat in the dark in our own ends of the boat waiting for the 'beep' and I don't think either of us slept a wink.

Our yardstick to indicate when we needed to pump was the height of the pump itself. When it disappeared under the water we turned it on until it couldn't pick up any more. Each time it filled I tasted the water and it was always brack, but that information didn't answer any of my questions. Once during the night, when it wasn't actually raining, we did our check and the level was lower than we'd become used to. Taking that as a promising sign we decided to leave pumping for another hour to see what happened. However it soon started raining again and at the end of that hour it was deeper than ever.

We went ashore in the morning with the miserable prospect of trying to light a fire in the wet, only to find Sue had already made a pot of tea and breakfast was cooking. That brightened things immediately and as soon as we'd eaten we crashed into the tent for some sleep, which brightened them even more. The weather didn't improve though, the wind stayed at twenty knots or more and the rain played tunes in the keys of 'downpour flat' or 'shower sharp ' on the roof of the tent all day.

Until the rain stopped there was little point in doing anything more than regular pumping. We did search out the locker lids to complete the forepeak bunks though, and took a couple of thin cushions to the boat to make the nights more comfortable. The ladies had spent weeks washing and drying cushions and the original forepeak mattresses had survived complete, but the boat was so wet and smelly we didn't want to put them in yet.

That night the rain stopped temporarily and an hour later we pumped out. All the rainwater that had collected should have drained into the bilge by now so we should be able to verify that the repairs were sound. It was bitterly disappointing to see the water still rising and in less than three hours it was over the pump again, and now it tasted strongly of salt. The patches looked good so there had to be a hole we'd missed.

However life had to go on and to make things a bit more liveable we searched out the windows and put them back in place, temporarily at first as we had just enough sealant to do the job once and it needed a cool, dry day to work properly, and the difference they made was dramatic. Without the rain driving in there was a distinct 'inside' to take shelter in and it felt a lot more like a boat.

Although it was like acting out a sick joke to mount solar panels in the pouring rain, this job had a high priority as we needed the power for the bilge pump as well as for lighting. The wires from the solar panel terminals on top of the cockpit canopy to the battery compartment had been cut in the rush to get everything off, a fate shared by a lot of the wiring, and were now too short. For the moment we simply pulled them through far enough to make connections and plonked the batteries down where the other ends finished up; the battery compartment no longer existed anyway. We could sort that problem out later.

Now it was back to searching for the leak. We were taking in about three hundred gallons a day so the hole had to be quite small. Having examined every inch we could see without finding any clues we had to accept that more of the floor had to be removed. The water was building up in puddles on top of the ballast encasement and draining from there into the bilge, which indicated that the problem was up towards the bow, so the next victim to the woodsaw was the forepeak.

Here we found water trickling backwards from one compartment to the next and, from judicious mopping and watching, concluded that it had to be coming in somewhere between the first and second ribs. A tiny stream appeared to flow from beneath a bearer and some interesting contortions with torches and mirrors allowed us to see the whole suspected area, but we couldn't see the damage.

Some time later, while Clive and I were mulling over this enigma, Hilary called from beside the boat. She'd been snorkelling round the hull looking for evidence on the outside and had found a suspicious bump, which she described as looking like a burst blister in the paint. From her description of the defect's position, one and a half cubits down and three back from the bow, it sounded as though it coincided with the trickle inside.

A quick trip ashore for mask, fins and hammer and it was into the water for a more detailed investigation. I tapped all round the blistered spot to break away the paint and as one large flake fell away it took with it a lump of cement some two inches across and half an inch thick, leaving behind a pocket the same size with almost clean edges. I worried away at those edges with a screwdriver to remove any crumbly bits and was left with a neatly undercut dent. Thank goodness it didn't go right through.

Back on board and towelled down I was amazed to see the leak had stopped. All I could think was that a dislodged particle had been sucked into a pin hole and, temporarily at least, solved the riddle. Several hours later we still had no need to pump out and the problem was reduced to finding a way to repair the hole without putting *Vespera* on the beach again.

With a full-size bunk each and some cushions, plus a jury rigged light to read by and windows to keep out the wind, the next night was positively luxurious. We even rigged a tent arrangement under the forward hatch, which now leaked, to keep our beds dry. Tina and Sue attacked the 'wreck' smell in the morning by swilling buckets of sea water around and brushing the sand and other gunk down into the bilge.

At first there was so much sediment that they shovelled it into buckets to take it out, but after the better part of a day's work the slurry was fine enough to be handled by the bilge pump. This made it much quicker as the pump could remove the waste as fast as they could wash it down. When they finished that evening the worst of it was done and it only needed a good rinse with fresh water.

The surface of the lagoon was much friendlier the following morning and Tina and I thought to dinghy across to Takamaka to meet the people on *Sgothlong*, a yacht that had just arrived from the Maldives. Before leaving we checked the bilge and found, in spite of the hole in the bow still being dry, that we'd taken in some twenty gallons over night. Another disappointment.

However, we decided to go anyway as we were looking forward to meeting these people. Not only had they brought some important supplies for us, and others, but we'd heard how kind they had been to Ted during his stay in Gan. Sue volunteered to swim out to *Vespera* every now and then to pump out if necessary and make sure nothing more serious took us by surprise.

Peter, Wendy and their son Troy greeted us like long lost friends, sat us down with cups of our favourite tea and regaled us with confidence-building stories. They had lived through a similar experience when their boat, also of ferro-cement, suffered a heavy encounter with some rocks off the New Zealand coast. But here they were now, several thousand miles into their cruise, with *Sgothlong* as good as new.

Their repairs had been done professionally, in fact by the same yard that had built the boat, and 'good as new' is the right expression. It was heartening to hear how closely the yard's repair process resembled ours. Of course they had rather different conditions to work with but the basic principle was the same.

Peter listened to my story with great patience and gleefully knocked on the head all my doubts and fears as I voiced them. He seemed almost to enjoy my final tale of woe, told, I'm sure, with the grim tone of despondency, about the pin hole, or holes, that were still leaking. As I stumbled into silence his face broke into a huge grin, one that filled his beard completely, and he told me he had the best news I could hope to hear.

He delved into his tool locker and produced a small tin of magic powder, or so it seemed to me. In truth it was a commercial mortar specially developed to plug holes in leaking concrete water tanks. Another God-send. The instructions on the can said to mix up just as much as could be placed in one go and that it had to be done quickly. You had only three minutes from the moment you added water to the time it set and it had to be in place within the first ninety seconds. That didn't sound too arduous. Then at the end of another fifteen minutes it would be hard enough to chip into shape if necessary.

Peter had used the stuff before and had some extra information to add to these somewhat terse instructions and we sorted out a procedure that ought to work under the sea. This was valuable stuff indeed, in more ways than one, and for the run home we double wrapped it in plastic bags and put the whole package in a bucket with a waterproof lid, just in case.

The trip back to *Vespera* was a much more light hearted affair as fresh, positive, thoughts over-rode the gloom that came with the leaks and, whether it was real or in response to our state of mind, the sky was brighter, the wind a bit less, and the lagoon calmer. Even better, about half way home, while crossing some deeper water, we saw a white flash under the dinghy and stopped to watch an underwater flying display by a young manta ray.

Still in lighter mood we took the rest of the day off and enjoyed a game of Trivial Pursuits with Liz and Russell, which we lost in spite of some uproarious cheating, followed by an evening at a fine disco in the Mediterranean camp. The crew of *La Bamba* had decorated a makeshift bar with palm fronds and rigged a generator for lights and music for their farewell party. The setting was straight from a fairy tale, the company was great and the evening superb. As splendid as any Boddam evening, but strikingly different.

Enthusiasm to try the magic powder overcame my desire for a recuperative lie-in and Clive came over very early next morning to help. To start with we had to borrow a scuba set as the 'one-and-a-half cubits down' put the hole about six inches further than I could reach without putting my face under, and I couldn't hold my breath long enough to let the mix set.

We performed some dress rehearsals against a stop watch to make sure we could do the mixing and placing in the required time and I'm glad we took the trouble. We tried mixing the stuff in my hand while I sat in the dinghy, then getting into the water and putting it in place; but all we gained from this was howls of laughter as getting into the water wearing scuba gear doesn't lend itself to careful husbandry of the magic powder. Next we tried mixing it in my hand while I was already in the water, but the gear is still pretty cumbersome when you're half in and half out of the water.

The best compromise was to tie the breathing apparatus to a rope and suspend it beside the hull ready for use when I got there. It seems an awful fuss for a mere six inches, or thirty seconds, but without it the hole might as well have been on the moon. The next run was done in earnest and we mixed a tablespoon of powder until it heated up, the sign that it was working, sealed it in my hand with a plastic bag and down I went. And learned that the disturbance made by taking the plastic bag off caused the mixture to disintegrate before it could be placed.

A second attempt, using the plastic as a slip sheet instead of a bag, was better but still not entirely successful and we thought it worth trying without any seal other than my fingers. The quantity we were mixing was so small I could envelop it completely in a clenched fist and probably keep the sea water out just as effectively as a plastic bag. This approach worked a treat and three more runs had plugged the hole completely.

The good weather of the previous day had allowed the inside surfaces of the boat to dry quite well, showing up a couple of other spots that were weeping. One was at the point where the log transducer fitted through a new part of the hull and was a result of over-enthusiastic plastering on my part. It had been particularly hard to push the mortar through the mesh just there and I'd worked at it too long, finishing up making it too thick. Afterwards I chipped the excess away so the transducer would fit, but the surface I left didn't seal round the unit too well. However, once known, the problem was easily solved.

The other weep was not so easy. There was just enough water oozing from a microscopic hole in the side of a rib to leave a damp trail down to the bilge. We took a painstaking look in the same vicinity on the outside and there was no evidence of damage at all. At this we returned inside, chipped the surface all round the hole to clean it up and cured it with another spoonful of powder.

As the boat steadily dried out more of these little weeps became visible and we cured them all the same way, eventually deciding we were chasing rainbows when we measured the rate of flow at barely a quart in a day, a lot of which was probably condensation, and the lid was put firmly on the powder tin.

But that went on over several weeks. For the present, now the major weeps were attended to, all our attention was focused on the upcoming Brits' visit. It is most unusual to know in advance when they expect to come but this information was the one good thing to come from speaking to them on the radio. For once we had sufficient warning to get our letters for home finished in time.

I don't know who it was but one of the ladies who helped retrieve stuff on Anglaise had dried enough note paper for us at least to write to our other daughters. The news had been transmitted to Tony, the man who operates the East African radio network for cruisers, and he had phoned them from Kenya to tell them about the mishap and that we were safe, but letters would give that news a bit more substance. But we sat and pondered over the pages for hours and words wouldn't come. Describing what had happened was easy, but communicating how we felt about it and the scale of goodwill and support we were getting from our fellow yachties was beyond us.

There was a ship off the pass when we woke in the morning and, shortly after, we saw the bow waves of the landing craft tearing across the lagoon. We were so anxious to see if the replacement engine bearings were going to fit that our patience was truly tested when they visited fourteen other boats on their way to us.

Then as they approached we saw a group of friendly and familiar faces. Most of the party had been on the visit two months before and were visibly upset at our misfortune. From a distance, now that she was floating, *Vespera* looked battered but no more so than many neglected boats; it was stepping aboard that dismayed them most. They hadn't seen the work that had been done to get this far so all they saw was an instant transformation from a warm and cosy home to a bleak and dreary hulk. It was revealing to see our status through their eyes.

Anyway we soon got down to the all-important mail, sadly not over the chocolate biscuits and decent English tea they brought with them as we had no stove, and they had a great pile of letters for us, but no bearings. There had been a lot of radio traffic to make sure they came from Malaysia in the quickest possible way and three weeks had passed since they were sent, so this was a big disappointment.

Later we took our bundle of letters to the French camp and planted ourselves in deckchairs to read the news. Somehow, with all the interruptions, we had to take most of it back to the boat unread when it got dark. I did manage, though, to arrange with the chap in charge of the landing party, known to all as Murdoh, for the necessary faxes to be sent to withdraw from the expedition next year. This left a bitter taste as we had re-arranged our future round it, but of course that was quite irrelevant now.

In the afternoon, while the party were lifting garbage into their landing craft for disposal, we told them of our 'irretrievable' heap left behind on Anglaise and learned they would be returning the next day with some of the ship's crew and would take a landing craft over and collect it then. That didn't sound much of an itinerary for a great day but in fact it turned out to be a splendid one.

I think its primary function was 'Rest and Recreation' as, along with a fair number of the crew, the ship's captain sent ashore a couple of chefs with the makings of a huge barbecue and all the yachties were invited. It was great fun and both Tina and Sue were treated to a high-speed run around the lagoon. Locating the Anglaise rubbish was all the excuse they needed to worm their way aboard the landing craft as guides.

There has to be a moral here somewhere but it eludes me for the moment. These two ladies usually finish an excursion round the corals with faces drawn and nerves in tatters, in spite of the fact that we travel at minimal speed. Today they came back wreathed in smiles after zooming round the shallows at thirty knots. I can only imagine it had something to do with the Royal Marines.

On a more serious note I spoke to Murdoh about the possibility of flying out from Diego Garcia if *Vespera*'s repairs didn't work. So far the hull looked promising but nothing else had been tackled. We knew the engine was unserviceable, but could probably be got going again, and everything else had a big question mark over it.

I still wasn't prepared to risk three lives for the sake of getting *Vespera* home, and I knew without asking that Tina wouldn't accept me sailing her away on my own, so my first priority was to confirm a safe passage for Sue, and the next was one for us in case I decided that sailing would not be safe.

There were a number of difficulties involved here, all of which apparently revolved around unauthorized people not being allowed on Diego Garcia and the problem of civilians flying on military aircraft, especially those of another country. Anyway, all Murdoh could do was raise the subject with the powers that be and we would see what happened.

Another thing of note happened on this day. Not long after the discussion about flying out, the three of us were at the French camp talking over the ramifications when a young man with a pronounced military gait approached. He was spokesmen for the men and women who made up the naval party, sailors and marines alike, and presented us with a bottle of rum 'from the lads' to keep up our spirits. Let me tell you there is nothing like rum flavoured with generosity to settle down a day.

After they left it was back to serious planning. The projection that they would be back in four to six weeks had to be considered a possibility rather than a probability and even this delay in getting the bearings would significantly affect the way we approached things. The dilemma was whether to assume everything would work and build up the inside woodwork to make it liveable, then shoe-horn the engine in afterwards, or simply delay everything for six weeks until the engine was in place and working.

An important consideration was that in six weeks most of the people would have left to continue their voyages. The monsoon had already established in favour of those travelling to Africa and the seasons have to be taken advantage of as they come. This could leave us with a shortage of muscle power when it came to manhandling the engine and that thought tipped us towards leaving the maximum amount of room. But then things that might happen six weeks in the future were largely out of our control and probably wouldn't happen the way we thought anyway, so we decided to start rebuilding a home straight away.

That decision proved premature when we got down to thinking about it properly. To begin with there was a patch that still needed regular wetting on the inside and, until that was finished, putting in floors and so on was out of the question. There was also a sound argument that we would do better to finish the really dirty work, like sorting out the fuel tank and lines, before we attempted any rebuilding. Then there was the knotty problem of what, exactly, to do.

Whenever we debated a plan of action we found ourselves at cross purposes. Tina and I certainly had different visions of what the outcome was likely to be and Sue, if she had any strong feelings on the matter, was wise enough not to say much. In stark reality what we could or couldn't do was governed by the resources we had, but our differences of opinion were about the target we should set ourselves.

In quiet retrospect it was the principle of setting a target at all while in a situation demanding flexibility that was the problem. It had been much easier to stay flexible before *Vespera* was refloated, but just seeing her on the water was enough to start trains of thought which, with so much unknown, could lead anywhere.

However, the grubby jobs gave us a bit of a planning respite and those that might pour fuel everywhere were obviously the ones to get done first. In the bustle and confusion of lifting the engine out the fuel cock had been used as a step and the copper tubes leading to it had collapsed. The kinked portion of one pipe had to be cut away and the other, very short, pipe had to be replaced.

Scratching through the boxes of spares which the ladies had oiled turned up enough tubing to do the job but the fittings needed had all been lost; they were somewhere on the bottom of the lagoon. Fortunately John had some of the right size and cobbling together a workable pipe was quite straightforward. Next was cleaning the fuel tank, a job I had been procrastinating over since the day of the floating but now couldn't think of a single excuse to put off any longer.

Access is through a small port in the tank top, just large enough to get your arm in, and you get to it by crouching under the companionway steps. The gymnastics required are exactly the same as those for taking out the generator, which under normal circumstances would have to have been removed as well, but here you have to reach even further.

The tank was built with four compartments and the port allows access to the front two only, the others having to be cleaned by pushing rags through holes in the baffle with bits of wire. There was perhaps a gallon of diesel left that we hadn't been able to get out when the boat was on the slope and I took this out now with a sponge. The slop bucket showed plenty of slimy jelly when I squeezed out the first spongeful so it was going to have to be a careful and thorough job.

I spent an entire day poking around with rags and flushing with clean fuel before I was satisfied it was as clean as I could get it. There are places in the back compartments that can't be seen, even with the most elaborate system of mirrors, so deciding when the job was finished was largely an act of faith. Unfortunately I had no more biocide to sort out any remaining bugs so that act of faith was a big one. When I refilled the tank though I ran the fuel through Mark's filter again to minimize the risk.

Now it was the ladies' turn and their job was the big interior clean up. The day they spent washing the insides with seawater had succeeded in removing the sand and most of the offensive smells but everything was covered with mould and it still smelled musty. My role in this was simply supportive and all I did was ferry fresh water from the well. The 'rinse down with fresh water' we thought would finish the job went on, in stages, for more than a week, but when they finally put away their scrubbing brushes the mustiness had gone and you could touch things without them feeling sticky.

In spite of this there was plenty of time for fun. One day I went fishing to the west of Boddam with John and caught a couple of nice tuna while the ladies took advantage of a spring low tide to walk along the reef from Boddam to the smaller islands. When we went to Ile du Sel to fetch them we took along a picnic basket and relaxed on this most beautiful of islands for a few hours. Shipwreck couldn't have been further from our minds.

The evenings were great fun now with so many musicians. Mike had a fine repertoire of songs and tunes for his harmonica and Brian was another accomplished guitarist. Usually the musical sessions were left until after dark and the earlier hours, around sundowner time, were spent playing games. 'Hoarse' is an uncouth card game that exercises the vocal cords more that one's cranial ability, its mental demands being about the same as for 'snap', and I can imagine it being a roaring success at a birthday party for five-year-olds. It was a huge success here too; but that probably had something to do with the pineapple wine.

Alan and Philippa came back from a visit to Peros Banhos in time for one of those hoarse (coarse?) musical evenings and had enjoyed such good fishing that they provided fish for everyone's supper. Heidi had an interesting 'exhibit' taken from one of the fish, a perfectly formed and undamaged baby turtle.

When cleaning the fish Alan had taken it from the stomach and preserved it in a jar with some spirit, where it served to illustrate how vulnerable the young turtles are. After much checking in reference books about breeding seasons and body sizes we concluded that this little fellow hadn't been hatched very long, and it was obvious the fish had taken him in one swallow. If each turtle represents just a single tasty morsel it's a wonder any survive to get big enough for the fishermen to kill.

Whichever way we tackled the rebuilding, whether as a one-time permanent fix or a makeshift affair to get us to a proper workshop, we had to have floors. It was dangerous enough climbing round the uncovered framework with the boat moored and would be impossible at sea. The original construction method using the floors as support for the other woodwork was by far the strongest way to do things, but it also meant all the wood we'd removed was damaged, or at least cut into small pieces.

Most of this was now in a heap in the shed and differentiating between what had been floor and what had been furniture, and indeed what had come from other boats for patches, was, shall we say, interesting. Some of the pieces had been cut to specific shapes to fit over the holes and the off-cuts were no special shapes at all. It was like inheriting three jigsaw puzzles, each with missing pieces, that had all been kept in one box.

One floorboard panel from the main cabin was missing but we could account for the entire forward section, though all its supports were gone. Someone remembered that the missing board had been wedged under ropes to provide a backing during the attempt to use inflatable dinghies to seal the holes, but no-one could recall seeing it after that. We had a good scout around Boddam for suitable timber to use in its place but the only planks we found were rotten, all the sound ones being structural parts of the buildings. Then, just in case the original had washed up there, we walked the entire beach of Anglaise looking for it, but no luck.

This loss pretty much defined how we would set about the job. We would cobble together a loose floor by cutting up other panels, but that wasn't at all suitable for a permanent job. In some ways, though, not being able to build a permanent floor worked to our advantage as the loose boards meant we had direct access to the patches.

The main cabin was comparatively easy. We sacrificed three cupboard shelves, unfortunately of different thicknesses, to replace the lost piece and supported them on hardwood strips left over from some work we had done in Thailand. The missing framework and sawn-away bulkhead made the support a bit flimsy but the furniture was still intact, and the chart table and ice box in particular made it stronger than it looked. I wedged a couple of props underneath while we were working on it and it seemed safe enough for now.

The forward section was a different story altogether. The first thing I had to do was adjust the shape where it sat against the hull. The builder had obviously gone to considerable trouble to shape the plywood edges so they sat snugly against the slope all along their length. Much of this workmanship had been damaged by the impacts and, more significantly, our cement work varied a bit from the original, just enough to make every board wobble.

After cutting away the splintered sections I laid the

boards in position on bits of coral and driftwood so I could juggle them to get the best fit. Then, after trimming them to the best of my ability, I had to find a way of supporting them that would keep them at the right height and be strong enough to work properly as a floor.

The original bearers had been bolted to holes drilled in the ribs and grouted to the top of the ballast, but we had facilities to do neither of these things. The best we could do was cut blocks to the correct heights and angles and screw them to each board, like the legs of a stool, then place them in position loose. Getting the lengths and angles right and fitting them so the board didn't tip when you stood on it took a lot of trial and error, mostly error, but when it was finished it fitted together quite nicely. Well, it fitted together and at least the boards over the patches could be lifted out readily.

Sue found the amount of time I wasted trying to make the best of this sort of job rather stressful, in fact she sometimes became quite angry at how little was achieved. I could also get pretty wound up about it as I really don't enjoy doing things that might prove a waste of time, except having fun, of course, but doing makeshift repairs isn't fun. All told it was a good thing that Sue had enough to do on the shore to stop us getting in each other's hair.

She actually had a rather demanding job to do. Retrieving our food stuffs had taken on a new level of priority as some of the containers holding dry goods, ones that had seemed okay when first examined, were showing signs of failure and this was worrying. Our most immediate concern was for Jess. Since her 'hairless' period in south east Asia her diet had been mostly dry food, or 'crumbles', and our stock of tinned food for her was strictly limited, only enough to give her a treat every now and then.

Somehow sea water had got into all the jars of crumbles, not a lot but sufficient to make them go mouldy. Sue spread the crumbles out in the sun to dry then spent many, many hours sorting the 'not too bad' from the 'very bad'. Jess would have to make do with the 'not too bad' ones or eat the same food as us, and she wasn't impressed with either option.

A much more serious problem developed, from the human point of view anyway, when rats got into the barrel of flour Sue had saved earlier. She arrived at the shed one morning to find flour all over the place and a substantial hole chewed through the barrel lid. Very bad. There were only two courses of action to choose from: we could throw the whole lot away or save as much as possible, but both choices were essentially wrong.

Instinct and training told us to discard it but it represented almost our entire stock of flour, so we had to try the alternative. Sue took a spoon and carefully removed the top few inches and it appeared that the remainder was good, but as an extra precaution she sifted it through a baking sieve and checked it grain by grain, or so it seemed. When it passed this test she transferred it to a sound barrel and whenever we cooked bread afterwards we tried not to think about it.

But her time wasn't all spent in difficult decisions and painstaking labour. In the course of one morning's work collecting firewood she witnessed a moray eel catching a crab. While walking along the tide line she disturbed a crab, causing it to scuttle off over the rocks towards the sea. A small eel, which must have been lurking in a nearby pool, shot out of the water and skittered right over the rocks, grabbing the crab in passing.

It appeared a lopsided battle as the crab was well armoured and very large compared to the eel, but the amphibian attacker had an unstoppable tactic. Once he had the body of the crab securely clamped in his jaws he threw an overhand knot in his tail and drew his head back through the loop. This action stripped the legs and claws from the crab and within seconds all its flesh had been eaten. This sort of violence is quite disturbing and the gentleness of a fluffy baby fairy tern, perched in a fork high in a casuarina tree, was just what she needed on her way home.

The anchorage at Boddam was quite uncomfortable now. The easterly winds had the full fetch of the lagoon to build up waves and these broke continuously on the beach. Travelling back and forth between boat and island became a penance as it was impossible to make the trip without getting soaked, the basis of good-natured humour on bright sunny days but under the more typical grey overcast that humour can be trying.

Except for a few die-hards everyone was planning to move to the lee of Takamaka and some boats that had returned from there for the Brits' visit were most anxious to get back. All of a sudden it felt as if the Salomon interlude was coming to an end and many of the long planned for, and dreamed of, ventures had not been achieved. No-one, for example, had walked on the reef at night; the planned video of coconut crabs was still a blank tape and few had fully explored the islands.

Most of these things could be done equally well from Takamaka but the reef is more accessible from Boddam and at low tide one moonless night a group of us donned our shoes, and our courage, and set out to walk to Ile Diable. This part of the reef was on the lee side of the lagoon and the shallow water easily foiled the waves from inside and the ocean swells were barely discernable ghosts far out in the darkness. Batteries were at a premium by this stage so the torches we had with us were for emergencies only and the principal illumination came from a paraffin pressure lamp.

Years of watching documentaries about living coral led us to expect that even those reefs that appear inert in daylight would spring into life at night with fluorescent polyps and anemones glittering in the lamplight, but we were in for a disappointment. We did learn that the cooler colour temperature of the lantern improved the reds and purples, though at the expense of the blues and greens, but the only activity we saw was the same as in daylight; the rocky corals seemed just as lifeless.

Thinking this was perhaps confined to the very top of the reef we edged our way towards the deeper water to see if things improved. They didn't. Obviously we had a great deal to learn before we would find where the lovely night-time corals live. A superb aquarium in Thailand had shown us, close up, exactly what we were looking for and we pondered over the significance of their display being lit with ultra-violet light, but the discussion didn't help as you don't get much ultra-violet from an oil lamp. We hoped the coconut crab filming would be more successful.

To those people who had arrived here via the Pacific the notion that coconut crabs are scarce enough to be protected was strange, but on Boddam we could readily see the reason for it. There were very few of them and, considering the abundance of food, that doesn't make sense. We could only think that the prodigious rat population was consuming more than its fair share, but whatever the reason they are indeed scarce.

They are nocturnal by nature and my night-time journeys during the wetting down era gave me a distinct advantage in finding them, and I only knew of two. One lived in a hole under a fallen tree close to our camp and another lived near the shed. Consequently when Liz and Russell came ashore armed with lanterns and a low-light video camera it fell to me to lead the expedition, which quickly grew in numbers as other people expressed interest.

I felt a bit let down when the crab that lived by our camp was missing. We scratched around in the undergrowth but found no sign of him. It was quite possible that the commotion had scared him away so our approach to the domain near the shed was more stealthy, well, as stealthy as bright lanterns allow. Russell had the camera poised in readiness while those carrying lights worked out to either side of where we expected the crab to be, but there was no-one home here either. So much for my expertise.

Not willing to be defeated we carried on past the 'watch your head' club towards the church and were lucky enough to find a fully grown specimen standing in the path, quietly minding his own business. He seemed quite oblivious to all the noise and took no notice of the lights at all. We gathered round for a good look at him, most of the party having never seen one before, then eased back to give Russell room to frame his shots.

I suppose it was us edging out of the light that excited his instincts. With the enormous contrast between the light and surrounding darkness, everyone but Russell, who was crouched at the edge of the illumination, was lost to his sight. Suddenly the centre of our attention lunged into life and off towards the safety of the night, straight towards Sue.

Now a fully grown coconut crab is a formidable animal, the claws on this chap being about the same size as Sue's forearms, and it moved surprising quickly, making plenty of noise as its legs fought individual battles with the undergrowth. Sue let rip with a loud squawk, which detracted rather from the studious theme of the video, and crashed off into the darkness.

When she convinced herself she wasn't about to be eaten, and recovered her dignity, we returned to the French camp reasonably content to have at least some footage and here we were in for a pleasant surprise. While Liz and Brian were rounding off the evening with some gentle guitar music we heard a sharp scuffling from the wood pile, and there was another crab. This was the little one that lived close by and before he slunk away to his hole he performed beautifully for the camera.

But as well as these fun things there were matters of a more practical nature I wanted to address before everyone left. I was particularly anxious to get the HF radio working as communication would make the voyage much safer. Russell had cleaned and dried the circuit boards, lubricated all the moving parts and put them together again so it only needed connecting to its antenna coupler and a battery.

The meter unit in the coupler had corroded into a solid lump, which would make tuning the antenna a bit hit-and-miss, but all the cables and plugs seemed to have survived. As with the solar panels we had to do some juggling with wires that were too short but I was quite excited when we turned on the power and heard a babble of voices from the loudspeaker.

My excitement didn't last long, though, as that was all that happened. The transmitter wouldn't switch on and the tuning unit on the set didn't work. Nevertheless it was a promising start; some of the circuits were obviously working or we wouldn't get the voices. With power on we could see that the relays were working and confirm that all the functions were getting the right voltages, so it was probably only a salt deposit or some sand somewhere upsetting things.

I stripped it down again and wiped the contacts meticulously, then cleaned the circuit boards again. Russell jury rigged a small lamp to replace a dial indicator that had succumbed and I did battle with the tuning unit. Being an old-fashioned set this was an intricate mechanical device and for some reason didn't want to turn through its full range. At one stage, while I had it upside down to brush its gear-teeth, there was a satisfying 'plink' as a small particle fell out and suddenly it all moved freely again.

When it was back in one piece I repeated the tests but there was little improvement. You could now turn the tuning control and the new lamp showed you were doing so, but that was it. The receiver still worked and the stations could be clarified by adjusting the controls but the transmitter didn't want to know. Still, I would be able to receive weather forecasts, which was the most important thing. Then suddenly the voices collapsed into a faint background hiss.

I spent a couple of days poring over circuit diagrams and building and rebuilding the thing but to no avail. I had a reasonable idea what was wrong but without equipment to trace a signal had no way of proving the point; but we had no spares anyway so the HF radio was declared officially dead.

There were other projects on the go that were treated as incidental to working on the radio which I suppose, seeing that they were more successful, should take preference in the story. Most of the folk who had packages of our things on their boats were preparing to leave so creating storage space on board *Vespera* was important, and urgent. With everything now squeaky clean the quickest solution was to remake the quarter berths and main cabin settee with the locker spaces underneath them.

We dug back into the wood pile and sorted out the bunk boards but only four had survived, though a fifth was present but in several pieces. When the complete ones were put in their original places we discovered that immersion had swollen or distorted the frames to such an extent that we really had to start from scratch.

Fortunately there were enough off-cuts left from Thailand to reinforce the framework and we found sufficient unrecognizable, and therefore homeless, pieces of plywood on the pile to make up the boards. As it happened we would have needed to do a similar job even if all the boards had survived because the drawers under the bunks would no longer open and the loose boards on top were the only way to get into them.

So, while I was playing radios, Tina and Sue made inroads into moving our things back on board. I still hadn't thought out a reasonable plan for the galley so none of the usual storage space was available there but, by leaving the more durable things ashore, they managed to relieve everyone else of our mess.

Two weeks after the Brits' visit we were enjoying a quiet breakfast when Russell came bounding up the beach with the message that the M/V *Anderson* was approaching and would be sending a landing party in with supplies in an hour's time. Immediately the plans for the day were discarded, well most of them, in anticipation of what might happen.

We would probably find out today whether Sue could fly out, whether the new bearings would fit and whether Murdoh had managed to organize some other vital things we'd asked him to look for. The day was loaded with possibilities and we were nervously aware that its outcome would have a profound effect on our lives. Fate had dealt its hand and the cards were face down on the table.

There were so many combinations of unknowns that all we could do was contain our hopes and fears as well as we could until the shore party arrived. Our biggest fear, that the authorities wouldn't allow us to stay and sort ourselves out without a seaworthy craft, was allayed by the advice that they were bringing supplies, but for everything else we had to be patient.

The landing craft came ashore with just three people aboard, a Captain of the Royal Marines and a couple of seamen, one of whom had experience of operating yachts. The young captain was an accomplished diplomat and in a very short time, without revealing his brief from the British Representative, he ascertained that we would be able to pay our way if they flew us out, that we understood any such flight would strand us in Singapore, and that we wouldn't be able to take anything more than a normal airline baggage allowance.

However, his enquiries were made with a view to ensuring that we were not pressurized into sailing away in an unseaworthy boat and not, as we feared, to put pressure on us to leave. Later in the day he took the experienced yachtsman from his crew and checked the repairs that had been done to satisfy himself that we were at least in with a chance of recovering *Vespera*.

When he asked me, forthrightly, for my assessment of the situation I was obliged to explain my doubts. The hull repair was better than anything I had envisaged, in fact with a couple of days in a proper yard for finishing touches she would be as good as new, but I wasn't prepared to commit us to an ocean passage without an engine. Sailing without a reliable engine is one thing in a boat that's known to be good in all other respects, but if there are any doubts it is not acceptable.

The result of these talks was that Sue would leave with the Brits when they next visited the islands, in two weeks' time, and we could stay and continue working on *Vespera*, essentially until either we sailed her away or decided it couldn't be done. He had brought with him flour, sugar and such to last us until their next visit and would make arrangements with his quartermaster for sufficient stores to keep us going to the end of the season to be delivered to us then. He also brought some filters, battery cable connectors and sealer that Murdoh had arranged. All in all this was about the best possible outcome from our viewpoint, except there were no bearings.

This unexpected visit was good news for others too. Ian had a damaged tooth which was giving him a lot of pain and a few days before, having run out of both pain killers and gin, had radioed Diego Garcia for permission to call there for medical attention. This was not forthcoming and *Cruise* left Peros Banhos to sail to the Maldives for assistance. Fortunately they called in at Salomon on the way to collect some of their belongings and happened to be on Boddam when the landing party arrived.

After sorting out our business the Marine Captain enquired of a group of yachties if the chap with the tooth problem was around, and Ian stepped forward eagerly to own up that it was him. 'I've got a bagful of assorted tools and thirty minutes training in combat dentistry. If you're game…' At this point I wondered if Ian hadn't wished he'd kept quiet, but it was obviously more painful than I imagined as he immediately agreed and submitted to the procedure.

Amid much noisy encouragement, and not a little

heckling from the gallery, he lay full length on the table under the palm trees while the 'combat dentist' struggled into surgical gloves. 'Wait, please. We really should record this for posterity', and an urgent scurrying for cameras and video stretched the moment of terror interminably.

Eventually, with cameras rolling and an enthusiastic audience, the battle commenced. Full marks to both perpetrator and victim for just getting on and doing the job in spite of the flow of conflicting advice. Half an hour later both faces were smiles and by the time the landing craft left to rejoin the ship Ian was back to his normal resilient self.

It took the rest of the day for the ramifications of all our news to sink in. Each of us had lone chores planned and we kind of drifted off to our respective places to ponder on things, Tina to the shed, me to the boat and Sue, who got the rough end of the stick, to the bakery. She really had the most to come to terms with and, to make it worse, the oven was in a particularly obstructive mood. It was after dark before she escaped its clutches and she just made it to the French camp, carrying two lovely loaves on an open rack to cool, when the heavens opened.

Another full-blooded Salomon squall with the wind screeching in the tops of the trees and blustering in every direction. The rain attacked the shelter, blasting fusillades of water in from all sides and threatening to put out the fire and ruin our dinner. We hastily put a cover over the bread and hung the oil lamp as high under the roof as we could to keep it out if the wind, then huddled together on the driest side. Not an evening conducive to calm and collected reasoning at all.

Ten or fifteen minutes after the rain started a ghostly shape flitted past a spill of light and disappeared into the blackness beyond the table before suddenly materializing beside us. Liz, clad in full sea-going oilies and a big grin, had given up the losing battle to row out to *Bob*, seen our light as the only downwind haven and come back ashore to wait it out. We were unsympathetic enough of her plight to just be glad of her company.

Sue was victim to many conflicting emotions. I know she'd been hankering for the vibrancy and friendships of young life in the cities and the shortage of mental stimulation from being so remote was problematic for her, but I also know she enjoys the beautiful places and changing horizons as much as, or more than, we do. She'd worked ridiculous hours to save the cost of going travelling, then walked away from a thriving career to do so, and now it was going to end in two weeks.

I'm sure she was also nervous at the prospect of starting over again. Whether she chose London or Johannesburg to return to, getting off the plane would present her with the problems of no home, no job and no transport. Nothing but a few old friends. She was not new to this situation, having moved between those cities several times before, but that merely exacerbated the problem because she knew how hard it was. She also had to decide whether to follow her heart or her head.

Her heart was in South Africa with its big skies, magnificent countryside and warm, friendly people; but burgeoning violence, crime and unemployment were putting those warm, friendly people at risk and common sense told her it wasn't the best place to be. Anyway she didn't have to make the decision before she got to Singapore and it seemed a much better idea to ignore it and cram as much island fun into her last two weeks as possible.

During the night the weather cleared and our first view of the morning showed wisps of smoke in the trees by the cooking fire. Sue had already put the pan on for tea and collected an armful of wood, which was steaming gently beside the fire by the time we got ashore. Wet firewood, the boy scout's nightmare, was a curse that bedevilled Boddam and without us being fully aware of her efforts Sue had established a routine of collecting, drying and storing wood that we would miss terribly when she left. Tina also did more than her fair share of wood gathering and struggling with damp cooking fires, but it was Sue who developed the expertise that served us so well.

We'd been pondering on what to do for the best about Jess. Up to now we'd kept her in the tent as we thought it less stressful for her than living aboard. Also, she was company for Sue who had a strong aversion to the idea of moving onto *Vespera*. Strangely it was only Tina, the one usually most susceptible to misgivings and intangible feelings, who felt comfortable on the boat. I found it distinctly depressing and unfriendly, threatening even, and Sue went out of her way to avoid even coming aboard.

Back to Jess, though: after Sue's departure she would have to live on board anyway so we decided it would be better to re-acclimatize her to it now while we were all together. But we were going to have a day off and, as we expected ructions, deferred the event to tomorrow.

The couple from *Aradonna*, a boat that had just arrived, came to us during the day and told us they had put a box, containing some things that they thought might come in useful, in the shed with our other belongings. In it we found a variety of goodies that we now considered luxuries: toothpicks, cotton buds and that sort of thing, together with a selection of good books and some edible treats.

We were enjoying a cup of tea with these people the following afternoon when rapidly deteriorating weather goaded us into the 'cat transfer'. Solid black clouds oozed over the trees to fill the sky then came lower and lower and if we didn't move her now we wouldn't do it at all. Tina clipped a short lead to Jess's collar, something to grab hold of if she ran away, and cuddled her close as she took her to the dinghy.

Sue stayed ashore to get the supper fire lit before the rain came and we motored the few hundred yards to *Vespera*. Poor Jess was frightened to rigidity. I stepped on deck first and reached out for her but she was most reluctant to come to me. Tina's face froze in shock as the claws went in and Jess just hung on. She struggled and struggled until we pried her loose and I put her down on the deck as gently as I could.

I don't think she recognized it as her home. There were still ropes all over the place and many of the familiar things from the topsides, the splashguards, liferaft and so on, were missing and obviously there were no familiar smells. Her hackles stood straight up and her ears flattened as she crept forward to investigate, which in itself was out of character, and it was only the first drops of rain that finally urged her down the companionway.

She edged her way down very nervously and the foot of the steps was the limit of her unassisted exploration. The original floorboards received a thorough sniffing but the make-shift boards were too much. Nothing would induce her to stand on them, let alone cross them. To add to her confusion she could see forward into the galley where her litter box, food and water bowls normally live and there was nothing there, just the bare hull.

This mixture of strange and familiar, after the upheaval of the last few weeks, was more than she could assimilate in one go. Tina approached her gingerly, her claw wounds still smarting, and managed to gather her up in her arms and carry her over the wobbly floor to her bunk. Here our poor confused cat prowled back and forth, sniffing and sniffing, before curling up in a tight ball and shutting out the world.

She didn't even stir when we both left the boat to join Sue at the French camp, but we didn't linger over our meal. Experience had taught us how to group our seats away from the worst roof leaks but we could do nothing to improve the ambience. And the ambience around our camp was just as gloomy. Rain hammered in the tree tops, coalesced into streams that ran along the palm fronds and cascaded all around. The tarpaulin over the tent merely concentrated the flow and a golf umbrella under one corner was all that averted a flood. Sue weighed up the pros and cons, or really the balance of cons, and opted to sleep on the boat.

We found Jess still curled up like a hedgehog and she took no notice of us at all. It was a strange experience to be all together again on board and we also had to grapple with the strange and familiar. It should have been a regular evening, like any of the hundreds we had enjoyed, but the routines didn't work.

Our customary deck shower was quite ordinary, in fact above average as standing in the driving rain left you tingling all over, but after that it fell apart. Our habits were to play a game, cards or Scrabble or the like, then maybe read for a bit before turning in. We tried to fall straight back into it and struck an immediate hitch. So far I had only rigged a single light in the forepeak and that was only bright enough to read with if you held your book close to it.

Nevertheless the three of us convened in the forepeak with the cards and played a few hands of dimly seen canasta before twisted limbs put an end to it. The forepeak consists essentially of two narrow bunks, joined at the foot to form a vee, with sufficient headroom to sit up only at one end. Jess didn't take up too much space as she had chosen the narrowest, and lowest, part at the foot of the vee but even so we felt like kids playing in the broom cupboard.

In spite of the aching legs we procrastinated over putting away the cards. Dictates of habit suggested we retire to our bunks with books and cocoa, but we had no cocoa, no means of heating water and not enough light. We did however have some coffee on board and a flask of hot water brought from the shore and whether we consumed it now or kept it for the morning was hotly debated. The morning won.

Without the soporific of a few pages of book, sleep took a long time coming. Then, at five o'clock in the morning, a monstrous clap of thunder woke us, startling Jess out of her ball. Huge eyes peered out under flat-back ears until she realized we were not abandoning ship again, then she curled back up and clamped a paw over her eyes. Obviously the world still wasn't worth looking at.

This and the next few mornings promised excellent low tides and to take full advantage of them we were going to go reef-walking at every one. It was still wet and blustery when we went ashore for breakfast though the sky showed evidence of a quick, if temporary, improvement. Sue chose as the first venue a stretch of reef off the southern end of Anglaise that none of us had yet explored and, with a couple of hours left of the ebb, we fired up the outboard.

Again we were a little disappointed with the coral. Our footing was on an irregular but relatively flat surface, uniformly covered with an almost velvety coating. I don't know how to describe this coating but it covers most of the level reef, certainly all the places that are shallow enough to walk on. It is neither hard nor soft, grey nor pink, nor purple, but it is, at the same time, all of those things. If you rub it it feels slippery but it doesn't come off the rock. If you stub your toe on it it doesn't yield yet it cushions your feet when you walk on it; if you look at it against the sun it's almost blue, away from the sun it's pink and in shadow it's muddy grey. It is exactly the effect you get if you use all the colours in the paint box and wash the brushes out in the same jar, recognizably the same but always tangibly different.

Whatever this layer is I'm sure it's what stifles the active polyps we went looking for at night. Now, in spite of the nondescript overall appearance, we took time to turn over the loose pieces and disturb the waters around bolt holes just to see what came out, and this was most rewarding. Almost every stone produced a different crab. We found brown ones with red eyes, green ones, some with two big claws and others with one big and one small. There were mottled crabs, crabs the same colour as the film on the rock and even one with dark brown and white stripes.

More plentiful still were the water hermit crabs, quite different from Hermie in that they live their entire lives in the sea. The first tiny shell produced a chap with bright blue knuckle joints on his legs and the next a very active little fellow who was hairy all over.

But a shell was the highlight of the morning. We picked it up from a patch of sand and found it still occupied by its original owner, not a hermit. It was an Ecclesiastical Mitre all of six inches long, twice the average size according to our reference book, and a perfect specimen. Shell fish are so sparse here that we only saw four perfect specimens in a year; even the hermit crabs pass shells on from generation to generation, so Sue took a couple of photographs with the one camera we thought had survived and popped him back in the sand.

It was with less enthusiasm that we made another encounter. Crown of Thorns starfish are notorious for the way they destroy coral, to the extent that they're generally considered a threat to Australia's Great Barrier Reef, and we counted twelve in an area no bigger than a hundred yards square. We hadn't seen them in Salomon before and neither had anyone else. Most unwelcome newcomers.

Our absorption with the reef got the better of our other senses and the weather caught us out again, leaving us to chug back in the rain, but as we arrived at the French camp the squall passed and presented us with a unique spectacle. We watched as the rain drifted across the lagoon and the islands eased back into view, one at a time, then, quite suddenly, a double rainbow formed.

Both arcs, one inside the other, stretched complete from horizon to horizon and the colours were sharp and intense. This was the only time any of us had seen such a thing and it sounds silly now to admit that, after admiring it for some minutes, none of us can remember which way round the colours went, only that one was a mirror image of the other.

My tentative plan for repairing the engine entailed installing the bearings and giving it a trial run on the beach before mounting it in the boat. Once on its mountings it would be impossible to get to the crankcase to correct anything so it seemed sensible to make sure it was working properly first, but transporting it as a single large working piece depended on having plenty of able bodies available, and the prospects of that were dwindling rapidly.

A revised tentative plan was to remove all those parts that could easily be bolted back on with the engine in situ and only transport the main part in one piece. If I made sure everything was completely ready so I only had to slip the bearings in and tighten the bolts the main part could be ready to move an hour or so after the bearings arrived. If there were no other yachties around then I could probably ask the Marines who brought the bits to help me lift it. The repair wouldn't be proven but if I did it properly, and could turn the engine by hand when I'd finished, there was no real reason for it not to work.

With this on my mind I felt I ought to forego the following morning's expedition round Boddam and make a start. In addition to exercising the new plan I had to rectify an earlier mistake. The engine had a hydraulic chain tensioner as part of its workings and with the oil pump out of action it had drained dry. Unthinkingly I had turned the crankshaft backwards and the slack chain had jumped on its sprocket. Now the all-important valve and injection timing was lost and re-doing that instead of walking on the reef was my penance for being so stupid.

When the ladies came back they were full of themselves and couldn't stop chattering about a lucky find. Where the reef stretches out towards Ile Poule they had chanced upon two small turtles foraging in the coral. Except for a fleeting glimpse of one while snorkelling off Ile Sepulture two years before and an occasional sighting of the single resident near the jetty we hadn't seen turtles here. These two were so busy with their foraging they took no notice of the approaching humans. We surmised that they might not have known what people were anyway.

The more we talked about that the more we realized it was probably true. Sue was able to walk right up to one and extricate it from the coral so it could be examined properly, and the other one didn't even swim away. They were hawksbills, maybe ten inches or a foot long, and the captured one put up with all sorts of indignities under examination with no apparent display of fear.

Further round the island, after making sure the released prisoner and his mate were happily munching sponges again, they found evidence that a large turtle had laid eggs on the beach. At first it appeared that several had done so as there were three or four large depressions in the sand, all surrounded by tracks, but a more careful look at the flipper prints revealed that a single animal had made them. She had left the water as the tide was falling and dug all the depressions herself before leaving as the tide rose.

The fact that the tide hadn't long turned and the exit tracks lead right to the waters edge gave rise to the thought that mother turtle had left only minutes before they got there. From the position of the depressions along the high water mark and the distance up the beach that the incoming tracks started it seems that spring tides are important to the process and three hours into the ebb was when it all began. Tomorrow's tide was expected to have the same range and the advantage of being a bit later so an immediate plan was laid for another visit in the hope of witnessing a similar event.

As luck would have it three hours into the ebb coincided with dawn so the walk round to the beach was something of an adventure. Liz and Russell joined us by the shed an hour before sunrise and, wearing almost forgotten shoes against the unseen rocks, we set off along the water's edge. High water and darkness made the familiar journey one of discovery as we found ourselves up to our waists in the sea or fighting our way through the undergrowth.

The first hint of lightness in the sky saw our string of lanterns bobbing over the rocks and the moment it was light enough to extinguish them we stepped out onto turtle beach. For once the tide tables, the clock and my arithmetic all agreed and the waves were gently lapping at the sand just where yesterday's tracks started.

Providence had deposited an enormous piece of driftwood, actually a twenty-foot-long hardwood log, right beside a springy coconut stump and, between them, they made comfortable seats for us to watch the proceedings from, and we settled down for our turtle vigil.

We watched a spectacular sunrise. High puffy clouds, barely discernable earlier against the pre-dawn sky, blushed strongly at some impropriety of the Sun God before regaining their composure and posing haughtily before the blue intensity of day. We enjoyed fine conversation that transported our minds to the edges of the universe and back. We just revelled, in fact, in the sheer joy of being surrounded by such beauty. But saw no turtles.

Later in the day, after a pleasant walk back across the island, there was still plenty of time for a visit to the boats at Takamaka. With *Vespera* progressively drying out we discovered the source of another weep and intended to swallow our pride and ask Peter for more of his magic powder to fix it. The trip would also give us an opportunity to wish God-speed to Jim and Joy whose departure for Madagascar was imminent.

Then the last few days of Sue's current cruise flashed by. All too quickly the calendar showed that tomorrow the Brits would be coming. She had packed, re-packed and packed again to squeeze her surviving mementos into carriable luggage and down to a reasonable weight. All her clothes had been stowed away in reverse order of how she expected to need them in her new venture, and her nerves were wound up tight as a spring.

She was most reluctant to be leaving us here when we still didn't know if *Vespera* would sail away. We would probably know the answer to that within a day or two of her leaving but she wouldn't find out until we could get a letter to her, and Salomon mail is very much a this year, next year, sometime, never affair. But the island cure-all for uncertainty and nervousness is a party and Sue's farewell was a prime excuse.

There were four boats of the 'old guard' and a couple of newcomers to make the evening memorable and the island did everything in its power to assist. The breeze played softly in the trees and millions of stars twinkled overhead, their reflections sparkling on the surface of the lagoon. Yoav filled Sue's emotional cup to overflowing by weaving a coconut palm sun shade for her to take with her then, as we paddled back to *Vespera*, we saw the lights of a ship standing off the pass.

The lights were still there when we woke and Sue scrambled to pack the last of her toiletries. It was still early when she finished and the tide, although not particularly low, was low enough to stop a landing craft coming ashore without the benefit of overhead sun so we decided on a final walk to turtle beach. All three of us were having trouble with our emotions and conversation was as stilted as at any other family parting, but somehow the setting and circumstances made it more poignant than ever.

When we returned we couldn't see the ship. It had probably tucked into the lee of an island to launch the boats and we opted to make a cup of tea at the 'watch your head' club while we waited. During the previous days I had stripped the pipes and valves out of the galley stove to clean and de-rust them and had succeeded in getting one of the burners working. This was connected to a gas bottle in the shed and making tea without lighting a wood fire was now a designated, and rationed, luxury. This morning definitely qualified for such a treat.

After a second cup we began to wonder where the

landing party was. With the majority of boats now anchored in the lee of Takamaka they would probably go there first but we hadn't seen any signs of activity. Even at that distance the bow waves put up by these little craft are clearly visible. To be sure it was comparatively early, barely nine o'clock, but when the weather is nice, as it was, they usually like to get the formalities over with as soon as possible to make the most of the snorkelling. Good basic common sense.

An hour later we still hadn't seen the boats and the ship hadn't reappeared from behind its island. Conversation became desultory and over-charged emotions chipped at the edges of anger. Yet another hour passed and we had to accept that they wouldn't be coming today. All was not quite lost as we understood they sometimes varied the order in which they visited the atolls and they had been specific about the date they were coming. It was quite possible that the ship we'd seen had launched its boats into Peros Banhos. Maybe tomorrow.

To take the edge off the disappointment we spent the afternoon snorkelling over a lovely coral outcrop close to where *Cairngorm* was anchored. It was a full expedition with plenty of people and the camaraderie worked wonders. The mind-set that had governed the last weeks underwent an astonishing metamorphosis. Instead of our thoughts being concentrated on 'the last few days' we now looked on the extra day as a bonus. All the packing was done so any extra time could be spent enjoying.

Next day there was still no ship. Brian and Trine brought *Born Free* across from Takamaka with a line of dinghies in tow. A number of yachts had been delaying their departure specifically to wait for the Brits' visit and, the promised day having passed, could wait no longer, so the mini-flotilla had come to say good-bye.

Within a day or two all the boats that had been here at the time of our accident, with the exceptions of *Cairngorm* and *Cruise*, would have left. Most of the offers of transport back to Africa would go with them. Our option ran out today and we were still lacking the information we needed to make the decision.

I honestly don't know whether it was the imagined difficulty of getting our things back together after they arrived at assorted African ports, the certain knowledge that such an action would further impose on these over-generous friends, or sheer funk, but the moment came and went and I did nothing.

Vespera now either sailed home or we had to abandon her complete. It was all down to the same throw of dice that we experienced when the wreck was on the reef at Anglaise. Then I considered it not worth the effort to pick the dice up and roll again, but our friends rolled for us and in doing so reduced the odds considerably. Fate was rolling them again now and odds are odds, whatever.

I suppose, in retrospect, it was simply a case of a decision making itself. I had been hanging on to see if the engine would run before stripping the valuable fittings, like the windlass and winches, off the boat. I felt it would appear dreadfully ungrateful to set about removing those parts just as the hull floated, tantamount almost to betrayal.

The hardest part to accept was that getting the engine running was only the next, and not the final, step. All those things that had been deferred until events proved the task worth while were still there waiting. Certainly if the boat would eventually be abandoned the few days it would take to get the costly fittings off the mast would be better spent doing that than wasting them re-fitting the galley; but it seemed equally silly to strip everything off then find the engine was okay and face putting it all together again. Anyway lack of hardware to put it together again made that choice a non-starter.

So nothing had been done. All the fittings were still on the boat, the engine was still unserviceable and the possibility of transport had now fallen away. It was sail away or fly away empty handed. That is not entirely true as several of our friends took such things as photograph albums for us but the generality is correct. And it sat in my stomach like a stone.

Another metamorphosis. The following morning brought no Brits and the weekend was approaching so a visit in the next few days was most unlikely. The waiting days became periods of raging uncertainty with Sue living out of a permanently packed suitcase. She could easily find herself in the situation of having to leave at an hour's notice, and shuffling her 'island' wardrobe to keep it both ready to wear and ready to go was a pain.

My outlook also changed. There was now no point whatever in moving forward one careful step at a time. The option that influenced my original decision to leave *Vespera* on the reef, specifically that my friends would take anything salvageable back to civilization, was defunct and any decisions taken in the future would be based on a much simpler, and infinitely more worrying, set of parameters. But I had changed my mind then and missed the opportunity.

I don't remember making a conscious plan at this time, I just pottered with fixing whatever happened to become top priority of the day. Often, if my fixing was a bit tardy and another priority slipped into first place, jobs would be stopped half done, which became a source of endless irritation. But the changing priorities were driven by circumstance rather than logic so I suppose much of the irritation was unavoidable.

The afternoon saw an assortment of frame components from the galley furniture go aboard and be balanced together to see just what would be involved in the reconstruction. Two principal elements had to be accommodated, the stove and the stainless steel worktop–cum–sink, both of which required the frames to be square. There was a little room for adjustment in respect of the stove as it was mounted on removable gimbals but the sink unit was immutable.

With the frame loosely screwed together and offered up it was possible to imagine a system of props that would, I thought, allow the whole thing to be suspended from the lone surviving bolt hole in the rib and still accommodate removable floor boards. It meant taking the floor up again, trimming it and redoing the supports but that was the way we had to go. Now, with a scheme fixed in my mind, the framework was dismantled and taken ashore to make room for the work to be done.

The alteration did not get done quickly. The weekend weather was glorious so we spent a lot of time snorkelling with Sue. It was 'the last few days' all over again and Tuesday was the next most likely day for her to go. But Tuesday dawned and no Brits, none on Wednesday or Thursday either then, bearing in mind it's a hundred-and-twenty-mile sea journey from their offices in Diego Garcia, it was weekend again.

Conscience wouldn't allow all the time to be simply frittered away and, with an hour or two here and a morning there dedicated to the galley, the main frame was eventually screwed together with the sink unit reasonably well supported. The weekend promised a spell in which I could start in the morning without threat of the emotional upheaval of Sue's departure dropping on us at some inopportune moment, such as when work pieces were balanced in place, or tools were all over the place and a supporting hand needed right now, so I tackled the problem of locating the loose water tank.

I was reluctant to put it back in its designed spot as it would cover some of the patches and I wanted to be able to get to them easily. About the best I could think of was to transport it empty, suspended in the place where the cupboard ought to be. Certainly the propped and wedged frame wouldn't support it full.

The tank is an irregularly shaped and singularly clumsy device and by the time it had been trans-shipped from the shed, scrubbed clean of spiders' webs and other nasties and balanced on a lath behind the sink, the first day of the weekend had devolved into snorkelling time. By the time it was actually held in place with suitably screwed down brackets and supports the whole weekend had gone the same way and it was 'the last few days' yet again.

Tuesday morning came and went and Sue was still with us. This daily uncertainty was having a marked effect on her equanimity. Every morning she looked at the sky and looked at her watch, carefully balancing the odds against them coming in the afternoon and wondering if she dare wash her clothes. These little things seem so trivial yet they controlled our daily lives.

Several of the people who'd given up waiting had left their mail with us to post when the Brits came, a decision they would possibly regret as the faster boats were already a thousand miles away and likely to beat the letters to their destination. Boddam was becoming more remote by the day, though, happily, far from lonely. Our company was mostly temporary visitors from Takamaka braving the elements to have a look at the old settlement. It was indicative of the sea conditions in the lagoon that yachties who'd sailed half way round the world to get here would spend the days ashore to escape seasickness from the awkward motion in the anchorage.

A lot of the mundane tasks also fell foul of the uncertainty syndrome. Sue didn't feel like starting anything she couldn't just walk away and leave if the call came and as the days were passing the list of appropriate tasks to choose from got shorter. She used some of the time putting finishing touches to her food retrieval programme.

While oiling the tins she had selected and packed away sufficient to provide the basics for a hundred days plus a few to spare, not too far adrift from the original stocking plan. Now, as she was leaving, this could be adjusted to last the two of us longer but the mix would need some attention to achieve a reasonable balance of protein and vegetables. Unloading the bags and shuffling the tins kept her occupied for ages and she finished with a neat pile that would keep us going until the end of November, except for Jess.

This gave us a fair margin in which to make plans. The south easterly trade winds were now blowing strongly, more than was wise to tackle with untried repairs, and would continue to do so for some while. The gentlest time of year, statistically, to cross to Africa is during September and the run down the Mozambique channel is easiest in November. If we could get sufficient dry staples to go with the cans and find some food for Jess we were okay.

Equally important to our thinking was that, with no options left, the quality of the engine repair should be as good as possible and I agonized over whether or not to ask Sue to organize a more comprehensive set of spares. The epoxy oil pump was a fine job but a genuine replacement would give more peace of mind, as would new main bearings to go with the big ends. The last day of August was our new target date and this might, might, give Sue enough time to arrange things. But the cost of the spares and freight would go a long way towards paying for an evacuation flight and it would possibly just be money down the drain.

Wednesday came and went. No Brits. It had to be tomorrow. Certainly one member of the last contingent had intimated they would be back in four to six weeks and, even though that information had been contradicted with a specific date, the six weeks may have been correct and it ran out tomorrow. Sue took particular care that everything was ready for a quick departure, but by Thursday noon it was obvious it wasn't going to happen this week. On Saturday it would be July.

Kay and Clive had progressively postponed their departure hoping to see *Vespera* in suitable working order to get us to Africa before they left and were already substantially late for their journey. On Tuesday morning they came to visit with parting gifts of beer, a Thai good luck charm and a large bar of chocolate. They were off to Takamaka for a few days to take advantage of the shelter while preparing *Cairngorm* for the trip. It didn't stop us making a plan though for a picnic expedition with them to Ile De La Passe, if the Brits didn't come, the following day.

During the afternoon I installed the stove alongside the new framework in the galley. The gimbal supports needed some modification but eventually it sat reasonably straight and level and connecting up the supply pipe took a matter of minutes. We turned on the gas and struck a match but the burner wouldn't ignite. This wasn't entirely unexpected as it has a long pipe to fill first but half the match box later we realized it wasn't going to light.

A few days earlier I'd blown through the pipe with a borrowed bicycle pump and all had seemed in order, but obviously something had escaped detection. Fortunately the first fitting I opened was clogged with something that must have shaken loose in the hose and a few prods with a bit of wire was all that was needed. A giant leap forward – we could now make tea on the boat.

No ships on the horizon in the morning but a beautiful day so we bundled the fishing tackle, snorkels and picnic plates into the dinghy and left for Ile De La Passe. On the way across our lure attracted a lovely frigate tuna, perfectly sized for our lunch, and we enjoyed a superb 'Salomon day' with our friends before more emotional farewells.

Next day was back to work and the woodwork progressed a little, far enough to permanently fit the sink unit in fact, and the galley, even without cupboards, looked more comforting than before.

I was under some slight pressure from the ladies as the finals of the Wimbledon tennis championship were due to be played at the weekend and they wanted to know if our portable radio could be got to work for them to listen. Reception had never been very good in Salomon (I suppose the broadcast engineers don't give much priority to the middle of the ocean when they do their calculations), but it was worth a try.

The good news was that the set had survived and worked as well as ever though the antenna was a bit 'iffy'. By whizzing the tuning dial backwards and forwards across the bands searching out the signals that were propagating well at any time we managed to get the gist of both major games. The world didn't seem quite so remote.

With nothing to provide clues as to when she might leave Sue had unpacked everything except the few mementos she was taking and day to day living returned to normal. The 'last few days' approach had worn decidedly thin; indeed the emotional let-down and renewed uncertainty tended to make it a trying time rather than a bonus.

Planning our days around 'ifs' and 'maybes' caused a lot of tension and tempers ran hot too much of the time. I was convinced that this would stop Salomon from imprinting good memories in Sue's mind and her lasting impressions would be of strife and disharmony in spite of the tranquillity the place exudes (though I've since been proved wrong). Then, before we could think of a plan to counter the negativity, we heard the Brits on the radio.

They called with a general enquiry about the conditions in the atoll and Ian reminded them that Sue was waiting to be picked up. The weather was being particularly mean and didn't allow the landing craft to be launched from the ship but the forecast was for it to ease over the next twenty-four hours and, after asking if any yachts were leaving and passing Diego Garcia, they said they would come for her then.

Panic stations. Sue began a frantic re-packing and all

sorts of hare-brained schemes were proposed to get her washing dry so she could get it finished. It was, of course, pouring with rain. The concept of winding up her cruising days on a high note had really gone for a loop. The island was being lashed by strong winds, lines festooned with wet clothes filled the boat and rain made cooking at the camp fire miserable.

And suddenly it was over. During a lull in the squalls the ship, the M/V *Cpl. Louis J. Hauge Jnr.*, succeeded in launching the boats and they bounced and splashed their way across the lagoon. Conditions dictated that it be a quick trip and while Sue passed her bags down Murdoh passed the mail up, together with some beautiful fresh fruit from the ship's captain for distribution among the yachts. I hope someday this gentleman finds out how much pleasure that kind gesture gave.

But there was another disappointment in store for us. Murdoh's opening statement was that he had both good and bad news, the good was that they had our engine spares, the bad that, in the turmoil of launching the boats, they'd been left on the ship. It was not possible in the prevailing conditions for them to make a second trip so they would bring them next visit.

Just a few minutes after they arrived we waved goodbye to Sue as the boats sped off into the gloom. Great gouts of spray burst from their bows as they bashed into the waves and we didn't envy them the passage through the pass at all. Long before they got that far they were lost from sight and it was only when we saw the *Hauge* get underway that we knew all had gone well. Sue was now on her way to a new phase of her adventure.

It was an auspicious day in other ways too. Chrissy was celebrating one of life's more significant birthdays and a lot of tactical and logistic planning had gone into making the day memorable. Weeks before, Ian had surreptitiously removed a bag of flour from their store and given it to Sue with a request to use her skills in the bakery to bake a special cake. This she'd done while *Cruise* was exploring Peros Banhos and, knowing the Brits were coming, had risen early this morning to ice it.

There were only two boats with us at Boddam, *Delight*

which had just arrived, and *Summerwind*, and the plan called for Ian to bring *Cruise* across for the party, but the dreadful weather and poor visibility forced a different decision. The celebrants opted to cocoon themselves in oilies and come over in the dinghy, brave stuff in twenty-five knots of wind.

The party was exactly what we needed. *Vespera* was engulfed in an aura of sadness but familiar friendly company chased the blues away. Chris, the young man single-handing *Delight*, hailed from a town only minutes from our old home in South Africa, indeed his studies had been concurrent with Sue's at the same university, and now with other South Africans here for the day it seemed more like a reunion than a day of parting.

The celebrations eventually broke up in the early evening leaving just enough time for the *Cruises* to get back in daylight and we settled on board with our mail. After a cheerful afternoon swapping stories of home it was depressing to read of the problems being imposed on our family and friends by the political and economic collapse there. Fortunately there was a lone item of positive news to round the day off: Vanessa's career had taken a good step forward.

Poor Jess found it difficult to accept that Sue hadn't come back with us in the evening. Once she realized the dinghy had been tied up for the night and Sue wasn't here she prowled around the boat sniffing and searching for a reason and didn't settle the whole night. We know because we couldn't settle either and kept her company. In the morning we heard that Ian's outboard had shed its propeller half way home and they had to paddle the last mile, against the wind and in the dark. Certainly a birthday Chrissy wouldn't forget.

Delight and *Summerwind* both spent the day preparing to move and we did some last minute trading for essentials. I'm sure there was nothing very fair in the bartering and from our viewpoint the few cups of rice swapped with Chris for flour to make a couple of loaves was an excellent deal. We had run out completely about a week ago.

Next day saw an atoll re-shuffle as Ian brought *Cruise* to Boddam and the other two slipped over to Takamaka. Then, within three days, everyone except *Cruise* left for Africa, and they could only stay a few more days due to the same constraints. In fact Ian was stretching his luck further than he should, primarily to give me a hand with the engine.

The Brits had given no real indication of when they would be coming again and their fall-back phrase of 'about four weeks' was all we had to go on. If that turned out to be the truth Sue would be hard pressed to get the parts in time, but if they were delayed much beyond that we would be into the cyclone season. Ho-Hum.

One thing was sure, we had to strip the engine down into parts small enough to handle on our own and get it all aboard. It would have to stay in pieces until the parts arrived then we could rebuild it in place. We must just be careful when we took it apart not to damage vital things like the cylinder head gasket.

I could only guess at what the parts would weigh but I remembered seeing a document quoting a weight of four hundred pounds for the bare engine. All the auxiliary bits were listed separately and the drawing looked like the lump we had left after taking everything off, so the figure probably referred to that. In a fit of enthusiasm Ian and I tried to lift it and came to the conclusion that it was about right.

Taking the cylinder head off wasn't too daunting as it was familiar territory, but that wasn't enough. We still couldn't lift it, let alone manoeuvre it around. The next heavy part to come off was the flywheel and that was a bit more concerning. Immersion in the sea had coated it with rust, effectively obliterating any balancing marks, and it was held in place with special bolts that the manual said had to be replaced and not re-used. We had no option but to cross our fingers and hope things would work out if we ignored that remark.

Soon the bolts were undone, and they looked alright, and with the flywheel off Tina and I could lift the rest without too much strain. So far so good. I'd cleaned off most of the surface rust and put a couple of marks of my own on the wheel so it would probably go together again okay.

We ferried the loose bits out to the boat and stowed them away in the lazarette. It was pretty damp and humid in there but we sprayed everything and wrapped them in oily rags and plastic so I thought it would be alright, especially if I aired it out whenever the sun shone. The remaining lump was trussed up in an overkill of rope slings to make sure we couldn't drop it and Ian helped me put it in the dinghy. Even so it took all four of us to steady it as we moved it and ten minutes later we swung it under the end of the boom, the same way it had come out, and lifted it into the cockpit. Another ten and it was sitting on blocks on the strongest part of the cabin floor where it could stay until repaired. A weight off our minds as well as our muscles.

Chrissy had been busy before we started playing engines and had transformed the 'watch your head' club back to its original function. It had been commandeered as a workshop while *Vespera*'s hull repairs were being done and hadn't yet recovered from the shock, but now she'd swept the floor, tidied up the fireplace, spread a decorative cloth over the table and generally spruced the place up.

There was a section of roof missing over the doorway facing the beach and south easterlies blew directly through the gap at the fireplace, making cooking impossible, so Chrissy propped a large driftwood panel over the bottom of the door aperture and used its mass to support a wall of palm fronds to cover the rest. This served well to keep out the wind and the missing roof section let in light and at the same time let out smoke.

This was going to make life much easier for us. Firstly it was a lot closer than the French camp and, with its functions re-vitalized, much more comfortable. There were even a couple of benches under a proper roof where we could eat our meals sheltered from the rain, most important with the wet season due to start. While there were just the four of us we used it every evening and, with a good fire burning in the fireplace and oil lamps in the dark corners, the place had a warm and gentle ambience.

But a week of these evenings was all the season would allow. Ian's cut-off date approached and, fortunately for him, the weather improved dramatically. The solid overcast broke under pressure from the sun and the wind, which had been blowing a steady twenty-five knots for days, eased to ten or twelve and steadied in a direction to put it right over the port quarter on their route to the Seychelles. Perfect, perfect conditions.

Like everyone else they went through their stores and passed on to us whatever they could spare. Then mid-day was upon us, and with it the best position of the sun for seeing their way out through the coral. A final cup of tea together and we were waving good-bye again.

We watched them safely through the pass then listened to their radio message that the sailing was idyllic, and all the time our emotions were doing cartwheels and handstands. The horizon looked very, very big when their sail disappeared and the islands changed their nature once more. We were singularly grateful for their complex mix of serenity and quietude to counteract what now seemed a much more threatening future, faced as we were with the reality rather than the forecast of being alone in Salomon with *Vespera* still unserviceable.

BOOK FOUR

IT WAS THE twenty-third of July and time to take stock of our situation. *Vespera* was afloat and the patches seemed fine. Other parts of her structure that had taken strain when bouncing on the reef, notably around the sharp corners on deck, were showing signs of spalling but that was more an extension of an old problem than anything new.

The rigging and sails were back on board and had suffered no visible damage, our only fear being that the stays might have been overloaded while standing her up. A façade had been created to make the interior habitable, if not exactly ready to go to sea, but it was apparent that with some determination and what we had available it could be made so. The engine, of course, was a major stumbling block and a few other things needed sorting out.

The steering, for example, was working but very stiff, probably resulting from a bump on the rudder, and all the wiring was in trouble but I didn't think there was anything wholly insurmountable there. If necessary we could travel without navigation lights; it seemed standard practice among the fishermen in the Malacca Straits after all.

Assuming we could meet our deadline of the end of August we had plenty of tinned food to get us to Africa with a margin of safety and Sue was organizing for flour, rice and so forth to be sent via Diego Garcia. We had plenty of containers to carry water and with twenty gallons in the remaining tank there was no need to worry on that score. All in all we were in good shape to get *Vespera* back to civilization.

The biggest shortfall was within ourselves. Both of us were scared by the thought of the ocean crossing in a below-standard boat and neither of us were really convinced it was worth the effort, so commitment was difficult, though more so for me than for Tina. Of course the voyage would save us the not inconsiderable expense of flying out and we could expect to recover the second-hand value of the surviving equipment when we got it to a market, but the nearest market was in Durban, three thousand two hundred miles of trade winds, strong currents and infamous south westerly busters away. On balance the prospect of risking our lives for so little was foolish, though we couldn't tell whether that was common sense or fear talking.

On a much more positive note we had, for the first time, our story book paradise to ourselves. The next weather window in which yachts might be expected was in September, when those en route from the Sunda Straits to the Red Sea might stop over. Of course there are people who choose to make unseasonal trips but most sailors prefer to make passages when the statistics are on their side so we didn't expect to see anyone else.

We had plenty to keep us busy but being on our own brought home just how high the price had been to be here and we became intent on enjoying our surroundings. Indeed, not to make the most of it would be unforgivable and probably harder to live with afterwards than if we hadn't come at all. So, with the proviso that we had to be ready on time, work was put firmly in its place.

The most important thing was to take advantage of any good weather. As it happened, the week that followed *Cruise*'s departure was the longest spell of bright skies and fluffy clouds we saw in a long time and we had to limit the hours we spent each day snorkelling or beach walking so as not to get burnt.

Guilt was the only spur that got anything done on the boat and it didn't make a good assistant. Doing makeshift repairs is always frustrating, but a lot easier to put up with when grey dreariness removes other temptations. When the lagoon was perfect for fishing or the sun just right for a walk, rusty fittings and frozen connectors looked especially ugly, and it was only the persistent 'you should be fixing the steering' or 'that drawer hasn't been made secure yet' tapping on my conscience that got me back on board.

The 'watch your head' club had established itself as more than just 'home', it was an easy place to relax in as well as the best place to prepare and eat our meals. Although we had a burner working on *Vespera*'s stove and plenty of gas left to last until October the fact that we could heat two pots at a time over the much larger fire ashore was attractive. Every day the south easterly winds delivered a few baskets of driftwood right to the door and Tina soon sorted out a working fuel policy.

We inherited a wood pile, just outside the doorway beside the fireplace, that would hold at least a week's supply of firewood and an old plastic basket was pressed into service as a kindling store and kept inside the main building along with a pile of coconut palm matting. This matting, whose proper name I don't know, is a cloth-like sheet of fibrous matter that separates the stems of palm fronds as they form then, as the fronds open, falls away and when dried makes an excellent fire lighter.

On fine days Tina would collect all the wood from the beach and spread it out to dry in the sun, then stack it in its appropriate place. For wet days that refused to fit in with her schedule we had a magic ingredient. When Mark filtered our diesel fuel he'd collected the contaminated stuff in a large jerry can and this we kept beside the wood pile. A roll of coconut matting dipped in this oil made a fiercely burning torch good enough to light the most reluctant fire.

One disappointment was that our superb Thai stove had given up the ghost. This stove was so effective, and burned so little fuel, that it had been in constant use at the French camp, often cooking half a dozen family meals in succession, and you can't expect too much from two dollars' worth of unglazed clay. But its demise was quite a blow.

A bigger blow was the return to my level of fishing skills. Ian had been catching enough every day to feed both their cat and Jess and he seemed to do it effortlessly. Apparently a few minutes with a hand line and whatever bait he could think of would yield a pan-sized fish at any time of day and at the outset I felt confident I could do the same. At anchor off Ile Anglaise we'd caught our supper most days and I imagined conditions would be the same here with no other boats around.

Silly as it may sound we were unhappy at the thought of catching any of the fish from our aquarium under the boat.

Within a day of refloating a couple of batfish had taken up residence and soon the couple became five. Then they were joined by some hump-back unicorns, a few yellowfin surgeons and a large shoal of fish we couldn't identify. Whenever we discarded the leavings from Jess's bowl they were all there waiting and would squabble over the scraps, gobbling them up before they sank.

This was a dilemma that had to be resolved or Jess was going to be a hungry cat. We pondered over it and decided that, as all those fish have small mouths, we could probably avoid catching them by using a large hook. I tied a 4/0 hook to my line, the largest I had left, and a heavy sinker to take it straight to the bottom.

In less than a minute I'd hooked and landed a batfish, the one we knew as 'white stripe'. How he managed to impale himself on a hook almost twice as wide as his mouth is a mystery, but he most definitely had. I removed the hook as gently as possible and slipped him back in the water before coiling up the line and calling it a day. That ploy was obviously not going to work.

Later I took my fresh water spinning rod to try for one of the trevally we'd seen from the jetty. I tried several casts with a nice shiny lure but the reel was sticking, in spite of being stripped and oiled, and my attempts at long casts only created tangles. Next I tried a winkle as bait on a very small hook among the little fish that always surround the stonework and immediately hooked one, a poisonous trigger fish.

I persisted until it got dark, determined to at least feed Jess, but all I could show for my efforts were two tiny unidentifiable fish. It's quite possible that between them they didn't weigh as much as the winkles I'd used as bait. Tina humoured me by cooking them as cat food but there was so little flesh Jess had to eat some of our supper anyway. Not at all like the fishing at Anglaise.

One afternoon while I was still trying to master 'Boddam' fishing Tina moved the last of our kitchen things, including the woodpile, from the French camp to the 'watch your head' club. Someone, probably from a 'Brit-ops' naval party, had left a tatty but serviceable wheelbarrow on the island and, although the wheel complained noisily and bitterly, its use saved a lot of work. One thing that took us greatly by surprise was that in only four days the pathway had grown over so much that it had to be cleared to let the barrow pass.

Another major job she did while barrowing wood was to sort out the best mix of fuel in the 'watch your head' and bakery wood piles. It was essential in the bakery to only use hard wood, like old takamaka, that burned down to coals, whereas the regular cooking fire more often than not needed flame, though sometimes coals were needed there too.

What had happened while a large group of people were using the oven was that great loads of assorted wood had been collected and broken up but only the good 'coal' wood had been used. Consequently there was a large stock of inappropriate wood by the bakery. Conversely most of the wood used at the French camp had been small sticks to fit the Thai stove so there was plenty of large 'coal' wood in that pile.

Tina blocked her mind to the dreadful squeak of the barrow and ferried different sorts of wood to the piles where they would serve the best purpose. To some extent this was a labour of love as we only had flour for two more bakes and I think her underlying reason was that those last ones were going to be good. She wanted our memories of baking to be of fine, crusty bread and not the wishy-washy half-risen loaves that sometimes happen when the fire goes wrong.

Even if we hadn't been in 'enjoy' mode Tina had earned a break after this marathon and a day or so later we took advantage of the tides for a walk round the island. There was tenuous evidence that we might see turtles hatching: we'd seen a green turtle returning to the water after laying some fifty days before, so we carried shoes to ease our way over the sharper coral and set off at dawn.

At the place we'd seen her tracks we found the shape of the beach considerably changed. The sand no longer swept in a smooth curve from the reef to the vegetation line but sagged in untidy runnels between stony outcrops. Sadly, at the very spot we assumed her eggs to be, we found a couple of soft shells with dried out embryos inside. They had been torn open, whether by crabs or birds we couldn't tell, and just discarded. There was nothing else.

Further round the island we were met with an extraordinary sight. A pristine harpa ventricosa shell, some two-and-three-quarter inches long, perched at eye level in a Scaevola bush. On closer approach the puzzle was explained by the appearance of a bunch of hermit crab legs clinging firmly to the branch.

This was a highly desirable shell, at least it was to us as we hadn't found another like it. Smaller harpa shells similar to the amouretta were common but we'd only seen the ventricosa before in Madagascar, and even there only for sale in a shop. It didn't take long to agree that if we could find a new home for the crab this shell would join our collection and we plucked it off the bush.

Hermie's old box was nothing like big enough for the harpa crab, who was almost large enough to just step over the sides, so we put him in the cockpit and made sure there were no loose ropes for him to climb up. A large chunk of coconut, a bowl of water and a slab of plywood for shade were put in with him and we set off on a 'home' search.

I've already said that empty shells are scarce on Boddam and empty shells of the right size and shape are about as rare as snowflakes. We still hadn't discovered how hermit crabs established their first homes, or even how they exchanged them as they grew, so had no idea where best to start looking. We found an endless supply of suitable shells already being worn by crabs but that was part of the problem, not part of the answer.

We shuffled along the up-coming tide line turning over every stone and piece of flotsam on the way, but to no avail. It was almost as though shells were born with hermit crabs in. When we got as far as turtle beach for the second time that day the rising water forced us to turn about and we returned along the new high tide line. Still no good.

There was one other possibility. The winds and currents were changing the distribution of sand in the lagoon and a new bank was forming between Ile Du Sel and Ile Sepulture. Tomorrow morning's tide was as low as it would get in this pass of the moon so we would give that a go. If we found nothing there our harpa crab would retain his desirable residence and we'd plant him back on his bush.

The trip across to the bank was uneventful other than for picking up a couple of nice mackerel tuna on our lure, by far our most successful style of fishing, and we anchored just inside the reef. In no time at all Tina found a magnificent cowrie that we hadn't seen before and I stubbed my toe on a tired old shell that was both empty and about the right size for the crab. What luck.

Having come over here we didn't feel like just turning round and going back so decided to explore a bit. We popped the cowrie into a bucket with some sand and water as we wanted to keep him long enough to see what he looked like with his mantle open, and carried on towards Sepulture where we found more evidence of turtles.

There were no obvious eggs, which we thought a good sign, but there were plenty of tracks on the higher parts of the beach and several nest-like depressions. On the way back to the dinghy we found a live seven-finger scorpion conch and popped him in with the cowrie.

Five minutes into the return trip the outboard started making an odd wheezing sound which drew our attention to the lack of water from the coolant tell-tale. Instant death for outboards if you continue so we stopped it immediately and paddled home. Thank goodness the wind wasn't blowing hard.

Back on *Vespera* we replaced the water in the shells bucket and put them in the shade to study later and offered the replacement home to the 'about to be evicted'. He wasn't interested. I picked him up to see how firmly he was lodged in the harpa shell and he let go immediately. By comparing the size of his body to the size of the shell and relating that to Hermie's experience it was clear that the pair were not well matched. The poor little fellow was quite upset at being undressed so we hid him under the piece of plywood with his new shell for company and left him be.

At nightfall he was cowering in a corner ignoring everything. He'd poked a claw inside his prospective home for a grope around then climbed over it a couple of times. He even turned it upside down and rolled it away before retiring to a neutral corner. Both the live shells we wanted to study were lying in the bucket inert.

The morning was most distressing. The empty shell was

still where he left it but there was no sign of the crab. We searched all the obvious places he might have hidden but he was gone. We could only think he'd climbed out of the cockpit and fallen in the sea, and we felt dreadfully guilty. The live shells did nothing to improve our feelings either as they simply lay under the water doing nothing. If I could repair the outboard we would take them back as soon as possible.

But that was not to be. When I stripped it down it was to find that the water pump impeller had lost all its vanes and we didn't have a spare. I had some thick rubber that I could try carving a new piece from but the chances of it working were close to zero. This was most concerning because as soon as the spell of good weather ended and the wind came back we wouldn't be able to go ashore. Paddling ashore with the wind behind was easy enough but getting back against twenty knots or more was impossible.

As an emergency measure we tied all our floating ropes together to make one long line and lashed fishing floats to it about a hundred feet apart. The idea was to rig a permanent handline from the boat to the shore that we could haul ourselves along, but when we paid it out over the stern we found it too short.

Earlier in the year some family folks had run a heavy rope from high up the trunk of a palm tree to an anchor out in the lagoon to make a slide for the children. We commandeered this rope, and the tree, and tied our floating rope to the end that had been to the anchor. Between them they were just long enough. This time we had to tow it out from the shore and it took a prodigious amount of paddling but we managed, eventually, to make the link.

With that problem solved we could take time to study our captive shells. The scorpion conch had an amazing way of propelling himself about with a large foot he could extend from underneath. He would roll himself over and push himself around like an inane clockwork toy. The cowrie was much more sophisticated, being able to wrap his strangely textured, multicoloured mantle over the top of his shell and still find muscle power to climb the side of the bucket. It was time for them to go back now but without the outboard we were unwilling to take them across to the sandspit so we found a similar area we could walk to and released them there.

That evening we ate our last onion. Soaking in seawater had severely reduced the keeping qualities of the ones we brought from Thailand so they were long gone but this was the last of several that had been given to us by generous people as they left. Tina waited for a perfect fire, cooked the precious vegetable most carefully and served it up separate from the rest of the meal so we could savour it to the full.

Our tongues had thrashed the topic of what we would do for fresh food almost to death without producing anything of substance. The breadfruit trees had to all intents stopped producing but, to be honest, it didn't make much difference. Given the choice between climbing seventy feet of slippery tree for a breadfruit or going without, I would go without. Around the breadfruit grove were several plants that looked like taro but everyone we'd asked, particularly those who had travelled through the Pacific islands, were certain they weren't. In fact the consensus was that they were poisonous and we lacked the courage to try them to see.

That only really left bilimbis to give variety to the endless coconut. We had been shown the trees and even tasted some excellent jam made from the fruit, but whether it could be used as a vegetable we didn't know. What we'd seen of the trees suggested they were not prolific bearers anyway but Tina thought it would be worth a try. She went off to do a survey and came back with several fruits and news that the trees were loaded. It was obviously their season.

The fruit roughly approximates a gherkin in that it's the same basic shape and ripe ones vary from an inch and a half to four inches long, but there the similarity ends. The bilimbi is much softer, much juicier and very, very sour. This we discovered by the simple method of biting into one, a mistake that exercised all our face muscles and drove us quickly to the teapot to wash away the acidity.

Our first experiment in earnest was at that evening's meal when Tina sliced a couple into a fried rice dish with some chunks of tuna. The fish and rice absorbed much of the acidity and the flavour was better than we expected, but it did need a lot of salt. However as a first go it was quite successful.

During the night we were woken by traffic on the VHF

radio between an American ship and a yacht. They must both have been close by for us to hear them, though we could see no lights, and at dawn there was a yacht at anchor in the pass. This was a real surprise. A little later there was more radio traffic, in French this time, and the signals were so strong we thought there must be another yacht in the lagoon that we hadn't seen. When the new arrival moved over to Takamaka we couldn't see him at all so an un-noticed newcomer was quite possible.

Not having the dinghy to get around with put a serious damper on our activities. The two most important effects were that lack of temptation made working on the boat easier and that we could no longer troll for fish. This was a great shame as we were just getting on top of keeping Jess fed with dried tuna and even managing to catch some for ourselves, but now it was back to my singularly unsuccessful bottom fishing.

Inside *Vespera* things were looking much better. I had put some rough shelves behind the façade and nearly everything that had to be stowed was at least put away. I'd started work on the wiring and although the fuse panel was completely unserviceable half the navigation lights and all the sailing instruments were working.

In this we'd been lucky as the meters had remained above the water level, but the engine gauges were not so fortunate. Along with the fuse panel they'd received a thorough dunking and corrosion had eaten them to bits. However, four panel switches and two fuse holders, out of fourteen of each, still functioned and that was a good start.

Our hand line to the beach proved invaluable against the steadily increasing wind. Going ashore had become an unpleasant ritual as it didn't matter how careful you were you always reached the other end of the line soaking wet. Fortunately we had a plastic bucket with a lid that clipped on to protect anything that needed transporting, like a change of clothes, and we continued to go ashore every day to cook.

Following on from the promising bilimbi experiment we decided to harvest some of the fruit and give it a proper go. We knew the trees were full so it was as good a time as any. There are four trees, three of which are tall and spindly and the fourth lower and more bushy. When we arrived at the first one we saw clusters of fruit, which grow directly from the trunk, reaching right to the top.

Our intention was to gather a few to go with our evening rice and, if possible, find enough to make some jam. We had three pounds of sugar extra to what Tina needed for her immediate baking and Sue was organizing more, so jam seemed the best way to utilize the fruit. This first tree had several fruits growing within reach of an outstretched arm but certainly not enough for jam, and visits to the other three only brought our ground-based harvest to half a saucepan full. Not really enough to justify a jam making spree so Tina, being the lightest, got a leg up into the least spindly of the trees.

Almost as her foot found the first toe-hold she was descended on by mosquitoes, not in the sort of numbers we were accustomed to by the camp but great swirling clouds of them. There seemed to be millions of the perishers and they were a very effective spur to action. Her picking arm swept around in a blur and seconds later she was back on the ground, well bitten but happy with a good bag of bilimbis.

Making the jam was hilarious. We had recipes for Seville marmalade and apricot jam but nothing that remotely resembled bilimbi. Our guess was that something between the two would be about right and we argued at length whether the term 'equal quantities of fruit and sugar' meant the same volume or the same weight. The same weight won the day, but how much does a saucepanful of bilimbis weigh?

We settled for a simple balance instead of trying to estimate actual weights and made a real Libran set of scales from a stick and oddments of string that pretty much conformed to the rest of the décor in the 'watch your head'. When everything was ready and the fire burning perfectly Tina put the pan on and boiled the fruit then added the sugar. At almost the same moment a heavy gust blew the driftwood and palm frond door down.

With half a gale roaring through the fireplace and up the makeshift chimney the ideal fire became a furnace and the pan bubbled and spat. We were most reluctant to abandon the effort as most of our sugar was in it so we had to do some fast thinking. The collapsing door had dislodged and broken the piece of wood over the lintel, which was its primary support, so a quick repair there didn't look very likely.

While Tina shuffled the pan in and out of the intense heat trying to keep things at a gentle simmer I rushed around collecting sheets of asbestos to use with the remainder of the door to make a wind-break. Under the circumstances I thought I did this rather quickly but by the time the breeze on the fire was sufficiently under control all the coals had burned away.

Now we had the other end of the spectrum to contend with. Even stoked with flame and coal wood there wasn't enough heat in the fire to keep the pot boiling and parts of the new wind-break were hurriedly removed to let in the draft. This construction and demolition continued most of the afternoon before a spoonful of the brew dropped onto a saucer was proclaimed to be setting and it was time to heat the jars. This we did in a similar fashion and finished up with three nice pots of jam.

However, our sense of humour was not made of the same stern stuff as the wind and the afternoon left us feeling a bit drained. Pleased with our success but thoroughly irritated by the performance we decided to cook our bilimbi rice on the boat as my equanimity wouldn't have stood another session with the wind-break. I'd also gone completely off balance when gathering the utensils used on the bilimbis to wash them up and finding the blade of our best kitchen knife deeply etched by the juice.

While on this domestic kick Tina put in an heroic effort at the bakery and to make the very best of our resources she planned her day like a military exercise. Her mission was to make a couple of loaves, a tray or two of castaway cookies and a chocolate cake. The cake would pinch a cup and a half of flour from her usual bread recipe so each loaf would be about five slices small but we thought the treat would be worth it.

Once again the principal consideration was getting, and keeping, the fire right and the schlepp of collecting proper wood argued strongly for cooking it over the same coals. In this case the cooking had to be done in sequence so she had to judge how much wood to use and the exact moment when the oven had cooled enough not to burn the cake which, together with the bread, would fill it for the first time, then get the cookies in as soon as the first load was ready otherwise it would run out of heat before they could cook. I'm glad she accepted responsibility for it all as judging the fire is as fraught as predicting the weather and by leaving her to it I could avoid any blame. Coward.

But there was no need to worry. Several hours after leaving the boat she walked triumphantly into the 'watch your head' carrying a really beautiful light and fluffy cake, two diminutive but excellent loaves and a week's supply of cookies, great stuff.

Overcome by these successes, and particularly that with the bilimbi jam, we thought it worth experimenting with some other creative preserving. There are two wax apple, or jack apple, trees on the island that produce a small, pale pink, bell shaped fruit with a very delicate flavour, similar in some ways to the water guava of Malaysia. We'd only ever seen a few fruits on the trees when the crush of people had been here but the same could be said of the bilimbis so we went to investigate with visions of wax apple jelly or something.

The first tree was a disappointment, only two of the lovely little fruit and no sign of flowers or other evidence of a developing crop. Not wishing to see them go to waste we pulled on the branches to bring them low enough and picked them. One each. Then to get to the other tree we had to pass some of the bilimbi trees and being in the mood, and reassured at the strength of the branches proved by Tina's earlier adventure, I shinned up the most heavily laden one.

I was pleasantly surprised to find well worn stubs and projections on the trunks at most of the places I needed to stop at to pick. Those little stubs were smooth and friendly to a bare foot and spoke eloquently of the numerous harvests the trees must have produced. The mosquitoes must also consider the well used foot-holds to represent a trap for ambulatory food as they dashed out in ambush exactly as they had when Tina tried. Anyway we managed to grab another good bagful before being carried away and this time we were going to try pickling some. Those that didn't come up to our arbitrary standard of conformity would be boiled down and the juice used to make a cordial. The second wax apple tree was bare.

While Tina had been performing her magic in the

bakery, I'd replaced the lintel in the 'watch your head' with a plank salvaged from the elevated floor in the shed and rebuilt the driftwood and palm frond door. It wasn't as decorative as Chrissy's had been but it was serviceable and the weird structure of overturned deckchairs and asbestos sheets that had been the fireplace wind-break could be demolished for the last time.

With the fire controllable again the 'juice' bilimbis were soon bubbling in the pot and ready to be mashed and strained. The first time we tried this we simply poured the contents of the pot through a nylon kitchen sieve and were quite pleased with, and surprised at, the deep red juice we collected. The following morning a substantial sediment had settled out in the bottom of the bottle and we decanted a bright, clear juice the colour of quality rosé wine from the top. This had all the acidity of pure lemon juice and even tasted quite similar. When diluted with sweetened water it made a most acceptable and refreshing drink.

The pickling experiment was equally successful and very easy. We'd recently finished the onions from a large jar that Sue had pickled in Malaysia and the prime quality bilimbis were simply soaked in salt water overnight, cut into bite sized lumps and dropped into the heated onion juice. A week or so was all they needed for the flavours to mellow and 'Paradise Pickle' became a firm favourite.

On board *Vespera* I was still trying to get the balance of the navigation lights working. The lights themselves didn't present too much of a problem as they had, presumably, been designed to be deluged in seawater but the wiring was a headache. I'd just given up on the existing wires ever working again and was cutting them away to replace them when I reached under the cabin floor and found 'harpa crab'.

Somehow he'd made his way out of the cockpit, down the companionway steps, round the main cabin and into the bilge. But however he'd done it here he was still cowering in a corner and looking pretty unhappy without a home. In this he struck lucky because the replacement he'd so steadfastly refused earlier was still in the 'home' box and hadn't yet been taken ashore. Shell collecting was not high in the priorities at the moment.

Using the same procedure of putting him in the cockpit with food, water, shelter and the new home worked like a charm this time. I think he'd been on the homeless and hungry list long enough and after an ecstatic five minute inspection of the shell he popped it on like an old overcoat and proceeded to attack a piece of coconut. Next time we went ashore we delivered him to the scaevola bush that had been in his territory and he scuttled off into the undergrowth a very happy crab indeed. Thanks for the Ventricula shell.

Over the next few days we got to know the people from the other boats in the lagoon and they were, again, friendly and generous in spite of an impropitious start, one that was entirely the fault of my big mouth. One afternoon, as the sun found just the right spot, we'd caught the glint of three separate masts near Takamaka and were more than a little mystified as we'd only seen two yachts come in. It goes without saying that we were intensely aware of any activity on our horizon and the realization that a yacht had entered the pass, crossed the lagoon and come to anchor with neither of us seeing it took some coming to terms with.

We eventually met everyone when two of the boats braved the poor visibility and coral minefield for a brief exploration of Boddam, and the crew of the third came across by dinghy to spend the day with them. In the natural way of things we congregated on the beach and, while trying to learn each others' names, I asked some questions about when each boat had arrived, freely admitting our concern at missing such an event now that the horizon seemed a mere extension of our optic nerves.

It was at this point that I tripped over my jaw. I spoke at length on the thought that no-one could be so foolish as to cross the lagoon at night. 'Don't worry', said François, 'Your observations are not at fault. The night you heard us on the radio our friends came to anchor in the pass and we continued straight through to Takamaka!' Ouch.

Only a beneficent quirk of fortune could have delivered such good natured people for me to stumble so in front of, and warmth bubbled up in a healthy laugh all round allowing me to pick up my jaw and set it back in place, ready to fall over again.

Later in the day they got their own back when we were talking about the failed impeller in our outboard. I explained I was trying to carve a replacement from a piece of rubber and made the mistake of showing them the outcome of my first attempt. In truth their laughter was quiet and well-mannered and not raucous as it might well have been. It was then that Frederick said he had an old impeller that had similar vanes, and Phillipe said they had appropriate adhesives to use them to modify my broken one. Miracle of miracles.

François and Phillipe took the remains of my impeller to their boat where they salvaged the all-important hub and in a very short time were back with a new part. The vanes were a little fatter but so what. Without further ado the outboard was taken ashore and humped up the beach to the 'watch your head' kitchen table, which we instantly transformed into its alter ego as a workbench, and the new part fitted.

The extra thickness in the vanes made putting it together more difficult but it turned out alright and we stood the engine in a bowl of water for testing. As soon as it started a bright stream of water jetted from the tell-tale. It made a bit of a noise that hadn't been there before but everything was working so we immediately bolted it back on the dinghy. For safety's sake we decided to use it only in emergencies and ruled out expeditions round the lagoon unless other people were around, but it was satisfying to know it was there if needed.

We had a disappointment in our dealings with these lovely people before they left for the shelter of Takamaka. Both crews came over with gifts of flour, pasta and other treats, even another spare impeller that could be modified if the first one failed, and Joel and Frederick brought their cat to visit. To our shame Jess doesn't take kindly to competition and while our guests were showering us with goodwill the junior members spat and snarled at each other.

All we could do was keep them separated and Jess, being in her own territory, got shut in the heads while the visitor had the run of the boat. This cooled the passions a little and when it came time to go our feline guest didn't want to leave. Joel called and clicked her fingers but all she got for her trouble was a set of bloody clawmarks down her arm.

Tina had an advantage here having had some experience handling lion cubs, though it seemed part of another lifetime, and with severe determination grabbed the furry cannon-ball as it followed a low trajectory towards a hatch. The poor little thing was really frightened and very well armed. Tina used all her skills to avoid the raking claws and succeeded in wrapping a towel round the moving parts before they got her, but she didn't escape the teeth and two full sets of puncture marks decorated her hand for a week.

Having such a disturbing effect on our visitors wasn't much fun and we finished the day with a deep feeling of chagrin though I think, I hope, the problem was mostly in our own eyes. But it got worse. At dusk the day before they left the atoll the menfolk dinghied up to *Vespera* to present us with a fish, and delivered it in a top quality frying pan.

Obviously in a great hurry to get back before dark they made moves to leave immediately. Tina was hurriedly washing the pan and calling urgently from the galley for them not to leave without it, but they protested that Joel meant for us to keep it and sped away. How could that be? Tina tried calling on the VHF but they obviously couldn't hear us and the following morning we saw them exit the pass. I'm sure there was a grave misunderstanding here, possibly from the language difference, but I can't help feeling we did nothing but give offence to these kind people.

The made-up impeller got used for its first emergency just two days later. Some sort of weather system moved over us during the night and very strong winds, thirty-five knots and more, swung right around the compass, turning *Vespera* completely around on her chain. Under normal circumstances this is of no consequence but the shore-line got in a mighty tangle.

Somehow the line had dipped under the self-steering gear as we turned, ridden up over the rudder and jammed against the shaft. Then, with the bow securely chained to the bommie and the stern captive to the land, *Vespera* couldn't align herself properly in the wind and became most uncomfortable.

The only thing to do was drop our end of the shore-line and let it pull through where it was jammed. It simply wasn't possible to move it any other way as the wind had stretched everything bar tight. The moment the rope was free the loose end whipped over the bow and a loud sawing noise, like a giant zipper, resounded through the boat as it dragged over the rudder until suddenly it was quiet.

The sideways lumpiness of the sea subsided as if by magic as the bow swung into the wind and the line, with all its fishing float buoys, whirled and twirled its way ashore. There the waves rolled it up and down the beach, but none of its parts seemed to go in the same direction at the same time and soon it was a two-hundred-yard-long knot.

It was a problem that couldn't be left as it was the lifeline between us and our cooking fire, so as soon as I could raise the enthusiasm we let ourselves be swept ashore in the dinghy. After hours of frustration and with miserably blistered hands we had the whole thing laid out in a straight line at the water's edge ready to be re-deployed.

We positioned the end that had to be towed out well up-wind and hoped to make use of its force to help us. If we paddled straight out the combination of wind on our side and drag from the rope as it peeled off the sand should take us directly to *Vespera*'s bow. At least that was the theory and at first it worked like a charm.

It was quite hard work paddling but the rope eased into the water nicely and all the relative movements kept it in a nice straight line that progressively moved out and along the shore. However, we were still twenty feet short of *Vespera* as we came to the end of the line and, try as we might, we couldn't paddle hard enough to stretch it that last little bit. The wind swept us back to shore in a long arc to finish up tangled round the jetty.

A few more blisters and angrily muttered words saw us back at the starting point ready to commit the outboard to its first real test. Everything ran smoothly until most of the rope was afloat, but this time we were badly positioned as we approached the boat and had to make up ground against the wind as well as put in the final stretch. The engine worked really hard for about twice as long as I can reasonably hold my breath, but anxiety stopped me exhaling until Tina clamped a hand round a stanchion.

Once she had a firm grip we could close the throttle and check the tell-tale and for a long moment we saw nothing. It wasn't until the engine slowed to idling that the stream restarted and we could breath a sigh of relief, though it was not clear why it had stopped in the first place. But with the shore-line secure again it wasn't too significant.

To take our minds off the morning's irritations we decided to give each other a haircut. Tina had first tackled this job under the patient supervision of a friend in Durban and, in spite of almost overwhelming trepidation, she did it well and has done so ever since. I, on the other hand, was not allowed near her head with a pair of scissors until she felt really desperate. Not having the vaguest understanding of ladies' hairdressing I suffered the same trepidation but we talked out a scheme that sounded idiot-proof.

On the basis that each hair should have grown the same amount since the last cut, and that the current style was quite acceptable, I only had to ensure that I cut the same length off all over. We reckoned that if Tina put rollers in, making sure every hair on her head was accounted for, I could undo them one at a time and simply cut an inch off each rollerfull.

So with noisily clicking scissors and a brash confidence that was a deliberate lie, I undid the first roller and combed the hair over my fingers. There must have been a hundred thousand hairs and all of them different lengths. With a slight gulp I guessed at the average and snipped off the predetermined inch. Then it was the next roller, and the next, and there was no turning back.

Fortunately Tina is blessed with nice curly hair that looks good whatever is done to it, and when the last roller was back in its box it only took a few strokes with the comb to finish the job. I was beside myself with pride and after the mandatory 'Can you just clean up these fly-away ends' Tina was quite pleased as well. It was a shame there was no-one else to show off to.

Only one more thing remained for the day and that was to replenish the coconut store. Behind the breadfruit grove is a group of trees that produce lovely big nuts that more than repay carrying them the extra distance when compared to the small nuts along the beach. On the way we would have a crack at a lone breadfruit that might be within reach of 'the pole'.

Brian and Trine had found this excellent bamboo pole in the Seychelles and brought it here for the express purpose of fruit gathering. It was very light, like an overgrown fishing rod, and the better part of forty feet long. If the fruit you aimed at was ripe a couple of deft swipes at the supporting branch was all you needed, apart from a little care to avoid the descending missile, but on this occasion the fruit was not quite at its prime and refused to be teased off its tree, so we contented ourselves with an armful of coconuts.

When we moved our everyday living to the 'watch your head' we had to devise a means of opening those nuts. At the French camp a previous traveller had set up a fine husking spike using an old fence post and this worked well, but a similar spike here had been broken, leaving us with a long walk each time we wanted a nut. We had brought a spike with us, having seen how easily the professionals cleaned nuts with them in Malaysia, but it had been lost in the upheaval.

One of *Vespera*'s anchors, a seventy-five pound plough, had been left propped against a tree when it was retrieved and the point on one of the flukes made a reasonable substitute. The first few nuts we cleaned taught us what was needed and, with the stock wedged under the roots of an adjacent tree and the shank firmly lashed to the tree against which it leaned, it worked as well as anything. In fact it performed better as a coconut spike than as an anchor.

Things were progressing well with work on the boat and all the navigation lights now worked. This was a big leap forward and instilled enough enthusiasm to tackle the steering. I took the whole mechanical system apart, cleaned off the rust and old lubricant that had solidified in the salt, and re-assembled it with new grease, and it felt a hundred times better.

The wheel was still stiffer than it should be and contact marks on the limit stops suggested that the shaft was slightly bent, a situation which we could do nothing about, but there were no particular points at which it stuck and no apparent leakage around the seal, so we pronounced it fit for service.

This exercise took a few days and we celebrated its completion by making afternoon tea on board. It was a miserable day with a sky like the inside of a galvanised bucket and the nuisance of hauling ashore to light a fire with damp wood didn't seem appropriate, so we wallowed in the luxury of simply turning on the gas, but the euphoria of surrendering to a good book and a second cup didn't last long.

Excited shouting in an unknown language had both of us out of our seats in a trice and we met shoulder to shoulder in the companionway. Right before our eyes was a small fishing boat with a gaggle of dark bodies on deck, all gesticulating wildly, but whether at us or among themselves we couldn't tell. They were several hundred yards away but the gap was closing quickly and they were heading straight at us. Our hearts sank. We'd agonized our way through similar encounters in the Malacca Straits but there we usually had other yachts in VHF range. Here there wasn't another soul and we were, frankly, scared.

Our tension eased a little when the boat changed course but it was a false signal as they'd merely side-stepped a coral head and resumed their approach immediately. They motored alongside then continued forwards a few yards to drop anchor, a sort of grapple made of rusty half-inch rods, then fell back to stop a few feet off our port side.

As the boat came to rest the shouted commands and counter-commands quieted and the crew, five in all, lined themselves along the bulwark to look at us. They appeared neither friendly nor particularly threatening, just seeming to want to examine us like exhibits in a zoo. Our attempts at communication elicited only two words, repeated over and over with different inflections – 'Sri Lanka'.

With the shamefully common, and arrogant, assumption that English spoken slowly and with suitable flourishes is understood by everybody, I laboured to express my concern that they were too close for safety. But it was wasted effort. That they were too close would have been obvious to a blind man, indeed such a man could have touched both boats with his stick, so the lack of understanding seemed deliberate.

The next act in this pantomime was for us to deploy fenders along our vulnerable side and, watched by lack-lustre eyes, I delved into the lazarette for some tyres. It was the wind that solved the immediate problem though. While I was passing up tyres the fishing boat slid gently astern and furious activity engulfed the crew as a huge, shallow and highly visible bommie lurked downwind.

They hauled up their anchor and made to motor between us and the shore, but this time they chose to understand my shouted warning that the row of buoys marked a floating rope. With a sudden change of heart they altered course to pass in front and re-anchored midway between us and the jetty. At least from there they wouldn't hit us if the wind swung.

Now it was my turn. Where they were lying put their stern just a few yards upwind of our shoreline and if their grappling hook slipped again, which I thought quite likely, the rope would finish up round their propeller – a situation that had catastrophe written all over it in both languages so, with great reluctance, we let the end free and watched our precious line coil itself up in another knot on the beach.

Later we were glad to have taken this precaution. When the night was at its blackest, about an hour before moonrise, we heard their engine start and rev up anxiously, accompanied by another round of excited babble. A brilliant searchlight flared into life showing that they'd dragged right across where the line usually sat and were drifting down on the same lurking coral. With a falling tide they were in a dangerous predicament.

We lit *Vespera* up as much as much as we could to give them a point of reference but without a common language there was little else we could do. In fact even had we been able to communicate I couldn't have led them through the coral in the dark as I didn't, and still don't, know it well enough.

But, in retrospect, our concern was unfounded. Either

they knew their way around or were on exceptional terms with their Gods as they managed to motor into the only reasonably open area in the anchorage and settle themselves down again. Only once had they been forced to disengage their engine and pole over a shallow patch.

This marked a change in the night's fortunes. The wind eased as the moon came up and at dawn they took advantage of the flat water to leave. We also took advantage of it to stretch the shoreline out without having to fight the elements and by breakfast time it was just another entry in Tina's diary.

Now that August was well under way we had to really come to terms with a voyage plan and being able to navigate was a primary concern. Our GPS receiver was working but had once, during a trial run, refused to switch on, so a backup was important. The sextant was okay and Sue had dried the almanac pages for September and onwards so as long as one of our watches kept going we could manage the hard way, but my calculator had been destroyed and without it I'm somewhat mentally deficient.

Clive had loaned me a simple calculator, of the sort usually kept in chequebooks, and we had a set of sight reduction tables torn from an outdated almanac so the manual backup boiled down to a refresher course in basic arithmetic. At the time it seemed easier to try the old satellite navigator.

At the outset it looked most unpromising as the aluminium case was corroded and the bolts holding it together were cemented in place by the oxides. But plenty of easing oil and patience did the trick and as soon as the bolts were out it came apart easily. For once the term 'marine' on the marketing package had been justified and, unlike most similarly tagged items on the boat, the electronic widgetry inside looked good as new.

With mounting enthusiasm we cleaned it up and put it back together and were most disappointed when we turned it on and only got an illuminated blank screen. However, we disconnected the power and fiddled with it, making sure that every terminal had been short-circuited to earth to drain off stray charges that might upset the computer, and next time we tried it cycled through its programme nicely.

Sometimes you strike lucky with this system and it locks

on to a satellite as you switch on, but more often you have to wait for ages. Naturally we fell into a waiting period so left the unit on while we went ashore for supper. On our return it was still scanning the heavens but nothing had yet seen fit to talk to it and we left it on all night. By morning it was clear that all was not in order.

Much later, in fact days later, I had reason to borrow a connector from its antenna lead while working on something else and discovered that the connector was faulty. Without further ado we repositioned the receiver to suit a shorter lead and – Bingo – it locked on as we powered it up. With two electronic navigators working, the sight reduction tables could stay in the grab-bag and the refresher course be deferred until I felt like it.

Sue had been gone almost a month and any day now the Brits would be back. Wondering whether she'd organized the parts in time was a thought process to be actively avoided. Like a bad tempered terrier if you dropped your guard for a moment it would jump right in and worry at your soul until you wanted to kick it.

Tina's way of keeping the beast at bay was to bash away on the typewriter writing endless letters to all and sundry. Ian had given the machine a thorough service and it was now getting the exercise it needed to loosen up its joints. This would be our last chance to communicate with friends and family until we arrived somewhere with a post office, so she was very busy.

One morning though, as a break from the repetitiveness of similar letters, she decided on a de-moulding session. Although the boat was drying out nicely the daily temperature cycle created a lot of condensation and mould flourished. Everywhere you looked tentacles of unwanted biology were expanding the blots in an apparent take-over bit for our air space. Bleach was the simple answer and a regular rinse down with the stuff would solve the problem for good, but our stock of bleach was limited.

Anyway, putting aside enough to treat our drinking water for the trip, she made up a strong mix and attacked the offending microbes. In fact she got a bit swept up in it and all her careful stowing was undone in search of the last molecule and when she eventually put down her cloth there wasn't a spot left anywhere. It smelt like a public convenience but that was easier to live with than the mildew.

While the housewifely vigour was pumped up she decided to polish the brasswork, a symbolic gesture of some significance. When *Vespera* was on the reef we'd discussed, briefly, whether to retrieve her brass nameplate as a keepsake and agreed that it was an integral part of her and should share her fate. Since then neither of us had wanted to tempt that fate by even touching the plate and it was looking pretty sorry for itself. Now the acceptance that putting a shine back on it was worthwhile seemed an important pointer to the future.

Not such a bright pointer was an inflammation of my right eye that had been niggling since the accident. Up to now it had been merely an irritation but lately the eyeball itself had started to swell and we didn't know what was causing it. None of the medication we thought appropriate had survived and the best we could do was make an eyepatch to protect it from wind and weather.

Fortunately the Brits' visit was imminent and we were sure the medic that usually accompanied them would be able to help, with information at least even if they didn't carry a full medical kit. In common with most people I find fear of ill health as difficult to deal with as the reality and was looking forward to some reassurance. Meanwhile the eye patch Tina made from a handkerchief, some cotton wool and a length of elastic from a cushion cover provided a lot of relief, especially as the weather had set in a bad mood.

A few boats had come into the atoll but all headed for the shelter of Takamaka, a wise move as the full strength of the trade winds across the fetch of the lagoon made *Vespera*'s location distinctly uncomfortable. Both of us suffered bouts of seasickness and going ashore was a miserable business.

To rub it in I was ferrying stuff from the shed to the boat one morning, an activity that necessitated using the outboard as the shoreline went to the wrong place, and the impeller failed again. The old hub had torn apart where the vanes were glued on. This time I did things differently and simply cut down Frederick's spare and adapted it to fit the shaft with a piece of plastic tubing. It worked quite well.

Speculation as to the day the Brits would come was our regular mealtime topic. We had deduced, rightly or wrongly, that their island surveys took about four days, usually weekdays, and were dependent on transport that seemed to have a fortnightly availability. I'm quite sure those deductions, when viewed against reality, would make the organizers chuckle but they were the best indicators we had.

Based on remarks made when they collected Sue we expected them sometime between the fifteenth and twenty-fourth of August, with Tuesdays and Thursdays as favourites depending on which way they travelled round the archipelago. The first Tuesday, then the first Thursday came and went with no sign of a ship but we weren't unduly concerned. Indeed each day that passed was a day extra for Sue to organize things, but at the same time a day less to get the engine together and running.

We kept ourselves busy through the intervening days making new doors for the cupboard in the head and the locker behind the saloon table, but when the next Thursday passed without a visit we worried on two counts: my eye was getting worse and the calendar was pushing me towards a bad decision. It was now less than a week to the end of August and every day we stayed after that increased the risk of sailing into a cyclone. From our observations it was most unlikely they would arrive on a Friday so the following Tuesday, the twenty-ninth, was our next gamble. It promised to be an awful scramble to get away safely but, with the exception of the engine and a couple of related jobs, we were ready.

The weekend disappeared under a spread of charts, cruising guides and pilot books while I searched for a compromise route, but it was only repeating the earlier work and our plan was already the compromise. No matter how we juggled the options, unless we got away in the next week we wouldn't get to the Mozambique Channel ahead of the season. However, according to the weather pundits, if we set out before the middle of September the chances of encountering a storm were only about three percent. It would run against the grain of my usual excessive caution but if we could leave by then, we would.

The sound of an approaching dinghy prompted us to

tidy away the books. Tony and Marjory from *Reveille*, one of the boats at Takamaka, had come to visit Boddam to have a look around. Earlier, during one of several long radio conversations, we'd asked if they had any excess flour or sugar as we were completely out of both, and their cheerful assurance that they did in no way prepared us for what was to happen. They'd got together with the crew on *Darius*, another yacht sheltering over there, and between them assembled a package of goodies that went far beyond our request. As they climbed aboard they opened a cavernous backpack and produced the flour and sugar, followed by books, chocolate bars, cheese and fresh vegetables.

Again we have this amazing circumstance where people who knew us only as voices on the radio, a means of communication usually as dry and impersonal as the telephone time signal, had joined with others, who didn't know us at all, to help. In fact not only to help with material things but with perceptive thoughtfulness that worked wonders for our morale. Small treats like candy bars gain enormous significance where there are no shops.

Next day we were able to thank Geoff and Penny, from *Darius*, personally when they brought their baby daughter to visit Boddam. We had even more reason to thank them as, having spoken to the *Reveille*'s and been told the nature of my eye problem, they'd discussed it with a medical student currently crewing for them and had brought with them a diagnosis, prognosis and all the necessary medicines.

They also brought disquieting news, though. They'd been in touch with Diego Garcia for their medical man to speak to his counterparts about treatment for someone else and had been told that, as far as their informant was aware, there were no Brit-ops planned for the next two weeks. We didn't know quite what to make of that but tried to rationalize it on the grounds that military people often know nothing of future plans until the orders are posted. We could but hope.

That same day a young man from our old sailing club in Durban came to reconnoitre a passage across the lagoon. He needed to take on drinking water and the rain water collected from the shed roof is far superior to the well water on

Takamaka. We thought this would be a pretty bold move as the endlessly disturbed surface made spotting bommies very hard, but next morning we saw him move off his anchor and weave slowly towards us.

It was good to have company for a few days, especially someone to reminisce with about familiar haunts and faces. We hadn't met before as Alex started his cruise before we even bought *Vespera* but there was plenty of common ground to foment a bout of nostalgia. Then, once his tanks were full, we went to show him the breadfruit grove but as a foraging trip it wasn't too successful.

Breadfruit were obviously not destined to be part of our menu but the taro controversy re-awakened. Alex's ideas on the matter were more than welcome as, having spent years in the Pacific where taro is a staple diet, he was certain that these were the right plants. So much so that he sliced a piece from a tuber and popped it in his mouth. Once he'd had a good chew he cut another sliver for me and I dutifully followed suit. Not knowing what to expect I munched for a second or two and swallowed. It was enormously bitter, but then many raw vegetables are and I was reassured when, after the tasting, he harvested a couple of tubers for his evening meal.

Walking back along the path the inside of my mouth started to burn as if I'd been eating uncooked stinging nettles, and before we reached the 'watch your head' my throat felt the same. Meanwhile Alex hadn't said a word. Copious drafts of water followed by numerous cups of tea relieved things a little but the sensation lingered for hours. If this plant was a viable vegetable it had to be a whole lot better when it was cooked.

Comparing notes in the morning we agreed that, although the plant was definitely taro, something had happened to it to make it inedible. The fact that we both survived the night indicated that it wasn't downright poisonous, but it wasn't downright palatable either. This was disappointing as it looked more and more as though we would be here a long time.

A huge yacht, *Cyrano de Bergerac*, came into the atoll while this was happening and called offering assistance as soon as she came to anchor. It was quite impossible for this large vessel, I should think thirty times the displacement of *Vespera*, to transit the lagoon so Gordon and Jenny zoomed across in a runabout to see us, immediately dispelling any residual gloom from the taro experiment.

The yacht carries a crew of eight and Gordon had put to them the question 'What would you really wish for if you were marooned here?' Their response was magnificent. In addition to things they knew we needed they brought gifts of sausages, real ones not out of a tin, an oven-ready chicken, a cold bottle of wine and a weekend 'Telegraph' with an impossible crossword puzzle. Luxuries beyond measure. They also took some letters which they would post in the Seychelles, where they expected to be in four or five days' time.

The morning of the day they left Alex moved to Takamaka in preparation for his own departure, also after squeezing his supply lockers to give us anything he could spare, and I'm sure some things he couldn't but gave us anyway. Then the next day we had the atoll to ourselves again. We treated ourselves to a walk round the island, just for the hell of it, and waved farewell to Alex as he sailed past the northwest corner of Boddam.

But we weren't to be on our own for long. The afternoon of the first of September brought two more fishing boats into the atoll. We assumed they'd come in for shelter as it was a miserable day, the overcast a turbulent exercise in grey tonality and the wind only dropping to twenty-five knots between squalls. The sea was so noisy that the fisherman took us by surprise and we only heard their voices when they were right alongside, too late to do anything about our shoreline but warn them it was there. Fortunately this time there was a crew member who could speak English.

In no time they were anchored, again very close, and a couple of men swam ashore for a look round. I was more than a little envious of their ability when we watched them swim back against wind and waves. It wasn't very far but the effort to overcome the elements would have represented a substantial day's exercise for me, all in one go.

By morning conditions were better and daylight saw both of them weigh anchor. Thinking they were going back to work we went on deck to wish them well, but in fact they were just coming to ask if it was safe to moor against the jetty. It quickly became apparent that my description of the hazards was only causing confusion, so I collected one of the skippers and the chap who could speak English and took them ashore to show them.

I pointed out the shallows and a rock outcrop that projects seaward from one corner and they gave the place a thorough inspection before returning to the boats. Consequently we were taken aback to go on deck after breakfast and find both boats tied bows-on to the jetty, seemingly right over the rocks. However on going ashore I saw they were sitting quite far out on long lines so didn't give it another thought.

I'd gone ashore especially to explain that the pile of things in the shed was our property and not treasure trove, but I was too late. One look showed me that not going ashore and staying there was a mistake. We'd kept these things stacked neatly on the raised floor and covered with plastic sheets, so 'private property' should have been reasonably obvious, but I found the sheeting strewn all over the place, cartons tipped over and rummaged through and all was in a terrible mess. My first thoughts were for the tools and precious engine filters which I left there because it was dryer than on the boat. They were nowhere to be found.

To put it mildly I was rather angry and the first person I encountered was swaggering along the path swiping at overhanging palm fronds with my machete, but all I got in response to my request to give it back was an arrogant sneer. He was shortly joined by a chap proudly carrying Tina's pegbag, now empty of pegs and filled with my sockets and small tools. His response was a blank, uncomprehending, stare.

The stand-off was ugly, particularly as I knew there were ten of them on shore.

Luckily, very luckily, the English-speaking chap and his skipper came along and between them defused the situation before it go any worse. There was considerable embarrassment all round and I felt it best to go back to *Vespera* while our things found they way back to the shed. Later, when we explained our circumstances more fully, the pendulum swung the other way and it would have been hard to find more generous and supportive people.

So much so they invited us to join them for a feast of Sri Lankan cooking at lunchtime. It was our turn to be embarrassed as they treated us like royalty. The feast was prepared and eaten in the 'watch your head' and they went to great trouble to lay the table using our plates and cutlery at places they reserved for us. At first we didn't fully appreciate this gesture for what it was but later, when we learned that knives and forks had no place in their culture, we were very touched. It's sobering to realize that we wouldn't have known how to show them the same respect.

At the designated time we were escorted to the places of honour and immediately the table cloth disappeared under huge bowls of food. Along with the inevitable cauldron of rice, several gallons of it, was a vast pot of curried tuna, an even larger bowl of assorted fish fillets fried with unknown spices and the most beautiful pot of cooked fresh vegetables. Once the initial shyness was overcome it was a splendid meal and, although all conversation was channelled through the one man who spoke both languages, it was a friendly and enjoyable gathering.

During it all we came to the conclusion that their venture was an exploratory one, even though a couple of crewmen had been here before. It seemed they'd chosen the venue largely on hearsay and had plenty of questions for us. Which way did the local currents run, what was the weather like and when did the seasons change?, and numerous queries about the other islands. Then, to make sure we were talking about the same places, one of them went to get their chart which soon took the place of the empty pots on the table. To say the least of it we were bemused.

The chart they'd used to find their way here, in fact the only chart they had, was of the whole Indian ocean and to a scale that fitted Sri Lanka into a circle barely an inch in diameter. Their voyage was represented by a track not six inches long and Boddam, as such, wasn't even shown, the whole island group being merely a speckle of dots. The only navigational tools they appeared to have was a set of school geometry instruments, so we thought anything more than pointing out the visible dangers would be out of place.

However, the following morning I went aboard one of the boats to look at a radio that wasn't working and found, to my amazement, a GPS receiver and a first-class recording depth sounder. This put a different complexion on things and at least we could give them coordinates of islands and reefs so they could avoid them at night. Unfortunately I couldn't repair the radio; it was a simple fault in a loudspeaker but we had nothing to fix it with.

Later in the day a third boat arrived but went initially to Takamaka. We couldn't figure out why he had come in as there was no cause to shelter from the weather. In truth we couldn't figure why the others were still here either, wasting their precious ice supply instead of working, but felt it was none of our business. The boat with the broken radio went to meet the new arrival to see if they had any spares then, as evening came, both boats came to join their colleague moored to the jetty.

First thing in the morning all three boats were alive with activity. The fishermen were learning why I'd shown them the rocks round the jetty as the lower tide was bumping them on the bottom. They hurriedly dropped their mooring lines to extricate themselves from the immediate problem, but one, in an extravagant manoeuvre to avoid a sandbank, drove hard onto a coral head. With much shouting and shifting of ballast they managed to get free before the tide set them fast, only to repeat the performance on another coral twenty yards away. Eventually though they were all safely under way and passed close alongside to hand across parting gifts of food and call loud farewells.

It was while we were preparing our evening meal that we noticed the first of the missing things. Tina went to the shelf where she kept the cooking utensils to fetch the kitchen knife but couldn't find it. Of course that's just the sort of thing easily misplaced when other people use the kitchen so we had a good look around, but it wasn't to be found.

The search revealed though that another knife, specially shaped for preparing coconuts, and our only working oil lamp were also gone. These were serious losses indeed as they were fundamental to our 'castaway' lifestyle. It got worse when we discovered that the tarpaulin Ted had given us and my machete had also gone 'walkabout'. We could only think that the crew of the third boat, or someone in it, hadn't been briefed by the others as, following the initial misunderstanding, they would have been mortified by such an occurrence.

The fickle weather Gods chose this moment to display their contempt and, now that the little fleet was back at sea, the period of comparative calm came to an abrupt end. All day the background wind increased and the convergence zone squalls marched past like angry soldiers. During the night we were woken by a loud bang, followed by an awful grating noise echoing through the boat. One of the squalls was working up to strength and we were getting the big gusts that precede the rain. It was a dreadfully familiar scenario that had both of us on deck, awash in adrenalin, in no time.

Our first look round with the big torch didn't tell us much. We still seemed to be in the same place but the trees were too far away to make an accurate assessment. Then, before we could locate ourselves relative to the bommies, the wind brought bullets of rain making it impossible to look in any direction other than directly at the shore. I rushed to the bow to check the lines and found the snubber rope on our anchor chain stretched taut and the other rope, the one to the old chain round the bommie, hanging straight down. Obviously the loud bang had been the old chain breaking and the grating noise was our chain taking up the slack.

Thank heavens for that second chain. It had been left deliberately long so its weight would absorb the shock in just such an event and it had worked well. We were anxious about how close the extra scope would put us to the surrounding coral but until the rain stopped we couldn't see anyway, so we ducked inside to make some tea.

Later, in the squall's dying flurries, I made a thorough check and the nearest bommie was still ten or twelve feet from our stern. Enough of a margin to let us defer sorting it out until daylight so we turned back in, but it took a long time for the adrenalin to subside.

It was quite simple to repair the break with a shackle and we did the job as soon as it was light enough to see. However, the chain was badly corroded and little strength remained; I felt I could probably snap it with my bare hands. But all the time it held it would take the load off *Vespera*'s chain and, like last night, give a distinctive warning of strong conditions, so we let it be.

On returning to the boat after breakfast we heard a garbled squawk from the VHF and Tina thought she picked out the name *Vespera*. There was a yacht near Takamaka, though it was no-one we knew, so a call seemed unlikely but Tina broadcast a response just in case. The yacht answered immediately but it wasn't them calling and they hadn't heard anything, so we put the squawk down to a vagary of atmospherics.

But half an hour later we were quite certain. "Yacht *Vespera*, yacht *Vespera*, this is the *Henry J. Kaiser*" (an American ship we had spoken to once before). Great excitement as we dived for the microphone. Here were the Brits with our engine parts and we still had a week before our arbitrary, but absolute, cut-off date.

As soon as we made contact and identified ourselves the radio operator delivered a message from the British Representative, "Your daughter Susan has arrived safely in London and your parts are in Diego Garcia. However, they are unable to mount a Brit-ops visit until November, but your permit to stay is extended until then, when they will bring you food as well as the parts!" November!

That our hopes could be raised and dashed in such a short time left me breathless and without a reasonable flow of words. I'm quite sure, in fact I know, that I was rude to the messenger, who was a very pleasant sounding chap, but it was quite unintentional. It was merely my reaction to the ramifications of what he was saying. After a hurried conference with Tina I spluttered some words of thanks to the Brit. Rep. for the message and signed off. November!

Jumbled and confused emotions were the order of the day. The one that came out uppermost was relief that I no longer had to make the decision to gamble with cyclones, but a lot of other thoughts bubbled away under that.

Food was the primary concern. We had started on the hundred–and–fifty–day supply of cans back in June but, luckily, our appetites had been subdued and we weren't using the packs as quickly as expected. At the current rate of consumption, provided the cans didn't rust through, we had enough to keep us going until Christmas, except for Jess, whose appetite was quite back to normal and for whom supplies would run out much earlier.

Sue had taken a shopping list to Diego Garcia to buy such things as toilet rolls and torch batteries as well as flour, rice and sugar but the quantities involved were only meant to compliment the cans until November, when we had expected to be in Durban. In the short term though the provisions given us by the yachts would see us through to the Brits' visit. We had flour for seven bakes, which meant bread every ninth day, and sufficient rice and pasta as long as we weren't greedy.

Now it was back to the routing charts to look for new options. Assuming the engine would be running by the end of November the next opportunity for a trip nominally free of headwinds or cyclones was to cross the equator in January and make our way to Kenya in the northern hemisphere winds. The only difficulty would be strong adverse currents as we approached Africa. It would be an uphill battle but was feasible. Another alternative was simply to wait and leave when the cyclone season finished in May next year.

There were, of course, other less promising possibilities but all involved tackling the trade winds head on and we only considered them as 'last options'. The best choice from the point of view of stress on the boat was to wait out the season; however, to do this we would have to stretch our food out to the end of June and even that wouldn't leave an over-large margin for sea time.

If we reduced our consumption from two tins a day, that is one each of protein and vegetable, to either one or the other we could manage a lot longer and we decided to start this regimen straight away. Whether we could stay till May or had to tackle the Somali Current would be decided by what Sue had managed to arrange with the Brits. Whatever happened we were going to eat a lot of coconuts.

Looking back on it that day was the beginning of an era. With the exception of the engine *Vespera* was ready to go and, now we had confirmation that the parts were available, anxiety on that front was reduced. We had sufficient food for the present and knowledge that more was on its way; and my eye was responding well to the antibiotic, so we had our health. And we had the prospect of time with our piece of paradise to ourselves and little more to do than enjoy it.

The corollary though was the threat of cabin fever, so the same day marked the start of 'The Book'. Very few, if any, of the people involved with *Vespera*'s salvage had resisted the temptation to say 'You should write a book about it', so the seeds of the idea were already sown, though until now most had fallen among stones.

From my school days writing of any kind has been indivisibly linked with punishment and, as such, something to be avoided at all cost. In those far off times the most minor misdemeanour resulted, if your were caught, in a five-hundred-word essay being added to your homework, and an accumulation of a thousand words in a term brought down the wrath of God.

I'd taken the trouble to check the word content of a couple of favourite books and was appalled to learn that, had I attracted the maximum punishment short of caning for every term since, I could still be scribbling now, long past my fiftieth birthday, and not yet written enough to edit a book from.

Not exactly overwhelming motivation with which to undertake such a venture but it seemed a tangible way to thank everyone and completing it became established as a debt of honour.

But staring at a blank sheet of paper trying to formulate an opening sentence flooded my memory with bleak Saturday mornings and the task of elucidating on 'the morality of obedience' or 'the importance of conformity in modern society' in a page and a half, but the rest of my mind was no more inspired than the water-stained pad in front of me. Nothing. Maybe tomorrow would be better.

But priority in the morning had to go to improving the way *Vespera* was attached to the bottom. The repaired chain was acceptable for the week or so we'd expected to be here but clearly wasn't appropriate for a stay of several months. The warp for our second anchor was mainly of rope, which wouldn't last long in the coral, and the chain portion alone was too short to go round the bommie. It wasn't until Tina remembered that Ian had left a chain on the bottom somewhere nearby that the solution came to mind.

Neither of us could remember Ian's plan for this chain, whether he'd left it here on purpose or simply forgotten to pick it up, but we didn't think he would mind if we used it for the duration then took it back to him in South Africa. It took half an hour of vigorous swimming to find it and another to get it ashore to sort out, when examination showed it to be far from perfect. Again it was in two pieces that had to be shackled together but it was infinitely superior to the one that broke.

Putting it in place round the bommie was easier than I expected. Tina fed it out of the dinghy while I laid it over the other chains and soon it was securely shackled and the bow line transferred. Even more peace of mind to add to our well-being.

I don't know if it was coincidence or simply that we had more time to observe things but the very next day nature presented us with a treat. Ever since first seeing hermit crabs and realizing the intense competition that must go on over the meagre supply of shells, we'd wondered how these guys organize larger shells to grow into. Today it looked as though they were going to show us.

Breakfast had been a leisurely affair during which we tried mixing coconut with our porridge to bulk it out, an experiment which turned out very satisfactorily, and we were comfortably settled on beach chairs in a spot sheltered from wind and rain, Tina busy with her diary while I pretended to write, when we noticed a crab in serious trouble with his health.

He was quite a large hermit, substantially bigger than Hermie but by no means a giant, and had just keeled over as he made his way across a clearing. He was now on his back waving his legs feebly in the air. Tina put him back on his feet but a few weary steps later he was down again, this time curled up in a more conventional defensive stance, so she let him be.

A minute or two later a similar sized crab edged up to the old fellow and rolled him over to investigate. There was a furious bristling of feelers on the part of the newcomer but it elicited no response. At this the strong one worked the 'feet' of a couple of legs under the curled-in claw of the other to get a good grip then just seemed to hang on.

During the next few hours a variety of different-sized crabs joined the fray and as each one arrived a most undignified scuffle would break out while a new 'pecking order' was decided. Essentially at the end of each scuffle we would see a line of crabs stretching out from the sick fellow, in descending order of size and each desperately clinging on to the one in front. I say essentially because sometimes there would be two crabs with the same sized shells, a dilemma which seemed quite beyond their ability to resolve, and until another misfit arrived the squabbling would continue.

At the end of one such tussle a second row of contenders formed and that evolution relieved the tension until there were simply too many participants for a sustainable peace. By mid afternoon the cluster of crabs resembled a starfish, but a very dynamic starfish as individual crabs would change queues like demented shoppers at a supermarket check-out. Surprisingly crabs much larger than the sick one also milled about the area and often took a turn at climbing over the assemblage, dislodging the grip of everyone they stood on and generally causing consternation.

As luck would have it both of us were by the fire in the 'watch your head', caught up in the ritual of tea making, at the critical moment. When we'd risen to the sound of a bubbling pot everything was as it had been for the past hour, with some thirty crabs waiting more or less patiently. When we returned with our cups all kinds of mayhem had been let loose and crabs were trying and discarding shells at a frantic pace.

The poor old fellow was lying in the sand and two of his legs were missing. Whether that was a function of his demise or if one of the bigger crabs had broken them off to get him out of his shell we couldn't tell; but the complete indifference of the others as they trampled him underfoot showed the grey side of Mother Nature's face and, while still wearing that face, she used her witch's cloak to conceal another of her secrets. We never saw what happened to the last shell. All that was left at the end of the day was the body of a homeless hermit.

We were learning that it needs selective and finely focused attention to enjoy living in paradise. Our years in Africa had taught us that peace and tranquillity in the wild is a thin, almost mythical, veneer overlaying a reality of savagery, but we hadn't thought deeply enough to expect to find it here. There are none of the dangerous mammals, snakes or reptiles that clamour for attention in the bush and on the surface everything is serene.

But a closer look reveals the savagery to be much the same, only the scale is different. The indifference to death of the hermit crabs is a mild example of the phenomenon; the delicacy of the noddies as they flutter and weave over a school of fish and the graceful swooping flight of fairy terns are only aesthetic masks covering bloody mutilation and destruction of equally delicate and graceful fish.

We watch the birds and exclaim at their beauty in exactly the same way that gentle people anywhere who, caught up in the excitement of things, wax lyrical at the sight of a lion kill or an eagle's deadly stoop. We give but brief thought to the fish, as those others give to the dainty gazelle or rabbit which, at other times, would invoke tenderness or compassion. Maybe God gave us this time in his Garden of Eden to watch and ponder on such things; but whatever He meant when He made it so is still beyond our understanding.

Eventually we learned the necessary lessons and applied a carefully selective vision. We could watch the play of light on the water without seeing the lurking hunters just as you can shut out the cries of animal terror at the sight of a bush sunset, or ignore the drizzly cold on an English country walk. This last was particularly significant during this monsoon as our imaginings of sun-drenched coral islands and gently waving palms were submerged in seasonal rains.

Occasionally we would catch a glimpse of yacht masts in front of Takamaka and, in truth, envied them their apparently less demanding view of things. Of course their rain was the same as ours but the thought of living without buffeting from the wind was enough to colour our minds green. Something else that maybe He gave us to ponder on.

We were soon reminded though that shelter is a comparative condition. Stan and his daughter Jenny brought their boat *Dionysis* in after a wild fairground ride from Cocos Keeling and came to anchor in our blustery anchorage with every sign of gratitude. Their arrival heralded the beginning of a time of cosy Scrabble games, beach walks in the rain and boundless philosophizing over glasses of good port.

To have such good company was a God-send for Tina as she suffered a particularly abject day about now. Far from pharmacies with HRT medicines and the like she was battling with the flushes and miseries that go with being our age, a Red Dwarf in Stan's terminology, and at the very bottom of a mood swing she discovered maggots had invaded her last, treasured, bar of chocolate. I suppose it was inevitable we would have infestations of this sort from the time everything was on the shore, but for a chocolate freak like Tina this was a bitter blow.

She spent a long time dissecting the bar, slab by slab and chip by chip, until the extent of the damage was defined, and threw the ravaged portion to the fish. The rest was shared out and eaten straight away before any more was lost. This incident, trifling under normal circumstances but catching Tina at such a low phase, lowered our morale dramatically and, as I said earlier, good company was a God-send.

Fortuitously we were to get more at this time just when we needed it. *Beaudacious* joined us from Takamaka and Milanke and Roger arrived from Cocos Keeling in their catamaran *Vakuta*. Roger, a vibrant Frenchman, celebrated his birthday that day by giving us presents of vegetable seeds; where else could this happen but in paradise?

Planting them out directly on the island was tantamount to feeding them straight to the rats but we had a couple of damaged plastic bowls, large ones of the sort used to carry washing, that we thought would make ideal plant pots. The holes and cracks in them should provide adequate drainage and the sides were high enough to hold plenty of earth.

To give the seeds a chance we roamed Boddam looking for good black soil, a rare commodity on an island of coral sand, then sifted it carefully over a base of small stones. Rows of tomatoes, beans, cucumbers and lettuce were tamped in at the prescribed depth and spacing and the whole garden put on top of a cable drum, beach-comber's trove from bygone travellers, to keep the rats at bay.

Joel and Hilary invited us to visit *Beaudacious* and share some of the beer that Ryan, their son, brews – at least, I think Ryan was their brewmaster but I may be doing Joel a disservice, though I hope not. Whoever was responsible, the *Beaudacious* brewery was a five-star operation producing crisp, cold lagers and strong, flavourful stouts. Tina was still in the dumps over her chocolate but I crave a good beer as much as she does her cacao beans, and I was in my element. I'm ashamed that we drank their entire ready stock leaving them with the dilemma of going without while the next brew matured or drinking it too young.

The night that followed was harsh, not from too much beer but from too much weather again. Tina woke to the sound of waves breaking heavily on the bow and the pitch of the wind in the rigging rising. All the boats were showing lights and they danced a rhythmless dance as the wind swirled.

While the squall blew itself out we both kept watch from the cockpit though there was nothing we could do without an engine. At one point we saw the lights of the three other boats moving past us together, giving the impression we had broken free and for a heart-stopping moment we waited for the drama to start again, then the pattern of lights broke up and we realized *Vespera* was only swinging in a different pocket of air.

Forty-knot winds with the beach only seconds away are not the greatest recommendations for an anchorage and the morning saw *Vakuta* and *Beaudacious* leave for Takamaka. Shelter may only be comparative but even so… However, it was barely twenty-four hours before the next boat arrived and I was starting to think my approach to the cyclone season was nothing but cowardice. It was already past my latest, latest possible date to leave and people were still arriving.

We had been round to the citrus grove at the southern end of the island with Stan and Jenny, where we found four lemons, and on our return discovered Marty and Steve relaxing in the cargo net hammock by the 'watch your head', while their boat *Cicada* bobbed at anchor beyond *Vespera*. They had also experienced a lusty trip getting here but were not in the least fazed by it. Indeed they were so relaxed they might have just sailed across the bay.

Then next day saw *Dionysus* on her way to the Seychelles; Jenny had a deadline to be back in Scotland for the start of the academic year and had a plane to catch. We were going to miss these two particularly as both of us had found kindred spirits and their generosity with goodies to ease the next months only made it harder. At least they had a reasonably gentle, if wet, start to their trip.

The seemingly endless rain was making cooking a drag. Although the 'watch your head' was partially roofed and the fireplace well protected from the wind it was as much as we could do to keep a fire going, let alone choose between 'flame' and 'coals' to suit the cooking. Even our trick of drying the next charge of firewood whenever we boiled a kettle wasn't working any more. Obviously a wood shed was called for that would let us collect wood on the dryer, or least wet, days and keep it under cover until needed.

Right beside the door by the fireplace, where we kept the wood pile, was a small clearing with a waist-high wall along one side. This wall showed promise as a support for a lean-to shelter, particularly as it would, of itself, provide a defence against the prevailing wind. More foraging supplied roofing in the form of corrugated asbestos shards which, when laid on a frame of logs from the pile we wanted to protect, completed the job.

Well, it almost completed the job; there was another vital ingredient that finished it off properly. Our jerry can of waste diesel 'firelighter' placed firmly against the frame served both to prop it up and inject some ergonomics into the arrangement. Dipping a couple of sticks in the goo on their way from shed to hearth was as close to turning on the gas as we were going to get. However, the temperature controls still needed work.

Two more westbound yachts arrived while we were doing this, *Tamar* and *Rouet des Jours*, then as dusk approached four fishing boats were seen heading for Boddam. Our losses from the previous visit still stung and, on the basis of better safe than sorry, we rushed ashore to collect the pots and pans and other paraphernalia of every day life. We snatched up a dinghy full of the first things to come to hand and unceremoniously off-loaded them on *Vespera*'s deck. Then we did it again before we felt content that the most important things were secure.

The approaching boats became involved in some intricate manoeuvring that ended with them in a huddle quarter of a mile from the local bommies, giving the impression they were rafting up to anchor in safe water, but they weren't. It was merely to allow a 'captains' conference' before carrying on, in line astern, to the jetty. We were most surprised to hear cheerful greetings shouted to us by name and a better look showed the third in line to be our friend with the defunct radio, but it was the first time we'd seen the others.

In the morning, while the crews were ferrying drinking water aboard, the English speaking man asked Steve about the radio and was delighted to discover that he had the necessary parts and knowledge to repair it. When Steve emerged from the wheelhouse after performing his electronic magic there were beaming faces all around, each clamouring for a turn at the microphone.

I think by the time watering was complete everyone from all four boats had spoken to home. Huge smiles and a monster red snapper for Steve in gratitude and they were on their way, their departure coinciding with the arrival of yet another yacht, *Mara* with Jim and Jean on board.

The social life of the anchorage underwent another metamorphosis with all these folks here. Whether it was simply the number of people, or the type of people, or that for the first time Boddam had a virtual monoculture we don't know, but whatever the cause we enjoyed it. Certainly a major contributor was *Cicada's* happy tank, a top-grade marine accessory that provided vodka on tap in a similar manner to, and in the same sort of quantities as, the more mundane running water.

The sound of 'Patonk' or 'Boulle' balls thumping into the sand like falling coconuts became a regular accompaniment to the clink of sundowner glasses. Jim had a set of very professional 'Patonk' bowls and the volley ball court, a reasonably flat rectangle of sand marked out with an old ship's rope, served admirably as a pitch. I think you call it a pitch.

In spite of Jim's short stay the game caught on to such an extent that an island set was made using husked and cleaned coconuts for bowls and a takamaka nut for the jack. The bowling nuts were carefully selected for weight and balance then carved with identifying hieroglyphs to prevent squabbling. However, it was as well that matches were played at sundowner time. The oddly shaped and liquid-filled nuts have the same dynamic stability as punctured rugby balls and this characteristic, after a tot or two from the happy tank, made for some uproarious competition.

Jim left another legacy of greater importance than this simple fun. The cut-down impeller in the outboard didn't have the same arrangement to retain the drive pin as the original and I had simply glued the pin in place. The glue was a well tried friend but this application put too heavy a demand on it and every now and then the pin would come loose. At one such failure it fell out in a way that damaged both the pin and its locating hole beyond repair. It so happened, as it often does in this story, that Jim had the appropriate materials, special drills and thread-cutting taps to modify the shaft and fit a permanent pin. Not long after discovering the problem all was fixed and working again.

Tina was not so lucky. Part of her regular routine was checking the stores to make sure they weren't getting wet or otherwise damaged; with every ounce of food accounted for it would have reduced us to tears to lose any through negligence, and she discovered a trail of maggots, like the ones in the chocolate, leading across a locker floor. She turned everything over, and over again, looking for telltale signs but nothing seemed to be affected. However she was loathe to put it all back in case she'd missed anything, and equally loathe to open any packets if they looked alright, sort of like sawing a leg off a chair to check for woodworm.

In the end she opted to seal everything up with a double dose of chloroform bombs, cotton buds dipped in chloroform and zipped into closable plastic bags. We used these bombs for weevil control but these grubs were obviously from something larger than weevils, so the dose was simply a guess. We could but hope.

Little irritations like this could assume ridiculous proportions if we let them and having company was a great benefit, putting a face on for other people helped keep things in perspective. It also helped us come to terms with a new nonsense with the outboard.

Somehow rain was affecting the brute and it had taken to stopping suddenly, invariably halfway between the boat and the shore. It could take waves breaking over it with impunity and, by its nature, spent a good part of its life half submerged with no apparent effect. But rain could infiltrate it and bring it to its knees. Whenever it stopped it stayed stopped until the carburettor was stripped and the water droplets blown away, then it would start and run perfectly until the next time.

As a precaution each time it happened we decanted the fuel from its tank and discarded the dregs then, when it became a regular event, checked the stock in the jerry can the same way but found no contamination. But it carried on raining and the engine carried on stopping, and I became more proficient at stripping the carburettor. Many were the occasions when a bit of cheerful ribaldry came to the rescue and kept the demon depression away.

According to the meteorological records published in the pilot books October and January were the rainy months.

If that was true we didn't even want to think about October. We were still far from the end of September and the pages of Tina's diary were so splattered with the word rain they should have dripped. On the positive side it had replenished the shower and drinking water tanks after the ravages of the fishermen, but it had drowned our garden.

All the seeds had germinated and the shoots grown to the four-leaf stage but the drainage system wasn't equal to the deluge. We tried covering the bowls with palm fronds in an attempt to reduce the flow but firstly I think we were too late, the seedlings having already succumbed, and secondly the fronds gave the rats highway access to the rat-proof table.

Before replanting we enlarged the drainholes and increased the thickness of the stone layer under the soil. We also raised the bowls off the table using bits of corrugated asbestos so the water could run out freely. This time we tried a different mix of seeds hoping they would be more flood resistant. There were no real grounds for that hope but we knew the first lot to be drowners and the second lot could certainly fare no worse.

One very depressing thing that even good company couldn't contain was a recurrence of my eye infection, this time in both eyes. Luckily we had a course of antibiotics left, different from the type I'd used before, which I started on straight away and the celebrations for Tina's birthday kept my mind off it.

Marty baked a nutty chocolate cake that couldn't have been more perfect for the occasion and each of the boats contributed a dish towards the feast. The term sundowner had become something of a joke but at sundowner time we arrived at the 'watch your head' to find the table covered with brightly coloured and beribboned packages. Rodney, Paula and Carl had gift-wrapped treats of drinking chocolate, braised beef and other luxury comestibles while Marty contributed such feminine boosters as face creams and hair treatments, even some frivolous underwear.

Whether it was entirely real or merely our perception of things doesn't matter but the birthday seemed to initiate a period of calm weather such as we'd almost forgotten. It still rained a lot, though not as much as we expected, but the wind dropped considerably. Often it would go for days on end without exceeding fifteen knots and sometimes even fell below ten. It was a little early for the monsoon change so we considered it a bonus.

It encouraged us to get on with some interesting projects. Rodney made his living with large electrical machines and had some ideas that might explain the lack of vitality in our generator, so we hauled it out and stripped off the covers. Between us we repeated the tests that had been done earlier and he did several more that I don't pretend to understand, then we ran its engine up to speed, but it still didn't want to generate anything.

At this point the attempt changed from something resembling a surgical procedure to something more closely akin to a post mortem. Our previous findings had been confirmed by an expert and, like the HF radio, the windings declared officially dead.

Steve was luckier with another venture. He'd seen Tina struggling with the fire in the 'watch your head' and had subjected the fireplace to some scathing, though genteel, criticism. One morning he set off to scratch in the tumbled down buildings for loose bricks, which he used to extend the chimney, and for anything else that might suggest a way of improving the draft.

The origin of the hearth is lost in antiquity but it consisted primarily of an open steel box standing on end in one corner of the room. A grate of bricks was built into its bottom and a hole that had rusted through its base let smoke into the triangular duct formed with the walls that made the smoke stack.

Adding three feet to the chimney made an immediate improvement. The fire lit more readily and the extra height deflected the smoke, or most of it, outside. However, Steve wasn't content with this and wanted a fire that would flame easily and generate more heat. The next modification was a sheet of soft aluminium, gleaned from a collapsed garden frame, folded to fit across the open face of the box.

He moved this baffle up and down until he found the optimum spot for draft and made a permanent fixture of it using a strand from a piece of rigging wire. Now the

performance improved a hundred-fold and a handful of
kindling, once lit, grew to a first class cooking fire in no time.
It meant though that we had to learn how to light it again as
the draft was so strong it sucked the flame off the match.

The weather continued to settle and the rainy spells
were interspaced with lovely tropical sunshine, so much so
that Tina managed to dry a few baskets of bilimbis, partly for
variety in our own diet but also with Christmas presents in
mind. We had learned that plenty of travellers are confident
enough of their weather forecasting to sail in the cyclone
season so it was quite likely we would have company over the
festive season. Indeed the Christmas spirit was already at
work. Tom and his family on the yacht *Hasty* stopped at the
islands for a couple of days, living up to their vessel's name,
and before leaving gave us a remarkable bag of provisions,
including some canned turkey that would look splendid on
the Yuletide table.

Steve, Carl and I were chatting one evening and the
conversation inevitably came round to boats and boating and
the different ways people equip their toys. They mentioned
that they were expecting a yacht from Cocos Keeling which
was skippered by an electronics wizard who carried an
oscilloscope as part of his tool kit, and all the other gear
needed to repair radios. This was most exciting as if it was
possible to repair the HF radio I really wanted to do so.

Next day I pulled out the set and stripped off the covers
in readiness, making sure that everything was were it should
be, and connected up. While it was in that easily accessible
condition I did my own basic testing again, just in case I'd
made a mistake, but still got the same results. Anyway with the
right equipment it shouldn't take more than a few minutes to
find out what was wrong and I laid it out carefully in
anticipation.

But time passed and the yacht didn't arrive and both
Tamar and *Cicada* were getting ready to move on. They had a
rather ambitious plan to dash down to Mauritius in front of,
or between, the early cyclones then straight across to South
Africa, so didn't have time to wait for their friend. One boat
did come in, *Veron* with Raoul and Danielle on board, but
they were farmers not electronic wizards.

Before moving over to Takamaka to wait for a weather slot Carl produced, like a conjuror pulling a rabbit out of a hat, three packets of dry catfood. What a blessing. Jess was very fed up, though only figuratively, with musty crumbles and the first meal from Carl's stock switched her purring into overdrive.

Communicating with Raoul, a Belgian whose mother tongue is Flemish, and Danielle, his French wife, was a constant source of amusement. If I try really hard I can dredge up a few words of French but it's a long time since I conjugated a verb and manufacturing a sentence is beyond me. Danielle's ability with English is about the same and, if anything, Raoul finds it even more difficult.

However, with a sandy floor to draw pictures on and plenty of extravagant body language we managed quite well. The first concept that Danielle conveyed that way was that our garden had drowned again, and without further ado she took the project in hand. By the end of her first day each bowl sported an individual asbestos roof and the seeds had been replaced with some of her own.

She was quite a hard taskmaster and we received instructions to remove the roofs for a few hours each morning and again in the late afternoon, but we had to make sure the seedlings were covered against the midday sun and any heavy rain. She was obviously quite right in this approach because the bowls were soon striped with strong seedlings but during those first few days our lives revolved entirely around the garden.

Before my morning tea I was chased ashore to uncover the little beauties, but as often as not rain made me cover them again before breakfast was over. With all this tender loving care the seedlings soon poked their heads over the bowl rims for their first taste of the wind.

To us the wind was so gentle we hardly noticed it but it caused the plants to put out distress messages the farmers understood. Raoul translated them into sand pictures and before the new crop could expire from wind burn the whole garden, rat-proofing cable drum and all, was moved into a roofless building sheltered from the south east. This didn't relieve us from covering and uncovering duty but some further improvement to the drainage, by the simple expedient of driving in spikes to make the bowls leak more, meant we could ignore anything less than a downpour.

With another miracle of languageless communication Danielle exploded the myth about bottling and preserving food only being possible with the appropriate equipment. She produced a fine meal using tuna she'd bottled in an ordinary jam-jar six months previously, proving her point beyond doubt.

We had a fair supply of jam jars as we used them to salt and store butter so decided to give this a try next time we had a sufficiently large fish to justify ninety minutes' worth of gas. The opportunity arose sooner than expected when a visiting fishing boat contributed enough tuna to fill both *Veron*'s and *Vespera*'s pressure cookers.

Tina selected jars of a size to make best use of the cooker and rummaged in the lid box for lids that both fitted and were free of rust. If this experiment worked feeding Jess would be much easier. Our cookery book went into great detail describing the use of proper preserving jars with cooking times, hints on correct cooling, when to tighten the lids and so forth, but Danielle's advice was to simply screw the lids on tight, use enough water to boil for an hour and a half and just turn the gas off when the alarm goes.

It went well, with one exception. We let the cooker cool overnight before opening it, when we found everything inside coated with oily froth. The first six jars lifted out looked fine, the fish was well cooked and the lids had sucked down to make good seals, but then the source of the froth became apparent. The seventh and last jar had cracked around the neck cleanly enough to allow the juices to escape then seal again as it cooled. It was only when Tina picked it up that it finally fell apart, luckily landing on the surface without breaking further.

Anyway, apart from this single mishap it was a great success. Each jar would provide one meal for us and two for Jess. What would have been a single gluttonous binge to eat as much as possible while it was still edible, with most of it being thrown away when it went off, had been transformed into six extra meals and enough to keep Jess for a week. As always with such revelations our first reaction was regret for all the food we'd wasted through ignorance.

It was mid-October before Carl and Steve got the weather portents they'd been waiting for and early one morning they radioed to say they would be starting their southerly dash that day. Raoul had already decided to stay a little longer but he was going to tangle with a different cyclone system. He was heading for Djibouti and hoped to skirt the stormy area by travelling west for a thousand miles before turning north.

During the morning we went ashore, primarily of course to check the garden but also to see what we could make of a huge red stain in the water close to the beach. We'd often seen the shallows turn into a sort of green algal soup and the occurrences appeared to coincide with spring tides, but this red bloom was something new. Discussions as to its nature had degenerated into an Anglo-French shrugging match when we noticed sails heading out to the pass. We just had time to return to *Vespera* to call farewell.

Back at the beach we resumed our investigation. We were concerned that it might be what's referred to as 'Red-tide' in South Africa, where the local radio stations broadcast details of outbreaks to prevent people eating shellfish at such times. Apparently it concentrates pollutants and feeding on it renders the shellfish toxic. Unfortunately many of the fish that might be caught here eat shellfish.

Altogether there were too many abstractions for mere body language and between us we were unable to reach any conclusions. To stay on the safe side we decided not to eat anything caught in the vicinity for a few weeks. However the episode brought us back to the topic, if that is the correct term for wordless communication, of food and Danielle showed us some agricultural pamphlets, in French, describing tropical crops, including taro.

Her interpretation of the pamphlets led her to harvest some of the islands' disputed plants in exactly the same way Alex had, but she had the advantage of a detailed description of how to prepare and cook it to avoid the bitterness. We made an eager audience for her practical demonstration of the prescribed way to trim the root for baking, how to cut and replant shooting buds, how to prepare the leaves for soup and all manner of interesting things. When all was ready Raoul collected a huge pile of wood for the bakery (obviously taro baking is a task to be taken seriously), and Danielle settled down to a long vigil.

We didn't see either of them for hours but when we did we were faced with two masks of despondency. In spite of the encouraging words baking the island 'taro' had simply converted the pale, very bitter, root into a darker, very bitter, root. Further reading suggested, we think, that the plants had grown wild too long and only recultivation over several generations would improve matters, but we were not inclined to experiment.

The fine weather persisted into the following day and we were still keeping a watchful eye on the horizon for the electronics expert, but were beginning to think he must have by-passed the islands. With such lovely, unseasonal, sailing conditions it would be very tempting to keep on going. Raoul was also having second thoughts about delaying any longer.

By late afternoon he made up his mind to take advantage of it and invited us to a farewell dinner on board *Veron*. They were most concerned at leaving us on our own with a still incomplete boat and insisted on giving each of us, in addition to some supplies, a talisman chosen from the excellent jewelry that Danielle makes. Then, first thing in the morning, they were away to Takamaka and the following day on their way to Djibouti.

At this point we decided that no-one else would be coming this season so I reassembled the radio and remounted it. Every time I saw the spread out parts I felt a twinge of disappointment so it was better hidden away. However, we had the islands to ourselves again, conditions were delightful and the overriding feeling was of contentment. Even the atmosphere caught the mood and treated us to another optical rarity.

The morning had been crystal clear and we were spotlit by a sunny gap left in a sky fairly crowded with light puffy clouds. As the day wore on it became progressively more humid and visibility changed until the sharp-edged islands became indistinct and blurry through the haze. Surreptitiously a faint rainbow formed that gradually strengthened in colour and intensity until it dominated the view. Seen from *Vespera's* cockpit it appeared centred on the bow with arcs on both sides dipping in front of the horizon, seeming to meet at a point under the forefoot. For a brief moment it was so intense that the horizon couldn't be seen through the bands of colour. We were convinced that God must have been happy to send us a second unique rainbow.

Tina's diary entered a phase of mundane entries that fully defined living on a desert island yet do no justice to the pleasure of it all. Simple statements like 'collected coconuts while Pete wrote' or 'Pete put the generator back on its mountings while I tidied wood piles' are really only the wrappings from bundles of gentle memories; of having time to stop whatever you're doing to watch a tropic bird; of the thrill of a hunting fish surging through the shallows; or of just sitting together by a fire sharing the glory of a sunrise.

I am trying to put into words the visions that fill my mind as I remember; some awe-inspiring, some magnificent and some as subtle as drifting smoke, but I find myself powerless to describe any of them. Like Tina I'm obliged to resort to the mundane. In reality the days were no different from any others except there was nothing to detract from, or in any way interfere with, the sheer luxury of being alive.

Actually, on reflection, there was an incident that detracted from Tina's enjoyment that I had forgotten about. It was a bread baking day and she'd started early to get the dough kneaded before the day got too hot, and breakfast at the 'watch your head' had been a hurried affair in order to get the bakery fire lit in time.

Leaving me in peace to write and keep the rats away from the rising dough she set off along the path. She had a long established routine for approaching the bakery which included clapping her hands and shouting to frighten away the spiders and scorpions that like to lurk there, and this was no exception. All went well until the kindling was ablaze and she reached into the woodpile for a log, disturbing a very large spider.

This creature was the sort we call a 'huntsman' and, legs

spread, was about the size of her hand. It got such a shock when she moved the log that it scrambled up the wall beside her, dislodging lumps of crumbling coral as it went. This was enough to get Tina, a certifiable arachnophobe, through the door and up to speed in a flash. Needless to say when I got there to take over fire duty there were no spiders to be seen. Unfortunately the episode put a damper on subsequent bakery stints though I think that was the only really big one she saw there.

As November approached we felt it wise to prepare for the promised Brits' visit. Even if you stay alert you only get an hour's notice of their arrival and unless we were ready with a list of things we wanted to ask we knew we would forget something and miss the opportunity. Most important was the question of food.

All the passing boats had been so generous with their stores that our circumstances were much improved from the last assessment. To put that generosity properly in perspective consider that even the largest yachts have limited storage space and all were more than a thousand miles into their voyages, with similar distances to travel before they could re-stock.

Nonetheless there was still a substantial shortfall and we had no idea what to expect. We did another detailed stock-take of every edible thing on board and assessed, or guessed, how long the packaging of each item would last. All the tins were rusting in spite of the careful oiling and many of the bulk things starting to go mouldy. We repeated the performance of separating everything into 'use first' and 'okay' piles and contrived a minimum list of what extra we needed to see us safely home. Our idea was that maybe we could arrange with the Marines for them to purchase those goods for us from the base and bring them when they next came.

We had barely finished the list when a different type of fishing boat arrived, much larger and more professional looking than the earlier ones. As it approached a crewman held their GPS receiver aloft and, from the downcast look on his face, it was clear he was asking for help.

When they were safely anchored I went to see what I could do, but with the dreadfully impotent feeling of one blind man offering to help another. An obvious place to start looking was a wet and untidy joint where the antenna cable had been cut to lead it through the cabin side and, with some trepidation, I peeled away the sticky insulation. Trepidation more from the encircling dour and silent watchers than anything else. With this expectant audience I was more than a little relieved to find a broken wire which, it seemed reasonable to assume, was the problem.

I cleaned the broken ends, adjusted the clamps to give the joint room to overlap and mimed a request for a soldering iron. This caused a frenzy of activity among the watchers and I was presented, in turn, with a pair of pliers, a 10-mm ring spanner and a large paper clip, but apparently they didn't have a soldering iron.

The trip back to *Vespera* to collect mine brought to my notice that the weather was deteriorating but it didn't seem important at the time. I was more concerned to discover that the fishing boat didn't have a suitable power supply for the iron. Neither, unfortunately, did I. So near yet so far.

In the end I resorted to twisting the ends together and taping over the joint but it didn't work very well. I don't know what the wire's function was but obviously it needed to be joined properly as with this poor substitute the set was still incoherent and no use at all for navigation. This was the limit of what I could do and I was probably more disappointed than the fishermen who, in spite of the gloomy looks, didn't seem too perturbed at the prospect of finishing their trip the old-fashioned way.

By the time I left to return the anchorage was very rough, a situation which led, indirectly, to a disaster. As I cast off one of the fishermen indicated a wish to visit *Vespera* for a look and I circled round in the dinghy to pick him up. Thirty knots of wind and a distinct chop on the water called for careful timing as he stepped down but a gust upset his balance and he stumbled heavily against me.

A number of events happened then in quick succession. I grabbed at the transom to steady myself and powered the dinghy away from the surging hull that could so easily tear it to shreds, while the fisherman groped for a handhold to regain his equilibrium. In the clash my glasses had been dashed from my face and now hung at my chest on their safety cord, but seconds later I saw that a lens had fallen out and was skittering along the far side air chamber. I lunged for it, but missed, and watched it flutter away in the tumbling water.

Since a débâcle with an optician in Thailand these glasses were the only usable pair I had and they covered two basic requirements, middle to long distance vision and protection from the sun. Given that we spend most of our lives outdoors these two functions are vital, and particularly so at this time while my eyes were still sensitive from the infection.

However, nothing could be done in the blustery conditions and the poor fisherman was distraught with embarrassment, to the extent that he pressed me to accept in reparation the silver crucifix he wore at his neck, obviously an object of great sentimental value, and was even more upset when I refused. It was just one of those accidents that happen. But looking ahead to months on a tropical island and essentially unable to go out in the sun was a bit grim.

The skipper only waited for the blow to dissipate before venturing back out to sea and as soon as he left I dropped a weighted marker buoy where I thought the accident had happened. The lens was a plastic one and weighed next to nothing so the tides would probably move it around all over the place, but the marker would give me some idea where to look.

Fortunately the water wasn't very deep, maybe twelve or fifteen feet at high water, but for the next three days visibility underwater was dreadful. In general you could see enough to locate yourself among the coral but you needed to get to within three feet of anything to see it clearly. All tasks other than the great search were simply dropped and I spent most of the daylight hours swimming funny patterns round the mark.

On the night of the third day it rained very hard, which improved the visibility enormously, and for the next couple of days conditions were ideal – clear water and a solid overcast to prevent glare – so I swam the same patterns until my fingers felt webbed. But no lens.

The search was interrupted at this point by the arrival of the yacht *Mystie* with Roger, Jacqueline and family aboard, also bound for Djibouti but travelling out of season as a result of being dismasted on their way to Cocos Keeling. They were so late that I think they would have skipped their island stop-over but for the emotional significance of visiting Boddam to complete a family circumnavigation of the globe. An achievement not shared by many.

Of course they couldn't stay long but notwithstanding this their son, Morgan, offered to spend some of his strictly limited snorkelling time helping with the search. We swam as a pair over the area I considered most likely without seeing anything, then split up to cover different patterns. I don't think we'd been in the water an hour when Morgan called 'Is this it?' He brandished over his head a small piece of plastic which I swam over to inspect and, lo and behold, there it was. Whole, clean and apparently unscratched.

Another stroke of luck was that Morgan's sisters, like Danielle, earn their spending money making jewelry and accordingly had the appropriate adhesives to both repair the broken glasses frame and hold the lens securely in place. Twelve hours later, when the resin was cured, I was back in the business of living. I could look around the skyline without screwing my eyes up against the sun and, better yet, actually see what was there.

That same day, a lovely calm one, grey but with the comfortable feel of polished metal, the Brits arrived. The landing party were a most cheerful and supportive bunch and brought with them a mountain of parcels and packages. Some were boxes containing things that Sue had bought in Diego Garcia on her way through: food, batteries, writing pads and such. In another box was the packet from Malaysia with the big-end bearing shells, six months to the day after David dispatched them.

Along with the boxes were two complete mailbags full of parcels from Sue and a great mound of provisions from the British Representative. Smiling faces passed more and more stuff over until the cockpit was full and in no time *Vespera* was in the cheerful shambles that typified her pre-accident cruising career. While Tina was spiriting a dozen cups of tea from her single gas burner the party medic took me aside to examine my eyes.

Our letters to Sue mentioning the problem, posted for us by departing yachties, had obviously got through and she had primed the people on Diego Garcia. Pete, the medic, had discussed the case with the base doctor and arrived well equipped with knowledge and medicines to sort out just about anything. As it happened the course of antibiotics I had recently taken had worked pretty well and for the time being my eyes were reasonably comfortable. However, he gave them a good once-over and was able to prescribe the final cure from his medical bag.

A little later another boat arrived from the ship bringing the Territory Administrator from the Foreign and Commonwealth Office, a charming man who'd travelled from London only a few days earlier and had brought with him a package of letters and photographs from Sue. We couldn't help wondering how many civil servants, or services, round the world would bother with such personal touches. Not many, I'm sure.

After a brief exploration of the crumbling settlement he invited us out to the ship, the M/V *Northern Desire*, to meet the captain and crew. She was a fisheries patrol vessel, newly on station and impressively equipped. We were shown over the bridge and other places of interest before being sat down to a delicious lunch. In essence it was an ordinary work-a-day lunch for the crew but to us, ten months out from the last market, crisp green lettuce and firm red tomatoes were food of the Gods.

During the afternoon we were made fully aware that this was a working ship and not just a means of transport for the naval party. They caught a fishing boat with an illegal long line set along the outside of the reef and all other activities, including returning us to *Vespera*, took second place against bringing him to book. We were taken by surprise because we had gleaned from earlier Brits visits that these chaps could fish outside the reefs but not inside the atolls. Obviously that information was incorrect.

It turned out that the arrested boat was our most recent visitor and as the afternoon progressed we became alarmed at the possible consequences. We learned that the probable outcome of the contact would be for the fishermen to have all their equipment confiscated and, if the timetable of events was looked at from their point of view, there was plenty of circumstantial evidence that we had called in the patrol. Roger and family were leaving that evening and the prospect of being alone and unarmed when *Northern Desire* left was unnerving.

The circumstantial evidence was strengthened when a squall came driving through while we were on our way back and the boat's helmsman was instructed to standby the fishing boat until it cleared. We finished up taking shelter on board, where the fishermen looked more morose than ever, while the fisheries men went about their work. In reality that work was now centred on repairing the GPS antenna that had beaten me before, but there was a noticeable tension in the air.

However, time passed, as always, and we were soon on our way again, passing the boats taking the naval party personnel back to the ship. We were disappointed that our extended stay aboard meant we'd missed the opportunity to thank some of the sailors and marines for their part in organizing the provisions. We thank them now.

At *Vespera* we faced a problem that twenty-four hours earlier would have seemed, at best, improbable. We had more food than we could possibly eat. Among the provisions were a large ham, several kilograms of beautiful vegetables and a big pack of beef. All frozen. And we had no freezer. Before Roger left we pressed half the ham on him and as many vegetables as he would take, but he didn't have freezer space either.

After a lot of discussion, argument really, we decided to try bottling the frozen beef in our remaining jam-jars. Nothing in the cookery book said you couldn't use frozen meat so it would probably be okay. It would consume some of the gas we were saving for the trip but losing this lovely beef without trying wasn't to be contemplated. Tina was busy until very late but before turning in had successfully preserved a dozen meals.

While she did this I unpacked Sue's parcels. She'd performed miracles on her arrival in England and had accumulated, within days, all the parts we needed, including some she had to import from Germany. Her homeward trip had been unexpectedly difficult and tiring but even so she had put the important things in motion before even looking for somewhere to live.

I found it particularly interesting that in a few minutes of discussion with a local dealer she had properly identified the oil filters, a task I had wasted days over, trudging around dealers in several countries and over several years without managing to achieve. Anyway the important thing was we now had new bearings, a new oil pump and new filters so there was nothing to stop *Vespera* now.

All through the night we were aware of lights near Takamaka. They were much too large to be *Mystie* and, as they were stationary, we discounted the possibility that it was *Northern Desire*. Logic, and I suppose a little fear, told us they belonged to the fishing boat. This was confirmed when, in the dull pre-dawn light, we saw the distinctive wheelhouse shape already on the move towards us.

We watched as they negotiated the narrow track through the corals and come to rest about half a boat length away. All was smiles and good cheer. With effective sign language they showed us that they had indeed had their lines confiscated and were now going home, obviously unable to fish any longer. We couldn't be sure but got a distinct impression that they knew they were in the wrong and felt they'd got off lightly in their clash with the law. All was peaceful and friendly and they passed over a large box of biscuits as a parting gift before waving farewell and leaving for Sri Lanka.

Following our success with the beef we had another lengthy discussion about the frozen vegetables. We had no more jars with metal lids and couldn't make up our minds whether it was worth risking the gas to try bottling in jars with plastic lids. Our worry was that we might not be able to tell if the bottling was unsuccessful and ran the risk of poisoning ourselves. Opening the packets and preparing to throw armfuls of broccoli, cauliflower and colourful mixed veg. overboard was the decider. Neither of us could bring ourselves to do it, so the pressure cooker went to work again and it was ten hours before we turned off the gas.

The authorities impressed us most favourably the following morning. The fisheries patrol had been aware of our anxiety after the arrest incident and, having made a quick dash to their base to land the naval party, came back directly to check that all was well with us. A brief and cheerful call on the VHF set their minds at rest and made our day.

Now it was time to tackle the engine but we were appalled at the condition the parts came out of the lazarette in. Knowing it was a dank and unventilated place at best we had taken considerable trouble to spray all the exposed surfaces with preservative, allegedly a better one than the type we used on the tins in South Africa, then wrap each part in oily rags and plastic before stowing it away.

First to escape its cocoon was the transmission drive plate, now a disk of solid rust. Next came the crankshaft pulley, same story, and the exhaust manifold and the water pump bracket. Mercifully the injector pump had been full of fuel and very oily when packed so escaped the 'preservative' but the starter motor almost brought tears to my eyes. I slipped it out of its plastic bag and unwrapped the oily rag to find another great glob of rust. It was not a good day. So much care, so much finicky attention and it had all been for nothing.

Everything got dumped in a big box and taken ashore for cleaning, a mind-numbing exercise that went on for days. The only wire brush to survive was a whiskery brass suede brush, normally used for cleaning electrical connections, that had no effect whatever on the rust, but I did have a selection of waterproof abrasive papers and a screwdriver was a good instrument for the initial scraping.

I learned a lot about waterproof abrasive paper, or 'wet and dry' as I usually call it, and the consequences of steeping it in salt water. Whatever the manufactures use to stick the grit to the paper is highly selective in the way it performs under these circumstances. On all the fine grades the 'stick' worked perfectly. On the general purpose grades it worked well enough but its life span was directly related to the grit size, and on the coarser grades, the ones you need to get heavy rust off, it was entirely cosmetic. The sheets looked perfect but a single vigorous wipe sprayed carborundum particles all over and, of course, Murphy's Law dictates that every one lands where it can do the most damage.

I soldiered on with screwdriver and fine paper and eventually got everything clean, or at least looking clean. At times it felt like turning half-crowns into sixpences with a nail-file but the end product, now glistening under a film of the ubiquitous sump oil, was quite satisfying. Thank goodness the major components had been kept in the cabin where we hadn't thought it necessary to 'preserve' them. In the end the only permanent damage we could see was a spot on the exhaust manifold that had rusted right through and we had to make a special plug to fix it.

The idea of assembling the engine in manhandleable lumps worked well and Tina and I could move even the heaviest parts quite comfortably, but Alain, who had arrived with his wife Claire on their boat *Edelweiss* just after the Brits' visit, gave me a hand and it dropped into place easily. Assembling the rest was routine except for the niggles, like broken fuel lines and seized cables, and next day it was ready for testing.

In my anxiety to make sure everything worked before using our limited resources to do the final fitting I had jury-rigged the batteries using the remains of the original wiring, but it meant bypassing the glowplug and starter switch for the trial. With my heart in my mouth I thrust the glowplug wire onto the battery terminal, using my thumb to make the contact, and when the resistors were smoking satisfactorily, replaced it quickly with the starter wire.

Nothing. Not a click, not a whirr – nothing. Disappointed I checked all the wires and re-tightened the connections but still got no response. It was possible that the batteries were not up to it but we were using them every day for our lights and the glowplugs seemed to work so, reluctantly, I concluded it was the starter motor.

Removed from the engine and connected directly to the batteries it worked a treat, bursting into noisy life as soon as contact was made. Back on the engine – nothing. I must have made a mistake with the wiring so I checked it all again but could find no fault. Out it came and again it worked perfectly on the cabin floor. Time for a conference.

Alain was beckoned across for a cup of tea and a brain-picking and I set things up to demonstrate the deviant behaviour. I clamped the wires on and made the contact – nothing. Oh dear. Contact again – whirr, and again – nothing. Obviously a conference wasn't going to help and our meeting degenerated to tea and grumbling.

The grumbling got louder when I took the end cover off and discovered the works to be as rusty as the outside had been, probably the result of more 'preservative'. It got worse when I pulled the brush holder out and a vital spring collapsed in my hand, having rusted right through. It took a long time to work out a jury rig for this and in the end it didn't help. When it was all cleaned up and re-assembled it still sometimes ran and sometimes didn't. The consensus was that the solenoid switch had also failed, a problem to which, for the moment, I could see no solution and without the starter it is impossible to start the engine.

Bitterly disappointed that all Sue's efforts had been for nothing and that we now faced sitting out the cyclone season with little to do but worry about making the passage without an engine, I put everything back in place and closed down the floor.

We woke the following morning to an awful smell. The hatches had been open all night so our first thoughts were that it was coming from outside, though we couldn't imagine what it could be from. Even on deck it seemed just as strong and it took a while to realize that the wayward ions, or whatever they are, had so permeated our noses that we were smelling our own nostrils.

Several minutes of fresh south easterly blew that away though and Tina plucked up the courage to go below and investigate. I listened as she clattered about among the shelves and cupboards then heard a dreadful oath, one that has no place here, and she bounded up the steps with one hand over her nose and the other clutching a jar of carrots.

A boisterous fermentation was going on inside the jar with bubbles rising to the surface like a good champagne and the plastic lid domed out until the seal leaked. Such a shame we could never achieve this vigour in our wine-making. Anyway this was obviously the source of the stink and, now with a towel over her face, Tina passed the other vegetable jars up for inspection. Lined along the coachroof they made a sorry spectacle. The crisp breeze eliminated the worst they could do but our eyes alone were enough. Half the jars had distorted lids and frothy contents and many of the others had turned sort of milky, but the rest looked alright.

But there was too much at stake and first to go over the side were the carrots, bright orange cubes drifted through our aquarium, but even the fish wouldn't touch them. Over went the lovely green peas, and the broccoli, and, possibly worst of all, was the thought of the wasted gas. Ten hours would have provided hot tea morning and evening all the way to Africa.

But such is life and the immediate problem was to make the boat liveable again. Now all the jars had been disturbed you could only go below for short sorties, certainly not longer than you can hold your breath. Even Jess slunk up the steps and oozed into the cockpit, wide-eyed and alert for whatever peril was causing this upset.

Earlier in the year Pom, from *Banana Moon*, had given us some incense sticks to ward off the stagnant smell inside *Vespera* after she refloated and Tina fought her way in to spread the left-overs around in the hope they would make things better. While she was busy with sticks and matches I grabbed the makings for breakfast and we evacuated our home for a few hours, leaving Jess, whiskers twitching and worried, on deck.

Alain and Claire had an infectious positive attitude to setbacks of this sort which helped whittle these disappointments down to size. It wasn't so much an attitude as a complete philosophy, encompassed by a wry smile and Gallic shrug. We never became true converts to this outlook, which is against my nature, but the realities of it made sense and improved our days no end.

We took time to go for walks, try our luck at fishing

again and generally just enjoy things. It was fun to show the others round the old settlement and pass on such information about the place as we had learned. Most cruising people, like ourselves, accumulate books and articles about interesting places along their routes and we had been shown many cuttings and photographs of these islands, some dating back thirty years and more. One, in a French or German magazine, I forget which, even included photographs taken when the copra plantation was still working. Looking at the ruins now it's hard to believe they were in daily use so recently, especially the jail with its overpowering aura of medieval savagery.

Nonetheless, for all our positive thinking and enjoyment of simple daily pleasures, the most significant thought in our minds was what to do next. We undertook yet another detailed stock check, with the inevitable arguments about exactly how much, or how little, we really needed to eat, and counting in the new provisions we could manage until the end of January. Almost enough to allow the option of crossing the equator to the cyclone-free area and going westward that way.

An additional attraction to this course of action was that by sailing due north to Addu atoll in the Maldives on the way we could pick up extra supplies and maybe get the starter fixed. But we were not sure we would be allowed to do this. The customs and immigration authorities are based in Male, three hundred miles further north, and getting permission to stop at Addu without going there first seems to depend on how the officer of the day interprets his duties. Several of our friends had made enjoyable stop-overs there – indeed that is where the cement and other repair materials came from – but others had simply been turned away.

Alain decided to call there on the off-chance as their need for provisions was as great as ours and he promised to write, via Diego Garcia, and let us know how he got on. We still had six or seven weeks to wait before the weather window to suit that plan so there was a fair chance that a letter could arrive.

This would be important information as without extra food we would be on strict rationing to make it to Africa, with little margin for safety. If we took the time to go to Addu though and were not able to stock matters would be worse. We couldn't help but remember that we floundered about for eight days in almost windless conditions covering that particular stretch of water on the way here.

In the meantime there were plenty of more mundane matters to occupy us. One of these was how to prevent the boat from smelling like a cat's midden. Right at the beginning of our sailing venture we'd experimented with beach sand, shells and other materials to fill Jess's litter box but no matter how often we changed it we were unpleasantly aware of our feline companion. Commercial litter was out of the question as it's much too bulky to carry.

The solution came when friends suggested using wood chips as an absorbent and these worked perfectly; what's more they compress easily for storage. Consequently one of our first expeditions whenever we arrived at a new venue was to locate a furniture factory to re-stock, but there are no furniture factories on the islands and we were fast running out. We were reluctant to use messy beach sand and the island's thin top cover of leaf mould and humus was pretty well infested with unwelcome bugs.

We decided to try recycling the chips. Each morning Tina poured the used chips into a plastic mesh bag which she hung in the sea for twenty-four hours. At the end of this wash they were transferred to a box and laid out in the sun on deck. Sometimes they were dry enough for reuse the following day but more often it took longer, so for the rest of our stay in the lagoon the stern of the boat was given over to the drying boxes of the cat chip reprocessing plant.

Another incident that taxed us was the failure of our 'dipper bucket'. We seem to use an awful lot of sea water one way or another, for washing and cleaning, sometimes even in the cooking, and the dipper was our means of lifting it aboard. *Vespera*'s dimensions are such that wherever you try from you just can't reach to fill a bowl by leaning over the side, so our carefully chosen and weighted bucket on a knotted lanyard was invaluable. One day the bottom just split away from the sides and it became nothing more than scrap plastic and string.

Having to clamber over the side into the dinghy to fill the washing up bowl or rinse out a wash cloth sounds such a petty irritation in retrospect but it annoyed us intensely at the time, and something had to be done. There was nothing among our things even remotely suitable for making a new dipper as all our plastic buckets had been sacrificed to mixing cement and such.

With the sole intention of finding a substitute we set out to beachcomb the island. Everything we came across was checked and its potential discussed: broken fishing floats, plastic bottles, flower pots, all manner of extraordinary things, but nothing was really what we were looking for. We carried the remains of a capless drum, brittle from exposure to ultra-violet light, for a mile or so while we thought about it but eventually discarded it as not worth trying.

By mid-morning we'd circled the island and had nothing to show for the trouble but an armful of old takamaka wood for the bakery. This, however, proved the making of the venture. Standing beside the oven, so blatant and familiar it was usually unseen, was an old plastic waste paper basket doing service as a kindling store. It had a split around the rim but, with the top cut off and a cats cradle of string to give it strength, here was our new dipper. In truth it can't be said it brought smiles to the washing up but it did lighten the load.

About this time, mid November, we felt the first breath of a change that significantly improved our quality of life. The persistent strong winds had become a bit variable in strength and one day *Vespera* swung her nose to the north west for the first time in months. It didn't last very long, a few hours maybe, but it was the harbinger of the changing monsoon.

Within a couple of weeks the new season established itself and getting ashore became a pleasure again. No more soaking wet backsides from the slop driven up by the south easterlies, no more total dependence on the outboard or shore-line to get to the kitchen, just a gentle paddle in calm water in the island's lee.

Soon we were confident enough to take down the palm fronds blocking the 'watch your head' doorway. The surrounding trees filtered the new wind leaving us just enough to keep the mosquitoes away and make the fireplace chimney work properly, while the extra light added a sparkle to the days.

One morning we were taken completely by surprise when the VHF chirped with a lovely clear signal from a yacht hurrying past towards the cyclone-free area. The call was directed at us by *Cillim*, a boat we hadn't met, to pass on a message from Diego Garcia that water samples taken by the naval party during their recent visit were contaminated and that we should take the necessary precautions. Unfortunately the message didn't include details of the contamination or what precautions we needed to take.

We mulled over all the pollution possibilities that came to mind and discounted the usual fears, dysentery, cholera and so on, because we couldn't imagine where it could come from. Heavy metal contamination was something we knew very little about and had no means of taking precautions against anyway. In the end we rationalized that we'd been drinking the water for nine months without ill effects and might as well just carry on. We did decide though to always make tea rather than drink it as it came.

I was still concerned about the engine. Even though there was no chance of starting it in the near future our experience so far had taught us to keep faith and I wanted to maintain it in the best possible condition in case a miracle happened. With images of all the corrosion fresh in my mind I thought to turn it over by hand every now and then to spread oil around the insides.

One morning I took the glow plugs out and, using a large spanner, rolled the crankshaft over for several minutes. Everything was fine until suddenly it locked up. I tried turning it backwards a few degrees and it turned easily, but when I changed back to the right direction it stopped dead. I could only think I'd left something loose, and that 'something' had now fallen off and dropped somewhere where it acted as a pawl, but I had no idea what it could be.

I took the top cover off to look at the valves and camshaft and everything there was in order. What could be seen of the drive chain and its tensioner also seemed fine and the exercise didn't yield a single clue. Next I took the drive belts off the front in case the problem was in a water pump or the alternator. No difference. It was slowly dawning on me that it had to be in the main body of the engine, which would mean taking it all out again. Or in the injector pump – an equally depressing thought.

After lengthy deliberations, and several cups of well-boiled tea, I stripped off the fuel pipes to remove the pump and soon the beast was on the cockpit floor. I wasn't sure whether to be pleased or otherwise when the crankshaft turned easily with the pump removed. I certainly wasn't happy when the pump turned freely as well, leaving me with no explanation for the stoppage.

I never got to the bottom of this enigma. The only other evidence that came to light was that, while adjusting the injection timing, I found one element of the pump not working. With moral support from Chris of M/V *Harmony*, presently spending a few days in the lagoon, I stripped the element as far as I dare, there being no way to re-calibrate it if I disturbed the settings, but all I succeeded in doing was destroying an important copper seal.

As luck would have it, again, Chris had a similar seal which I filed and sanded to fit, rectifying my mistake but not solving the problem. Everything seemed mechanically sound but it didn't want to pump. Our next thought was that an air bubble was trapped inside and the only way to dislodge it was with a good flow of fuel. Of course the only way to generate that sort of flow was using the starter motor, so I put it all together again, rolled the engine over by hand to stir up the oil and left it for miracle day.

In other respects things were improving with the weather. We referred to the new monsoon as 'Spring' though the temperate climate terms don't relate well to tropical islands. October had seen the sun pass overhead on its southern migration and March would see it back, so essentially we were in the 'short' period between mid-summers and the effect, in subtle ways, was like spring.

The bilimbi and wax-apple trees bore prolifically as the sun passed but as the wind turned both seemed to carry more flowers than fruit. Many of the other trees carry flowers and fruit all year round but now the path to the well was bathed in a wash of new fragrance from the mapou trees. These trees flower at night and the blooms rarely last a whole day, most dropping off a couple of hours after sunrise, complete and perfect, to decorate our morning walks. We made a daily ritual of collecting a couple of the flowers, each large enough to fill a hand with its four white petals and giant cluster of pink and gold stamens, to make the boat more homely. Arranged in half a cleaned coconut shell they made a most pleasing addition.

Coconut shells were one commodity that never ran out and, in common with island dwellers everywhere, we discovered numerous uses for them. Each day we consumed at least one nut each and, judging from the way the husk pile grew, often many more. As well as making attractive, if temporary, flower vases the shells were our primary source of light when we ate in the 'watch your head' of an evening. Once the meal was cooked and the fire no longer needed tending, half shells tucked in the embers would flare into intensely bright flames, each shell lasting three or four minutes, sometimes even longer.

For some reason shells that were still a bit hairy or, especially, those that had a residue of flesh left inside, were never as efficient. However to leave shells in that condition was sheer idleness as scraping the outside before opening them not only prevented loose bits finding their way into the porridge, the scrapings were excellent for smoking fish. Removing flesh was simplicity itself.

Broken shells thrown under the takamaka tree would be inundated with hermit crabs. Hordes of busy scavengers would latch onto and squabble over any flesh left attached. If you threw them far enough away the rats would get in on the act and great inter-cultural battles would rage. All that was left for us to do was collect the clean shells in the morning and add them to the 'light' pile.

Often we noticed a half-shell would disappear during the night and it puzzled us for a while. Then we witnessed a running fight between two rats, probably tug-of-war describes it better, when a shell was pulled hither and thither until it was lost in the undergrowth. Of course it was always the shells that were nicely shaped or had split cleanly enough to make a bowl that went. From then on if we wanted to reserve a particular piece but were too lazy to clean it ourselves we would put it under the tree in a basket. That way the creatures could get in to do their work but couldn't carry the goods away.

Such simple entertainment!

Things were not only improving on the weather front. Three boats were sharing the atoll with us at the moment, two only temporarily as they were on route for the next islands but the third was destined to stay a bit longer. In conversation with Tina one of the ladies explained that she had the remainder of a course of HRT medication which she'd purchased and then found unsuitable. It was not the same type that Tina had taken before and the instructions were written in German so it was something of an unknown.

However, when there are no qualified physicians around you are left with common sense as your only guide and Tina, really struggling with being fifty, flushed and fragile, decided to try them for a month. The effects were almost immediate and within a fortnight she was able to get a proper night's sleep and face the days with a smile. This medication kept her healthier and happier until she was able to replace it with her own, which was better still.

Another reason to smile was that Knut, of *Yebisah*, had welding equipment and sufficient electrical capacity on board to operate it and he undertook to weld up the cracks in our self-steering gear supports. These cracks had been worrying me ever since the gear had been re-mounted. I had sort of accepted, or rationalized, that the damaged legs would be in compression under normal circumstances and that, all being well, they should be alright, but I wasn't really convinced. The alternative, up to now, had been to remove the gear and take it home lashed on deck – and the prospect of hand-steering all the way was a miserable thought.

While Knut extracted the welder from its storage space, inaccessible enough to make me feel guilty for asking, I dropped the gear into the dinghy and stripped off the brackets. Soon it was finished and I was particularly pleased it had been done. A couple of cracks in the top bracket had escaped detection earlier and could have caused havoc had we sailed with them.

Then, still on a roll as they say, it was back to the engine. A few days earlier a combination of cyclones on each side of the equator had given up on the task of rattling the yacht *Heather* and let her owners, Eric and Robin, bring her safely into the lagoon. With them came a burst of inspiration.

Off came the starter for yet another going over though this time under Eric's watchful eye, an eye that enabled him to earn his living jousting with such things. To make it interesting for him all the individual parts, including the solenoid switch, worked perfectly when I set them up to demonstrate the problems.

Quickly, before they could renege again, I re-assembled it and bolted it back to the engine, where it worked perfectly. We hadn't done anything. Straight away we started work to rid the injector pump of its intransigent air bubble and all afternoon the starter whirred away whenever it was called on to do so. The cabin steadily filled with a fine mist of diesel fuel as the spinning engine pumped it out through the empty glowplug ports.

As soon as the bubble had worked its way out and all sections of the pump were operating properly, thank goodness, I re-installed the glow plugs, crossed my fingers and thrust the wires together. The shaft turned, grudgingly, through a few degrees and stopped as the end cover of the starter glowed red and sparked.

This time the strip down, while not providing a direct solution, at least defined the basic problem. All the windings seemed to be alright but as soon as the contacts were called on to carry a heavy current they broke down. The fittings were all pitted by corrosion in spite of my attempts to clean them and on this occasion there was enough resistance somewhere to melt the solder from a brush connection.

Eric had a remarkably well equipped workshop on *Heather* and was able to not only repair the broken connection but properly swage the new battery cables Sue had sent and, if we were lucky, refurbish the solenoid switch. Neither of us had ever dismantled one of these so didn't know quite what to expect and I confess to being reluctant about the venture because it was working, albeit intermittently, and dismantling it could easily prove permanent.

Having a somewhat more courageous spirit Eric embarked on the task of talking me into it and soon the switch was clamped in a vice on *Heather's* saloon table, while her skipper administered open heart surgery with a hacksaw and small cold chisel.

Once the workings were laid open it didn't seem nearly as daunting and the condition of the innards showed clearly that the step had been necessary. Wire brushes, files and plenty of abrasive were the order of the day and when the bits were offered up together again all the contacts sparkled. All that remained was to restore the sawn-off case and make it hold together again. With plenty of hands to hold the bits in line and some judicious work with hammer and punch, it was done.

When the bench tests were complete we made up the new battery cables before installing it so there would be no excuse for it not going, even if the key switch was hot wired. Now, with so many attempts to run the engine finishing in disappointment, I was nervous of trying again and went through my pre-start check list two or three times until I could delay it no longer. Oil level, okay; water level, okay; seacock, open; glowplugs, contact!

For several revolutions she ground over, audibly slowing as the batteries took the strain, then she coughed, coughed again, stuttered for a few seconds and settled to an irregular idle. But she was running.

I cracked open the injector lines, one at a time, to purge the last vestiges of trapped air and, as I closed the line to the troublesome element of the pump, she started to run sweet and clean. It is not possible to explain the feeling of freedom that sound evoked.

With renewed vigour, even enthusiasm, I tackled the peripheral jobs that had languished under the uncertainty. The key switch, for example, would make the nervous dexterity of juggling heater and starter cables redundant but for the moment it was seized up. Unlike the solenoid switch it was not entirely necessary so work could be done on it with a lighter heart.

It is a complicated mechanical device designed to be thrown away rather than repaired if it fails. The idea of sawing the case off in the same way was discarded out of hand; even thinking of the likely explosion of pins and springs was too hard, so the first step was to steep it in our corrosive 'preservative' spray. Maybe it would protect the harmful oxides the way it protected our valuable tins.

After steeping in this juice for a day the guck was flushed out with a mixture of engine oil and kerosene and the key, which was corroded in, subjected to a light battering. Ten minutes of bashing and wiggling and the barrel could be pushed in and out between the 'pre-heat' and 'start' positions. A significant improvement but far short of the easy spring return of a new switch.

The process was repeated until the barrel would come back out on its own and could be turned to its limits. It never relented sufficiently to let the key be taken out but you could feel the basic movements clicking inside and an ohmmeter showed that the functions were working without too much resistance. Things were going so well we even thought it worthwhile to try and revitalize an alternator.

The alternator that had been in service when *Vespera* sank was utterly destroyed but the spare had been washed off and dried, though at this stage not tested. Indeed, until the engine ran such a test wasn't possible and, like the starter, it had been stored for several months since cleaning. Eric concluded that the circumstances justified a full working-over before wiring it to the batteries.

He delved into the workings and obviously exercised his mind over them a lot because he was busy for ages, but I don't profess to know what he did. Whatever, the end result, when connected up with new fittings from his stock, was that we could start the engine using the key and generate electricity once it was running.

It sounds as though this was a period of nothing but work, but that's far from true. It was one of the most enjoyable times of all. Once the engine had run everything we did was lighthearted, the weather was as good as it ever got and the four of us had the atoll to ourselves, the other boats having gone elsewhere until Christmas.

Robin had a predilection for snorkelling and not a single day passed without her finding some new delight. To indulge this interest, and indeed our own, we made several excursions together round the atoll and shared some lovely discoveries. One such discovery, or revelation, was of a culinary nature and the setting for it as near perfect as possible.

We had trailed a lure on the way to Ile Fouquet and had the good fortune to catch a couple of mackerel tuna, the second coming to the hook as we arrived. Being close to lunch time fillets from the larger of them were seasoned and set to cook over hot coals in a beachfront glade. Meanwhile the smaller, and fresher, fish was prepared as sashimi and served on platters of palm fronds. The revelation came when Eric produced a dish of wasabi to go alongside the soya sauce.

Gourmets will know about this horseradishy taste that's a traditional accompaniment to sashimi in Japan, where it originates, but to us of more plebeian tastes it was something entirely new. The friendly warning from *Heather*'s chef didn't prepare me fully for the lightning storm that surged through my head at the first taste, but once my sinuses came back to life it was most enjoyable. We got our own back later by introducing them to raw bilimbis.

Another incident happened now that profoundly affected our stay in paradise, and it was based on a misunderstanding, or breakdown in communications. Robin was a keen radio ham and allowed us access to Tony's network to ask him to telephone Sue, from Kenya, with the good news about the engine. It sat heavily on our consciences that she had dashed off to the far side of the world, rushed about madly to get our spares and send them off 'express', then heard nothing from us for months. We were sure she would have had a first-hand report of our good health when the administrator returned but apart from that she might as well have sent the parcels to Mars.

Anyway Tony, obliging chap that he is, contacted Sue with the glad tidings and the next day forwarded a return communication, "Do you want me to send money for provisions with the expedition scientists?" This was a bit cryptic but during our brief discussions with Charles, the expedition leader, before we left Malaysia we gained the impression that the expedition would be provisioned from Diego Garcia, and this sounded like a classic opportunity.

With visions of a short list of requirements being tagged onto a comprehensive requisition against a military store, all paid for in advance by Sue, then a day's voyage alongside the expedition's supplies, our immediate response was 'Yes please'. This would allow us to stay until the best passage time without the worry of rationing and would cause a minimum of inconvenience to others.

Short-wave propagation was poor for a few days but next time we had good contact I passed our list to Tony for transmission to Sue. I should have realized then that things were not as I understood them when he said he would see what he could do. There was already some confusion as, from snippets of disjointed conversation, there was a suggestion that Charles, with whom Sue would probably have to arrange things, would join the expedition in Kenya and provisioning would be done there.

This needed clearing up quickly because, if true, he would have to leave England soon and there was a deal of urgency for Sue to deliver the list, and the cash. What was more Christmas, with its endearing habit of disrupting plans, was looming. Confused questions and obfuscation on my part clogged Tony's net for several mornings while I tried to find out what was happening, and regular reports of a boat on its way from Aden did little for my comprehension. Obviously I was missing something.

Eventually I cottoned on, to my embarrassment and Tony's enduring credit. Nobody was embarking in Kenya but one of the expedition's boats, owned and operated by friends of his, was scheduled to call in there on its way from England to the islands. He was simply waiting on its arrival to clear things with the skipper before taking any action. In the meantime, while I had been nurturing illusions of military simplicity he, and his very understanding wife Daphne, were planning to do all the shopping for us in Mombassa, putting up the money on trust, and deliver it to their friend's boat,

Inga Viola, as and where it called in. And that's exactly what they did.

Here, also contrary to my mental image of nestling beside tons of stores, our goodies made a significant dent in the space remaining on board, and the crew were stuck with it for weeks. I can imagine, only too well, what my own reaction would have been to a cavalier request, by persons unknown, to carry such an inconvenient cargo and the fact that Mike and Gitta would even acknowledge us when they reached Boddam speaks volumes for them. But I'm getting ahead of myself again.

One communication about which I had no pre-conceptions, and therefore understood fairly quickly, was that three boats were currently approaching Boddam from South Africa; one indeed should almost be in sight as we received the message. The yacht's name, *Glee + 2*, told us that the front-runners were old friends Glynn, Lee and son Matthew, with a new boat and a new daughter. The prospect of friendly small children on the island augured well for Christmas.

While they were threading their way through the corals Tina accompanied Eric and Robin on a breadfruit gathering mission. Her function was to act as photographer and she certainly had an unusual subject, for an island barely ten feet high, as they headed off for the grove loaded with ropes and climbing gear; like carrying skis in the Sahara. However, the fireside talk later of prussic loops and belays made sense beside the big basket of breadfruits they had to show.

Almost as versatile as the coconut, the breadfruit can be prepared in many ways. Ripe ones can be eaten just as they are by spooning out the flesh, which is a bit like stringy custard, and there are countless variations on the 'add them to something else' theme, but our favourite was to slice a hard, unripe fruit into chips and fry them.

The very best way is to deep fry them as you would potatoes, but using oil this way is far too extravagant for the islands. Shallow frying in a hot pan produces a fairly good chip though and until the oil ran out this was a special treat. We did some experiments in frying with a minimal amount of oil (none), with a singular lack of success, just to discover that simply dropping a whole fruit in the fire and leaving it until it's completely black works a treat. You just lift it out and break off the charcoal and the inside is delicious. It's as well we only discovered that shortly before leaving as I may have been tempted to try climbing a tree. Well, 'may' is possibly too strong a word.

Glynn brought three things with him that changed the island lifestyle completely. The most obvious was a substantial hard-bottom dinghy with an out-rigger and sails, but the most telling were a generous spirit and a love of fishing. Hardly a day would pass without 'Little Glee' venturing off to the prime fishing spots, many of which were outside the reef and not safely accessible to inflatables that depend on engines.

We had a clear display of our dinghy's vulnerability under such circumstances when, on the day they arrived, our outboard's starting mechanism broke. Happening, as it did, only yards from *Vespera* no harm came from it, other than that fixing it caused me to miss the breadfruit climbing spectacle, but the incident underlined the dangers of fishing outside on your own. Glynn's enthusiasm and generosity put paid to any temptation to take such a risk as most days he was happy to find someone to give a fish to.

Afternoons and evenings developed an entirely different character with a young family to consider. It was fun to eat together and best for everyone if we ate at an appropriate time for the children. This subtle change resulted in long sociable afternoons outside the 'watch your head'. Lee's first job on arriving had been to rebuild a table that had fallen victim to the workshop last season. There was another one at the tide-line but it wasn't so nicely placed and her new one, albeit built of old planks, driftwood and fishing net floats, became the focal point. It was just right for the backgammon games and large enough to seat us all. Set under a takamaka tree with a loose row of palms separating it from the beach it couldn't have been more perfect. There was even a swing nearby, for children of all ages, that an earlier visitor had made.

A couple of days before Christmas the second boat of the South African trio arrived and the same tide saw Knut and Renatta return from the other atoll. Almost before the sand settled over their anchor Knut was in his dinghy to come and fetch us for sundowners. Once they had us comfortably seated in *Yebisah*'s cockpit with ice-cold gin and tonics in hand, what heaven, Renatta ducked into the cabin to produce a Christmas present they didn't want to keep until 'the day'. The first instalment was a hanging basket, neatly cut from a fishing float, FILLED with shiny fresh oranges. However did they do that? Then came a pile of yellow coconuts that are especially good to drink and, to cap it all, a heap of carefully wrapped papayas at varying stages of ripeness.

We could hardly believe our eyes. We were aware of people finding fruit on the other islands but most of the forays had been, at best, only marginally successful. From this showing they must have found the mother-lode. We had lovely sweet oranges to eat and plenty to squeeze for juice. Tina carefully shaved the zest from the skins and sun-dried it to add to her cooking. The papayas provided handsome breakfasts right up to the new year and we have never tasted better.

Next morning the third South African boat came in, bringing the island contingent to seventeen souls for Christmas. Lee's table wouldn't quite stretch to this number so the celebrations were planned for the French camp. The cooking facility there was not so efficient but there was more room and the surroundings more amenable to partying.

December twenty-fifth was a lovely gentle, if cloudy, day and with the enlarged community the morning's social round was just like at home, Christmas cake, pressies and all. Completely unlike being at home though was an early afternoon snorkel over the coral when we encountered an extraordinary shoal of tiny purple-eyed fish tightly clustered around an outcrop. Even when we swam up close to them they stayed completely motionless, giving the impression of a huge, neatly coiffured, head of hair with purple highlights. Then, as a finishing touch, we found a friendly hawksbill turtle to play with.

Seemingly in no time it was mid afternoon and time to gather at the French camp, now festooned with bunting and tinsel, for the feast. Goodness knows how so many edible luxuries survived predation from hungry crews on their way here but certainly no-one anywhere ate better than we did. There was even a delicious leg of lamb that Eric roasted in the bakery oven.

Unfortunately our celebrations came to an abrupt end on Boxing day when we spoke to Tony to pass on seasonal greetings and for news of those friends who were staying in Kenya. We heard stories of grand parties and fun being had by all but also learned of the death of Chris, from *Delight*, who had been so friendly and helpful in Boddam. He was an enormously gifted young man with a big heart and had been killed in an accident while, characteristically, helping some local fishermen on Mafia Island.

This tragic news put a damper on our spirits but we were determined to enjoy the relative quiet while it lasted. The expedition scientists would be here in a few weeks and, though not actively involved, we had volunteered our services for the duration and didn't know what to expect. Whatever happened it would be a lot different from the virtual subsistence lifestyle we had adapted to. Then, we supposed, by the time they left the season for sailing across the Indian Ocean would be in full swing and the anchorage would be full again.

The week leading up to the New Year saw us snorkelling on new bommies and walking the beaches. There is always something new to learn and somewhere different to explore and the fact that it rained at least once every day didn't detract at all. There was consternation in some quarters though that the New Year's Eve party could be rained off, particularly as the records show January to be the wettest month of the year.

This was at least part of the thinking behind Knut's mission to repair the 'watch your head' roof though it was more a public-spirited action to benefit everyone; us in particular as we cooked there every day. I went with him on a couple of foraging excursions that yielded, from buildings that had already collapsed, some corrugated iron sheets in better condition than the existing ones, some of which had rusted right through, and a few lengths of timber that would do as supports.

The main task was to build a new section, about five feet by six, over the doorway where there was, presently, no roof at all but he also wanted to cure the worst of the drips. On reflection the drips were more annoying than the big hole. At

Île Mapo

Vespera *on the beach*

The extent of the repairs

Île F

Île Ja

Repairs get underway

Île Mapc

Île F

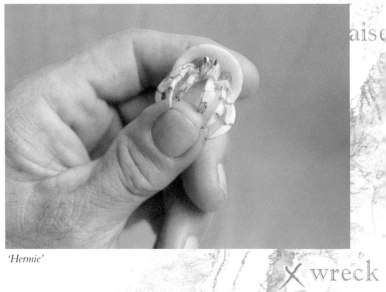

'Hermie'

Kay and Sue in the bakery

Coconut shell cleaners

Sue at the well

Vespera *ready for the final patch*

Preparing to refloat Vespera

Île Map

'Watch your Head Club' beach with Vespera *(Right) and* Heather

Île

Peter and Tina Lickfold

Jess

least with the big hole you knew to keep out of the way and the wet area was well defined. Under the rest of the roof it seemed that wherever you chose to sit the first rain drop would find its way either down your neck or into your dinner.

First thing then was to take off the worst of the existing sheeting and reposition the rest so that good metal would deflect the leaks to drip outside. Next was to build a frame with the lengths of timber, reinforce it with a couple of steel bars we found in the old copra yard, then nail the collected iron sheets in place. It sounds very simple but Knut was pushing and pulling sheets, cutting and wedging beams and driving nails for most of New Year's Eve before declaring himself satisfied.

It's not quite true to say we couldn't wait for it to rain to see how well it worked but we certainly looked forward to the first test with interest. Of course, in line with nature's immutable laws, the rain clouds that threatened all day dispersed with the setting sun and plans to sing 'Auld Lang Syne' under the new roof were scrapped in favour of the French camp.

Some of the Christmas bunting was still in place and a glittering blue 'Happy New Year' banner – compliments of *Cicada* – was strung between two palm trees. A unique benefit of being on a remote island became apparent later when the precise time came under friendly dispute. Not many people were wearing watches and those timepieces present didn't agree, so at an appropriate time in the festivities 'Boddam Standard Time' was decreed and the New Year welcomed in.

Reading through the diaries it appears we did little else but attend parties at this time. Only three days later Matthew from *Glee + 2* turned six and Mark, from *Dalkiri*, celebrated his twenty-first birthday. It had already rained often, if briefly, to prove Knut's workmanship on the 'watch your head' but again we found ourselves round a laden table at the French camp. Brian gave his son a short and very moving presentation before everyone settled down to serious feasting, an undertaking which was disturbed by an excited call from the darkness an hour or two later.

"Come quickly, quickly, there are baby turtles all over the beach." Robin had walked quietly away and only gone a few yards before stumbling into hordes of the little creatures scrambling down to the sea. Soon there was a circle of interested people with powerful torches to light the scene and we watched in fascination.

The turtles were appearing from under a bush barely ten yards from where we were sitting then heading straight for the water. The tide was well down leaving a wide beach with coral bits scattered on the sand. These obstacles, small to us, made a formidable barrier for these little fellows but their instincts hardly faltered. They would merely sidestep until they cleared the obstruction then carry on directly for the water. Only a couple seemed to lose their way and those had been subjected to strong video lighting while their antics were recorded for posterity.

Once or twice we witnessed a hiccup in the learning curve as the creatures reached the sea. On the way across the beach they moved the flippers on opposite corners together, like a dog or a horse walking, but as they entered the water their flippers worked in pairs, as though swimming breast-stroke. The hiccups came when contact with the water didn't switch them over immediately and they carried on trying to walk.

They could certainly swim alright but the funny cornerwise flipper movement drove them round in tight circles, always clockwise in those I saw, with the movements becoming more and more frantic as they apparently didn't understand what was happening. We found if we saw one doing this imitation of swimming down a plug-hole all that was needed was to pick him up for a few moments and put him back in the water, hold him still until you felt the movement change, and off he would go quite happily.

There was more activity on the landward side of the beach where someone had back-tracked the run and located the nest. Unlike nesting pits that have just been dug, which are basically the same size as the adult turtle, this appeared as a small hole, maybe only ten inches by four on the surface. Looking straight down into it you could see a writhing mass of bodies scrambling desperately to reach ground level only an inch or two above them. Every few seconds another would make it over the rim and start his journey to the water.

What a beautiful and memorable thing to see on your twenty-first birthday!

The following days brought us back down to earth with a series of radio reports from the BBC and others on the changing lifestyle back home in South Africa. We heard of ordinary suburban communities erecting city walls for protection against intruders and of burgeoning violent crime. Radio reports are not necessarily correct of course and in our own experience anything to do with South Africa was particularly prone to distortion but, for once, first hand news from the recently arrived boats confirmed the stories.

More and more the prospect of leaving our piece of paradise to return to such surroundings became hard to stomach. It was a reality we had to face though but, being so remote, any plans we dreamed up to counteract the perceived difficulties were based on conjecture and invariably dwindled away to inconclusive daydreaming. A far from satisfactory view of the future.

It should have been easy simply not to think about it but a negative frame of mind is an insidious thing that can worm its way under sunshine and white sands to flaw the most beautiful day. Our ill-formed fears for the future were becoming as real as our fears for the voyage and conscious effort was needed not to let it spoil things. The only redeeming quality of such worries is the heightened enjoyment of living when you escape them.

During one such escape we went for a swim over our favourite bommie and experienced some of the best snorkelling conditions ever. The water was as clear as could be and the sky bright, but hazy enough to eliminate reflections. The colours were sharp as paint and we were engrossed in the antics of some clown fish when a large shark appeared.

Large is an emotive word to use when describing a shark and many would think it out of place here, but to us who were accustomed to, and reasonably comfortable with, the three-foot-long black-tips that abounded anything much bigger was BIG. This fellow was about eight feet long, broad shouldered and very fast. More to the point he was much too interested in us as he circled closer and closer.

We edged towards the dinghy, which was at anchor over

a nearby sand patch, keeping a careful eye on our inquisitive companion. It probably took mere seconds to get there and scramble out of the water, but they were very long ones. Both of us flopped over the sides half expecting to find our fins shortened by teethmarks, but all was well.

The incident curtailed the swimming for a while and we filled our days with other pastimes. I enjoyed several fishing trips outside the reef with Glynn and Gert in Glynn's sailing dinghy while Tina, unhappily, was more involved with the daily workings and never seemed lost for a chore. She was still collecting bilimbis, though the trees were bearing fewer fruit now, and she made plenty of juice that would keep until we had a better supply of sugar. One day she returned from a fruit gathering expedition with the lone orange we'd watched ripen on a tree near the breadfruit grove. Boddam oranges are a great rarity and we treated the peeling and dividing of this one with due reverence and ceremony – and what a surprise!

Unlike the oranges from the other atoll, which were dark fleshed, this specimen was pallid like a grapefruit. But it wasn't a grapefruit, it didn't have the characteristic thick skin. It wasn't a lemon either, or a lime, and we didn't know what to make of it. The segments separated easily and were entirely free of pips. The flavour, when we tried it, was deliciously sweet and completely unique, certainly not an orange. We agreed it had to be a citrus but there was nothing, specifically, we could liken it to.

We felt rather guilty afterwards as maybe we'd eaten the last fruit from a tree unknown to science, the only salve to our consciences being that it had no pips anyway – but I wish we could find another one.

Still on a horticultural note we were now reaping a harvest from our 'washing-up bowl' garden. The bean plants had formed a thick covering over a framework of sticks stuck in round the edges and most days we picked a couple of succulent beans. There were rarely more than two ready at a time and rather than hoarding them and run the risk of them drying out we took to eating one each, straight off the plant, before cooking lunch. One of the other bowls produced a crop of strongly flavoured, and very hot, radishes and we had several servings of fresh greens from the chard and potchoi seeds.

On board we were about to experience the next episode of the engine saga. During a regular check for water in the bilge I noticed a rusty streak on the exhaust pipe jacket where the cooling water is injected, very close to a spot where the pipe had broken once before on the way to Thailand. A few days later the streak was worse and when I took the pipe off I found the jacket leaking water into the manifold as well as to the outside. By way of a change I had a spare pipe and something had gone wrong that I could fix easily.

A few hours of spanner-work and some shuffling of pipes to make them fit and the job was done. I just needed to run the engine to make sure everything worked okay, the spare being not quite the same as the original, and went through the normal starting procedure. I got a fright the moment I turned the key when the engine roared into life and raced up to maximum speed immediately.

Nothing I did would slow the wretched thing down. The throttle lever had no effect and the stop cable was firmly stuck. With some trepidation I put my hand over the air intake to stifle it and the racket stopped as abruptly as it started. The racket of my pulse didn't stop so quickly.

Thinking, hoping, that it was a problem with the controls I disconnected the linkages and worked the cable and levers back and forth. They were very stiff but nothing really untoward. I oiled everything that could be oiled, which made things smoother, and checked the pump movements before connecting them up again. Both levers were free and felt perfectly normal.

So, on with the key again and it was back to full speed straight away, but now I knew how to stop it. This was as depressing as a cold shower as there appeared to be a fault in the pump that I didn't understand. I had a pretty good drawing of its main workings but the governor, which I suspected, was just an enigmatic box.

Nevertheless something had to be done and the whole thing had to come off, undoing all the bodging that had gone on to get it going. My approach to stripping the governor was no more scientific than undoing the visible nuts and bolts to see what happened. It didn't achieve much other than that the case dropped open enough to give a tantalizing view of a complexity of springs.

Expecting something to unclip or disengage I manipulated the case every way it would move but it wouldn't open any further. I tried to see what was hanging up inside by poking a dentist's mirror through the gap but there was only room at the side for either my eye or a torch, not both, and the innards remained a mystery.

Eventually I noticed the control shaft, which traversed the gap and disappeared into the pump, didn't move however much the rest of the contraption was wiggled. And that didn't make sense. I took another cover off to see if the far end of the shaft was obstructed but there was nothing there and I could only resort to more shaking and wiggling, with a light tap now and then for encouragement.

After three full days of such attention the thing suddenly lurched in my hands and the gap snapped shut like a clam. The control shaft jumped forwards and all the pump elements rotated as smartly as a well-rehearsed chorus line. This was exactly what I was trying to achieve but I was dismayed to see it happen without knowing why, or indeed why had it stuck in the first place.

Anyway it was working now and delaying putting it back served no useful purpose so I re-fitted it directly. This time the job went easily and the engine was docile and started obediently. I still don't know what caused this misbehaviour and confess that, since then, I won't switch on the starter unless the floor is up and I can reach the air intake.

For a bit of light relief I joined the others to go crayfishing. Glynn had engineered an excellent shade for his pressure lamp so it cast a pool of light without blinding us and at the same time shone a bright beam forward to illuminate the prey. A moonless night had been chosen and the spring low tide was due around eight o'clock in the evening.

A few moments after dark Glynn, Gert and I met at the 'watch your head' and set off across the island. We had just passed the old hospital, where the path branches, when we saw a coconut crab, a tiny one. Controversy still raged about whether the big purple hermit crabs grew into coconut crabs and this sighting caused as much discussion as ever. The crab was a fully formed coconut crab with the distinctive shape and colouring of his big brothers, but overall he was smaller than the average 'big' hermit. One vote for the 'no they don't' camp.

We were lucky enough to see eight more on the way across the island, most of them equally small but two were a good size. The last took us by surprise by appearing at eye level rather than underfoot where we were looking. For a few seconds it stayed still, apparently mesmerized, then scuttled rapidly up the tree on which it was perched. It was rumoured that fully grown crabs climb the palms to collect the coconuts. We didn't see that but I can believe it.

At the end of the path we turned west and a few hundred yards further on came to an area of jumbled rocks separating the beach from the coral flats. It was a bit early as waves were still swirling around the rocks, telling us it was too deep and turbulent for easy wading. We parked ourselves on a couple of comfortable rocks and a bottle of 'ready mix', scotch and water, helped while away the time as the water dropped.

When the scotch ran out conditions were deemed good enough so we formed a line abreast and started along the flat. Every nook and cranny, even the slightest indentation in the bottom, was investigated and within minutes Glynn spotted a crayfish close to the line of breaking waves. We concentrated the light from the lamp and two torches on the crustacean to distract its attention while he sneaked up to grab it from behind. One in the bag.

Before moving on we pumped up the pressure lamp, which had started to dim, but during that exercise it suddenly went out. The mantle is usually hot enough to re-light it if you're quick, but it didn't work this time. Of course the matches and spirit had been left in a bucket on the beach with the other clutter so, leaving Gert to mark the spot, we took a torch and went back.

A sudden blustery wind told us a rain squall was imminent and before we reached the beach the first flurries arrived. The rain was ridiculously cold and fell in a deluge, huge dollops biting through our shirts as they landed. We clambered over the now treacherous rocks and huddled in their shelter until it blew over, thinking guilty thoughts of Gert standing up to his knees in the sea, surrounded by darkness and being blasted by the icy rain.

It stopped as suddenly as it started but enough had fallen to drown the matches so the pressure lantern was no further use. Gert's torch was a dull glimmer in the blackness and the batteries in the other would only last another thirty minutes. Time to go home. It was a wet, cold and disconsolate group of hunters who returned almost empty handed to our wives.

The squally weather persisted for days, giving us restless nights as *Vespera* bounced and slopped on her chain while the wind whistled in the trees. Tina retreated from shore-side chores and busied herself making the boat ready for the arrival of the expedition and the boat bringing our supplies from Tony.

One thing that had to be done before we could stow any stores was paint a cement slurry over the patches. There were several spots where the mesh had been inadequately covered and the surfaces were well streaked with rust. We hoped that a slurry of neat cement would stick well enough to seal the bad spots against further corrosion.

While clearing the way to do the job Tina moved the basket with our meagre stock of cans and in doing so heard one of them burst. It wasn't very loud but the sound was distinct and clear enough to make us line them all up for inspection. Every one was rusted to a greater or lesser extent and we checked them carefully, examining every spot minutely, shaking the tins close to our ears and squeezing the ends for signs of failure, but we couldn't find the culprit. Normally we would have discarded the lot rather than run the risk of food poisoning — there weren't very many after all – but we didn't think we could afford the luxury.

We'd become a bit blasé about determining the edibility or otherwise of tinned food by inspecting the inside of cans after we opened them. We thought we could tell the difference between an actual hole, that could be dangerous, and a surface discolouration, which we considered benign, and so far we'd been lucky. We would have to be very careful, and even more lucky, in future.

Tina was particularly deflated by the worry and only recovered her equanimity when she formed an eight letter word on a triple word score in a game of Scrabble later. David and Adela from *Malgre Tout* completed the cure the following morning with a gift of fresh eggs, tomatoes and vegetables. A most appropriate and welcome morale lifter, especially as we now treated all our food with suspicion.

There were now six boats in the lagoon and each, in its own way, was preparing for the scientific onslaught. Quite apart from our excitement at the prospective arrival of our stores we were looking forward to contact with people who could answer some of our questions. Others were not so enthusiastic, seeing the whole exercise as a threat.

This conflict of views was a source of lively discussion when we were all together. On the one hand was the concept that any increase in knowledge had to be beneficial, while on the other was a perception that the most likely outcome would be gross exploitation and restriction of access to an academic elite. Both views were valid and neither prevailed, though there was a general leaning towards pessimism.

Two weeks or so before it was all supposed to happen we enjoyed a Brit-ops visit, presumably to check on the island housekeeping before the commissioner came, and it was just like Christmas over again. Sue had mailed loads more parcels and piles of letters filled the spaces in the post bag. Alistair, the fisheries protection officer, added to the feeling by coming aboard *Vespera* with a gift of fish hooks suitable for angling in the lagoon.

Equally important was an opportunity to talk to the medic about my eyes, which were giving me trouble again. Sue had sent medications to treat all sorts of symptoms but I needed information as much as anything. This, fortunately, was not a lengthy business and there was plenty of time left in the day to show the sailors and marines where the best snorkelling was.

Not a lot was achieved in the next few days; the naval party had left some British newspapers and our mail contained several fairly current South African ones, so most of our time was spent kneeling over the spread out pages. Items were read and re-read; even the most mundane information was grist to the island mill.

The prices of groceries in Johannesburg: 'Look what your washing powder costs now', 'Just think about a braai when steaks cost as much as that'. The Sits. Vac. reduced to a scant page from the usual four or five. Armed hijackings, murder and arson were commonplace, simple robberies apparently no longer newsworthy, and hardly a mention of a good deed. In the end it was a relief to pass the wretched things on.

Chris and Louise cheered us up by bringing more oranges and a lemon from the other atoll, and before long we heard the expedition boats speaking to each other on the VHF. We first heard their traffic at four o'clock in the morning and the weather was being most unfriendly, in fact it was raining hard enough to fill all our jerry cans before it got light. But it eased at daybreak and *Inga Viola*'s sails could be seen silhouetted against a dull overcast outside the reef. Later they were joined by *Aztec Lady* and, taking the precaution of launching a dinghy to scout the way, both boats snaked through the coral to come to anchor near Boddam. By now the clouds had relented and a harsh sun burned ready for when the work started.

And work that first day was hard. The fisheries patrol vessel kept station a short way off shore while tenders ferried fuel from there to the beach. Thousands of litres of fuel were transferred in ordinary oil drums, horrible unwieldy things to manhandle in inflatable boats. When the bulk of this was finished we watched a tender leave *Inga Viola* and make its way towards us.

The helmsman introduced himself as Mike, the owner, and his passenger as 'Frog', the mate. Imagine our chagrin, mortification is a better word, when we learned they had come to apologize for leaving our stuff on Diego Garcia for the Brits to bring. They had so much equipment on board that our bundle, which now seemed ridiculously large, simply wouldn't fit anywhere.

These good people were kind enough to make light of the inconvenience it had caused all the way from Kenya, and the awkwardness that must have ensued when the scientists embarked to find their storage space full. Between them they managed to persuade us, almost, that it had been amicable and easily sorted out though I think we only heard part of the story.

Later, when the fuel and heavy equipment was safely ashore, they invited us to join them in a beach party and it was good to meet Charles and Ann, the expedition prime movers, and get first-hand news of Sue.

Next day was something of a red letter day. We cooked breakfast ashore in our usual style, at least Tina did while I sat under a tree to write more of this book, and the reason the day was special was that I reached the hundred-thousand-word mark of the first draft. I hadn't yet had the courage to re-read what I'd written and endless second thoughts told me most, if not all, of it would finish up in the shredder, but nonetheless it was quite a milestone. My original daily target had been halved, then halved again, but even so almost every minute not spent working on *Vespera* had gone into writing to get as far as that. Now, with more interesting distractions, progress was to get worse and the target halved again.

The first distraction was to watch the entomologists catching insect specimens. Preconceptions of smiling faces lunging through the undergrowth behind billowing butterfly nets are not entirely wrong, but they're not entirely right either. We were amazed at the number and variety of 'bugs' they caught within the radius of quiet conversation from our breakfast table.

To be honest it was a little hard on our egos as we consider ourselves reasonably observant and had gone to great trouble to make notes of all the insects, trees and birds we'd seen, where we'd seen them and when, with the intention of saving them some legwork. But in a few hours they had captured twice the number of varieties we'd noticed in a year and the stream of new acquisitions continued unabated.

The marine biologists were equally successful in that during their first dive, mere yards from the old jetty, they discovered a previously unrecorded blennie. It was likely to carry on like this too if the stories we heard of previous expeditions were to be repeated. A couple of decades earlier a similar party, including several of the people here now, had discovered new species on a routine basis.

The 'hundred-thousand word' day was memorable but the next one even more so. This day we celebrated spending a full year in the islands.

So many things had happened. Some exceptionally good, others rewarding or inspiring and others definitely not worthy of celebration but, all things considered, we had much to thank our Maker for. Looking back over the shared experiences of our thirty-some years together it's hard to find a catastrophe of similar proportions to being shipwrecked, but a year in a tropical paradise with the company, if temporary, of so many delightful people has a lot to commend it.

Then for a few days we were kept busy wandering the paths and open spaces of Boddam with an enthusiastic, if a little over-awed, young botanist, offering help wherever we could with her task of verifying the interpretation of some elaborate satellite images. We took our GPS receiver to confirm the image locations and were pretty upset when it started misbehaving only forty minutes after we switched it on.

It had worked perfectly when tested six months earlier and then we'd simply remounted it with a sigh of relief. Ian had restored my sextant and Sue had sent a copy of the current almanac and a spare wristwatch so satellite navigation was a convenience rather than a necessity, but what a useful convenience. For the moment it looked likely that we would have to do it the hard way.

On our return to *Vespera* I discovered the GPS batteries were completely flat. They'd been replaced that morning and are supposed to last for ten hours of normal operation, so whatever had happened to the set was making it draw a lot more power than it should. Plugged in to the boat's batteries it seemed to work well enough and there was nothing definite to indicate a permanent fault – another device that may, or may not, survive until we got home.

A week after the expedition arrived the Brits came, this time on a regular 'Brit-ops' visit, and in addition to bringing our stores brought mail and so forth. The morning was calm and transferring everything from the ship and then onto *Vespera* went well. With the whole load piled in the cockpit we had a better understanding of the problem it must have been for *Inga Viola*. We were now familiar with the boat and had seen for ourselves the prodigious amount of scientific equipment they had on board.

But red-faced or not we were very excited. Daphne had done a splendid job of translating our vague list into a well balanced mix of provisions, and had included a gift of beautiful fresh pumpkins. There were also parcels of treats from other friends; a bottle of wine, some jam etc. and a giant pack of toilet rolls. What bliss. With all this and a bagful of Christmas cards, a bit late but welcome as ever, we buried our heads for the rest of the day.

The most immediate effect of the store's arrival was on Jess's diet. Unlike us, who are quite content with the most extraordinary meals, she didn't understand when presented with a bowl of lentils or bulgur wheat instead of her usual fishy fare and, as often as not, simply wouldn't eat it. Most days someone caught a fish and the remains, after filleting, were usually contributed to feed her, but it didn't always happen. Daphne had made sure we had plenty of small tins of fish and Jess didn't go hungry at all after that.

The atmosphere of the islands changed a lot while the scientists were there. It wasn't so much the surge in numbers as the marked difference in outlooks that caused it. Most of the newcomers had stepped virtually from their offices to the beaches and, of necessity, brought the constraints and pressures of urban living with them.

Time, to us, was governed only by the rise of the sun, the onset of hunger, or tiredness. It was quite odd to watch people rushing from site to site in high-powered dinghies, working against a tight schedule and the unforgiving clock.

Strangely it seemed most were unaware of the irony in studying nature at such an artificial pace. Maybe that's an avenue of research for scientists of another discipline.

Soon, though, our watches were stowed back in their resting places and the expedition moved on to different horizons. They would be back in a couple of weeks but in the meantime living could return to its normal speed. Somehow though the mere fact that the outside world had reached in and touched us left its mark and in ways too subtle to explain, or at least for me to explain, our outlooks had changed.

Good conversations with people actively involved in the daily business of earning a living while pursuing their interests were opening doors in my head I had been trying to keep closed. They certainly didn't make planning for the unknown future any easier but some were stimulating enough to start me thinking it might even be fun.

But there was another more subtle change in the island ambience. The disruption of 'routine' and, I suppose, a measure of conflicting interests made the afternoon get-togethers somewhat heavy going and contrived. In a self-conscious sort of way the community split in two, one group using the 'watch your head' and the other the French camp. There was nothing unfriendly in it but, in some vague way, we felt that island life had been diminished.

Often though the smaller and more varied gatherings were more fun, and at one such the company was good enough to make us relax our guard against rats hiding in the dinghy. That particular evening we'd eaten at the French camp, so perhaps the lapse came from a break in habit, but the end result was waking next morning to find rat droppings on deck.

Oh dear. We'd been through this pantomime before. Jess had as much interest in rat-catching as she had in long-distance swimming and we had neither traps nor poisons. Our first thought was to find the brute. The droppings were centred around the lazarette hatch so we assumed, hoped, that he was lurking on deck somewhere. And we were anxious to keep him there.

We closed all the doors and hatches and blocked every access route that might allow it inside and started the search.

I armed myself with a stick to chase it over the side with and probed around the easier places, but he was nowhere to be found. We kept the boat closed at night for several days and put up with the sweltering temperatures just in case he came visiting again, but a borrowed rat trap left on deck remained untouched. Gradually we persuaded ourselves he'd dived over the side and a week later returned to sleeping normally and gave the trap back.

At the end of the couple of weeks the scientists' boats returned, but with an almost complete change of personnel. Ill health had obliged John, owner and skipper of *Aztec Lady*, to remain on Diego Garcia when they called in there to pick up a new group of scientists and, how she did it I don't know, his wife Joan had not only dealt with the hustle and bustle of embarking new passengers while getting her sick husband to hospital, she'd organized a tray of fresh eggs for my birthday!

The main thrust of the scientific work was quite different now and we were lucky to have a lot of contact with the new group. We were both able to go with them on visits to the smaller islands and the senior botanist I had the privilege to accompany opened my eyes to the way the forest must have been in the distant past, what had happened to it in the days of the copra plantation and the way it was recovering now.

Tina was in her element. As an avid birdwatcher she'd been feeling somewhat deprived since we started sailing but the expedition's ornithologist was a friendly companion as well as an expert in his field. Each evening she returned to *Vespera* to spend hours making notes of what she had learned during the day.

Obviously we gained a great deal from this encounter but I think the only honest contribution we made to it was helping with the garbage disposal. Getting rid of rubbish is problematic on the islands and however you tackle it someone will find it contentious. Our approach was to burn everything that could be burnt, leaving tin cans and the like in the fire to burn off any protective coatings then crushing them, and we gathered up waste glass and broke it into a container. Some years earlier the authorities had installed bins on Boddam in which visitors were asked to deposit the crushed cans and glass for disposal in the Diego Garcia landfill but the idea seemed to have fallen out of favour.

The waste that accumulated from the yachts over the year had condensed into a binful of glass and a couple of mailbags, left for the purpose, filled with crushed tins. Now, with the influx of people not accustomed to life without municipal services, the output mushroomed and the couple of bags became a heap. Even with the cans hammered flat, and a chunk of scrap iron from the old copra plant made a very efficient crusher, the bags filled up quickly. Each morning we lit a huge bonfire at the waste site when the crews brought the garbage ashore and 'tin bashing' was a regular chore.

In the expedition's aftermath the bags were removed to Diego Garcia amid deep murmurings and undercurrents of wrath from administrators unhappy about clearing up uninhabited islands, which is probably as it should be. Once it was gone we continued to burn and bash but, ignoring the bins, volunteers took the prepared rubbish out to the oceanic depths beyond the reef to dispose of it properly, which is definitely as it should be.

Mike's wife Gitta, the lady who had to create the space on *Inga Viola*, must have forgiven us completely for our imposition as she regularly gave us gifts of things notably absent from our stores, bacon to go with Joan's eggs, packets of biscuits and many more. She also made a point of including us in their hospitality and our time on board gave us a much greater insight into the academic community, something entirely foreign to us up till then.

But, as with all things, the expedition came to an end and the field party went home, the biologists back to their microscopes, the geologists back to their laboratories and the administrators back to their offices. Schedules, time restrictions and organizational plans dissipated with the breeze and the roar of powerful engines dwindled to the putter of small outboards. The reefs and islands closed the chinks in their camouflage, so rudely disturbed by prying minds, and serenity returned. For a short while anyway.

It was well into March now and west-bound yachts from Thailand and Malaysia were starting to arrive. Among the first was *Brumby*, who had helped so much bringing materials the year before, stopping over on another voyage. It was getting to be like old times and as the community grew the afternoon gatherings were a natural focus of attention for the newcomers, and the social whirl expanded rapidly.

In the nature of things groups of people with similar interests band together to exchange ideas, propound philosophies or generally chew the cud and here was no exception. Flashes of inspiration or thrashed out common sense brought many island projects into being. Some of these could reasonably be described as frivolous though they provided hours of fun for all concerned: experimental fishing tackle, beautifully crafted galley utensils and so on, but others were much more serious. In fact it's a blessing that these islands are here to provide a haven for yachts that encounter difficulties on the long stretch across the ocean.

One boat arrived with a non-functioning gear box and another with its self-steering gear damaged. The gear box was beyond repair and a replacement was necessary. Again the radio networks, following boats and dynamic friends came up trumps and a new unit was delivered. The steering gear was not so easy and substantial island engineering was required to fix it.

These sort of jobs plus the endless, and I mean endless, maintenance that goes to keep boats and their equipment operational in the tropics meant that the area in front of the 'watch your head' became pretty busy. We had overwhelmed the place the year before by strewing *Vespera*'s innards all around, but this year there wouldn't have been room. The dining area, now good and weatherproof under Knut's new roof, was a logical place to store tools and generators rather than ferry them backwards and forwards and the kitchen table reverted to being a work bench. As all jobs tackled under these conditions take longer than can be imagined from a civilized point of view, half-finished projects became our regular suppertime companions.

We were, at that stage, so acclimatized to living on our own, or with very few neighbours, that 'people pressure' was starting to tell. Tina has always been more gregarious than me but I know she found the restrictions imposed by simple good-neighbourliness almost as demanding as I did. Force of habit as much as simple expediency moved us to cook our evening meals in time to eat and clear up before the light failed. Of course it was equally logical for anyone repairing an engine or patching a dinghy to carry on working all the time he could see to do so. The two requirements of the 'watch your head' are mutually exclusive and more and more often Tina fumbled to cook in the dark.

The new season's volley-ball league compounded the problem. Several yards of rope and some guard rail netting from one of the boats had converted the 'patonk' pitch back to its intended purpose and sundowner time volley-ball became an everyday happening. Here I must confess that avoiding team recruiters was more significant to me than crankshafts on the tea-table and we usually avoided going ashore till the games were over, accepting the difficult cooking arrangements as the price.

While these social changes were happening we had two visits in the space of a few hours that can only be described as uniquely special. The first got off to an inauspicious start when an unknown yacht motored across the lagoon and anchored, in poor holding, close enough to cause concern. I'm afraid our reaction wasn't very friendly and we simply went below to grumble at each other about people imposing on our paradise.

Fifteen or twenty minutes later we heard the buzz of an approaching engine followed by a cheerful hail. We stuck our heads out and were greeted by two beaming faces. Roger and his son Morgan, of lens recovery fame, were helping the owner of the new boat sail from Djibouti to Reunion and had stopped at Boddam for the sole purpose of bring us provisions. They brought onions, butter, flour and sugar, and a huge bag of lovely crisp rusks.

When I say they came for the sole purpose of bringing us these things it is the exact and literal truth. We barely had time to help them collect coconuts for the rest of their voyage before they weighed anchor and left. They were going to traverse an area with a high risk of cyclones so every minute of good weather was precious yet, knowing this, they'd made this detour just for us.

Pretty overwhelming stuff but it wasn't finished yet. Tina

had been in the middle of making bread when they arrived and had quickly returned to the bakery when they left. The first indication that something else extraordinary was about to happen was a distant 'whup-whup-whup' of a helicopter. The only aircraft we'd seen in ages were an occasional American maritime patrol Orion and a Royal Air Force VC 10 that preceded a VIP visit with the expedition. The sound approached rapidly and a fire-engine red helicopter, its doors bristling with arms, legs and video cameras, swooped overhead.

Tina had chosen the moment for her stage entrance on this family video to perfection. Dressed in island work clothes she'd worked up a sweat breaking firewood, smoke and ash from the ill-tempered fire had covered her in soot and the bread was over-proving. She was not a happy lady as she turned to face the lens.

A little later, while I was writing aboard *Vespera*, I heard another cheerful hail, this time from the skipper of a smart high speed launch filled with more smiling faces. The caller introduced himself as 'Captain Nick' of the M/V *Maupiti* and explained that they'd come to invite us to their yacht, which was holding station outside the atoll, to make a telephone call to Sue. Well… !

Tina's embarrassment was complete when I led the party into the bakery clearing and found her still struggling with the fire, eyes running from the smoke and perspiration leaving stripes in the soot. But these people exuded charm and quickly put her at ease. After a hurried shower we were transported in style to another world. Their yacht, or ship, defies description and its accommodation was as different from our island home as it's possible to imagine. The satellite telephone link was excellent and our call to Sue as clear as a face-to-face chat.

It was our first conversation since she left in July and naturally she was anxious to know how things were working out but our immediate interest was to find out how the family were. Words fell over themselves in the hurry. When we eventually hung up we felt comfortably reassured that all was well with our off-spring and, I hope, Sue could pass similar assurances to her sisters. They were almost certainly more worried than we were as, for us, everything was pretty much back to normal. We weren't going anywhere and our standard of living had dropped a bit but habit was glossing over the less pleasant chores and the truth is we were enjoying the simplicity of living day to day.

For the rest of the day we enjoyed hospitality that was the very opposite of simplicity, in fact we were treated like royalty. The owners and crew had heard of our circumstances before leaving for this part of the world and had spoken to Sue some time ago. Then, out of simple generosity, had come to Boddam solely for the purpose of that telephone call... words fail me again.

A programme broadcast by the BBC gave us something to look forward to shortly after this. Astronomers were forecasting the arrival of a new comet, named Hyakutake after its discoverer, towards the end of March and predicting that it would be the largest of the century. They did say that it would be most clearly visible from the northern hemisphere but, as we were only five degrees south, we thought it worth looking out for.

Our enthusiasm was only slightly tempered by an earlier experience when the same predictions were made for Halley's comet in nineteen eighty six. On that occasion we'd joined a group of like-minded friends and, on the main day, armed ourselves with telescopes, binoculars and books of ephemerides and sought the darkness of the mountains. We searched... and searched, but most of the evening was spent round a chest of cold beers arguing whether a particular fuzzy star was the celebrated phenomenon or not.

This happening proved very different. Each evening after the waxing moon had set we gave the sky a quick sweep and a few days before prime time we saw the comet, as clear and bright as could be up near the star Arcturus in the constellation Bootes. We had the best possible viewpoint with wide open skies and no extraneous lights whatever, and the bright ball with its long fat tail appeared so big I was prompted to dig out the sextant and measure it. Seven full degrees from stem to stern. Enormous. And that was just the beginning.

We were really surprised to hear a report the following

morning that it was visible from Britain but only with binoculars. It didn't seem possible that such a huge thing could be disguised by, I assume, ambient artificial light.

The night before the predicted closest approach we had to wait until after midnight for a sky clear of both moon and cloud but then we were treated to a stupendous sight. The comet's head was close to the pipe in the Herdsman constellation and the tail stretched out past Berenice's hair. Through the sextant's telescope it looked even longer and the scale read forty-three degrees when I got the two ends to coincide.

That very evening we'd been aboard the Australian yacht *Tasman* with friends we'd first met in Malaysia eighteen months earlier, acknowledging, we couldn't really celebrate, the anniversary of *Vespera*'s sinking. I still ponder on the significance, or otherwise, of this brilliant comet appearing at such a meaningful time.

Two days later it was gone. It was a great disappointment to me to have observed such a unique thing with no functioning photographic equipment to record it. Russell had fixed a body but there were no lenses or film. Sue's camera, which we thought had survived, proved otherwise when she had a film developed later.

Ian and Chrissy from *Cruise* must have had an even more exciting view of it. They would have been a couple of hundred miles out from Salomon on a voyage from Kenya when the comet was at its best. Imagine experiencing such a work of creation alone on the ocean vastness.

It was even more like old times when they sailed into the lagoon. There were several fewer boats this year than when the accident happened but the 'old hands' imposed a sort of community continuity. The atmosphere was very similar, the parties just as exuberant, the bakery submitted to the same culinary experiments and fishing assumed the same commanding position on priority lists.

One evolution that was quite different was the development of the French camp social evenings. This may be entirely subjective as continuous proximity to the place the previous year could have distorted our memories, but these evenings became largely the province of the few 'old hands' and not the central focus it had been before. From an entirely selfish point of view this made the loss of our easy-going cooking at the 'watch your head' easier to accept. There always seemed to be room on the communal fire for our pot.

Another evolution was one of attitude. Months earlier, when we learned we wouldn't get the engine spares in time to leave before the cyclone season, the transition from atoll visitor to atoll resident had been conscious and deliberate. Now the transition back was much more subtle and, as time passed, being met with greater and greater reluctance. Fear was still a major factor; facing the ocean with compromised equipment was a bogey-man that wouldn't go away, but the prospect of sailing away from our island life had become a bigger concern.

Where else would we find a place so beautiful it could stop you in your tracks just because the light changed, even though you saw it every day; where else would the sense of tranquillity be so tangible you could wear it like a shirt, or the breathing of the trade winds overwhelm your mind with the perfume of flowers, or friendly dolphins load your emotions with gentleness. Where else would we be able to contemplate days without pressure from business commitments and unpaid bills, the threat of violence or restrictions of arcane laws. We didn't want to leave.

However, the sailing season was fast approaching and, to some extent, the hustle and bustle of people still in travelling mode was rubbing off and we started our final preparations. One outstanding task was to clear the remains of our junk from Ile Anglaise. This had been preying on our minds for too long and couldn't be put off any longer. We'd returned from an earlier foray into the 'beyond retrieval' pile, when searching for bottles during the frozen vegetable débâcle, with bags of sodden books and squishy toilet rolls ready to spread them out in the sun to dry before burning. In the first flush of enthusiasm we thought to turn the pulp into a kind of artificial wonder-fuel, but the attempt was a dismal failure.

Needless to say we approached the site with less enthusiasm this time but it wasn't so bad. Hermit crabs and other organisms were doing a great job of turning paper and rags into soil and the more durable remnants were separating out from the heap. Making a determined effort to avoid scorpions we picked out the solid bits, plastic file spines and so on, and bagged them for disposal with our regular garbage.

We'd gone with matches, diesel 'fire starter' and dry kindling intending to burn anything we couldn't move but after picking through it until our consciences were clear we decided a fire would only kill the beneficial bugs, so we settled on disguising it with palm fronds. It's not exactly on a well-trodden path so it was unlikely anyone would walk there within a decade and by then it should be smothered in greenery.

As a reward for the effort we treated ourselves to a day outside the reef. Ian had been extolling the virtues of a special place just north of the gap between Ile Anglaise and Ile Diable and persuaded us to join them snorkelling over it. Putting aside visions of sharks we'd seen caught out there we slipped through the gap on a rising tide and motored the dinghies out to the spot.

This was the only time we swam over the drop-off. We were always too nervous to venture out there when on our own as a single outboard and a pair of paddles are not sufficient insurance against a change of weather, especially if the motor is a doubtful starter. But we made up for it that day by drifting at least half a mile along the shelf.

The coral wasn't particularly attractive, certainly not like some of the stunning outcrops inside the lagoon, though it appeared to blossom into splendid arrays on the steep wall. Visibility was excellent and we could see sixty feet and more down but that only allowed us a glimpse of this alluring world. We contented ourselves with the shelf and spotted several fish that were new to us, clown trigger fish and an angular file fish among them. Ian gave us a surge of adrenalin by swimming down and tweaking the tail of a sleeping shark, only telling us it was a nurse shark later.

Then it was back to voyage preparations. Tina added biscuit making to her bakery routine, biscuits being the easiest thing to eat until you get your sea-legs, and stowed them away in plastic containers and tins. There was a brief flush of bilimbis on the trees as well so she picked a few jars to add flavour to the corned beef.

Two things happened while we were getting ready that made us think even the islands were telling us it was time to move on. First the drinking water tank failed, then the shed fell down. The drinking water tank could yet prove a disaster for future visitors. Although there are several wells on Boddam and the island seems to have a large fresh-water lens the water is not very palatable. The authorities have erected large notices by the main well warning that the water is contaminated and needs to be boiled before use.

Because there was usually enough rainwater in the tank to satisfy the potable water demand the well was only used for washing and was quite possibly polluted with soap. Bearing this in mind a group of us opened the next well in line, midway between the 'watch your head' and the French camp, and cleaned it out.

This was a laborious business entailing trimming away roots and stems that had grown in the shaft, stirring the mud and silt off the bottom, then hauling endless buckets to encourage a flow of clean water. Hours of pulling had no noticeable effect on the colour of the water so we left the bucket set up such that anyone passing (it was right beside the path) could spend a few minutes hauling in the hope that time would solve the problem.

It worked reasonably well but we couldn't get rid of a sulphurous smell and taste. Several filters were tried, some using sand and broken coral like one that had worked on Takamaka once before and one rather special one using commercial elements of porous limestone, but they weren't the answer.

A lot of creative engineering was lavished on the tank trying to repair the leak but the steel had rusted right through where the tap fitted and there wasn't enough metal left to hold it all together. An interim solution was to treat the shower tank, which wasn't covered, with plenty of bleach and use that for drinking while still using the well for washing. I don't really remember if the sulphur smell that stuck to your clothes when you washed them was always there or if we were particularly susceptible to it then, but pulling a clean shirt over your head made you shudder at the thought of a cup of tea made from the washing well.

The shed was much more dramatic. It was a black and rainy evening and we had left the die-hards sheltering at the French camp and gone home to bed. I didn't notice the time but not long after the rain stopped there was a thunderous roar that we couldn't place. We couldn't see a thing beyond a black skyline against an equally black sky, until a flicker of torches defined the French camp. Then our sense of direction told us the sound must have come from the vicinity of the shed and Tina commented it had probably fallen down. I disagreed but couldn't offer an intelligent alternative.

The torch lights dipped and bobbed along the path, mostly hidden by the trees, until we watched them congregate under the tall palms at the well and loud exclamations carried across the lagoon confirming Tina's supposition. Next morning we saw it for ourselves.

Fortunately the front portion, where the roof forms the rain water collector, was still standing and looked to be in fair condition. The back part, where until recently our self-steering gear, gas bottles and so forth had been stored, looked like the aftermath of a war. Huge timbers, some a foot square and ten times that long, were tangled together like pick-up sticks in a child's game and tie-bars, roofing sheets and purlins knotted them together.

Part of the old hospital roof had come down in strong winds before Christmas and the shingled roof of an adjacent building followed it a few days later but those events lacked the style and showmanship of the shed.

It was probably only coincidence but the night the collapsing shed demolished a chunk of the rat habitat the bell rang to open round two of *Vespera* versus 'Rattus'. Rat got in first strike and left his calling card on the galley draining board. This opponent was obviously of a more serious frame of mind than his predecessor.

This sent us scurrying to borrow the trap again and we set it, with a bait of succulent coconut, inside a cupboard so Jess couldn't trip it. When we checked twelve hours later not only had he stolen the bait but he'd chewed open a container of Tina's voyage biscuits and gorged himself. We were not amused.

One of the other boats offered us some rat-glue to back up the trap and we set both. Next night we were woken by the thump of a sprung trap but somehow he'd escaped. To rub it in he'd also managed to reach across the glue trap and pinch the bait without leaving so much as a hair. Later we discovered he'd been in the 'treat' drawer and eaten the last sachet of drinking chocolate and destroyed our Parmesan cheese. That was the last straw and our tempers were up and running.

We set the trap, set the glue and filled the cockpit with pitfall traps of planks balanced over drums of oily water. Jess had to be restrained as visions of our hairy friend tangled up in rat glue were just too dreadful.

This time we struck lucky. He must have jumped to escape a teetering pitfall and knocked against the glue board in his flight. There was a commotion of tumbling planks and scuffling feet and the glue board fell on top of him, allowing me to catch and despatch him quickly. Round two to *Vespera*.

Just as well as we would have been more reluctant than ever to leave if he'd still been aboard and time had caught up with us. Even here escape is illusory and I tackled the very last job, cleaning *Vespera's* bottom and changing the anodes, with a dull ache in my heart.

Usually the anodes, zinc plates mounted near the propeller to reduce electrolytic corrosion, get changed when the boat is out of the water for antifouling. Changing them in the water is a bit risky as it entails slackening bolts that go clean through the hull, but it had to be done as the existing anodes were reduced to powdery shells.

We were very careful and the change went without mishap. It went so well in fact I was able to scrape a fair bit of growth off the hull before taking a break. That this growth was mostly soft algae came as a pleasant surprise as we expected to find plenty of crusty coral and barnacles. The remaining antifouling paint was more than eighteen months old and for the duration of *Vespera*'s stay on the beach had dried, at least partially, with each tide. That is way outside the working conditions stipulated by the manufacturers and we were impressed.

I was more impressed when I came to the new, unpainted, patches. These were an entirely different kettle of fish. Here were the expected coral and barnacles and they seemed harder and more unyielding than ever. The overall velvety sheen of algae was interspersed with razor sharp nasties perfectly placed to slice careless knuckles, while jelly-like lumps in other spots hid hordes of little stinging things. Not so nice.

I was more than a bit alarmed when, while attacking an obdurate growth on the rudder, the scraper lifted a section of epoxy and a slab of plywood came off with it. I knew the area had been crushed in the accident and had studied it at length before the boat refloated, deciding at the time that the damage was superficial and the rudder was good enough.

For a while I wondered if I'd been right. It looked as though water seeping into the wood was making the damage worse and I gingerly probed for more evidence, spending a long time evaluating what I saw. In the end I couldn't make up my mind if it was really any worse or just looked it because I could now see it from directly underneath. I didn't find any more loose bits, at least none that I considered too serious, so we left well alone. There wasn't much we could do about it anyway.

Our plan was to leave Boddam and motor over to the lee of Takamaka and anchor on the sandspit for a few days. The primary reason was to test the engine and steering under circumstances we could control while still having time to do something about it if we found any problems. The other reason was that we both have a soft spot for Takamaka and wanted a last swim over its lovely corals.

The day for the great move was chosen with meticulous care. I wanted plenty of water over the bommies to leave room for error, the tide to be rising for the same reason, the sun to be in the best position and little or no wind to ruffle the surface. In reality there was plenty of room, well, enough room, around the bommies for *Vespera* to motor out without difficulty but I'd been worrying about it so long I found the prospect intimidating.

Any forecast of a day with the right wind was doomed to failure but May sixteenth would fit the bill in every other way. High tide would be five feet above datum and occur at one o'clock. Eleven thirty was the best time for the sun so everything looked great. If it was blowing too hard or if rain killed the visibility it would still be okay the next day. The decision was made.

We finished our preparations with a few days to spare, the jerry cans were topped up with water, every remaining plastic bottle likewise, oil levels checked, cupboards packed and 'de-rattled' and anything not needed on the trip hidden away. We talked for ages trying to decide which of the beautiful things we'd done on Boddam we most wanted to repeat before leaving, and couldn't. In the end we spent the days like all the others just taking things as they came, and it was perfect.

With the tides moving towards springs the reefs were ideal for early morning walks and we took full advantage of them. Even at this stage we found things we hadn't seen before. On our last walk towards Ile Poule we discovered a miniature coral that shone the most vivid lime green, the only live Bullmouth Helmet we ever saw and a pristine Seven-finger Scorpion shell. We tucked them away in less obvious crannies in the hope that more predatory collectors wouldn't find them.

That evening would probably be the last on which we could enjoy a Boddam sunset in private as our friends had invited us to a special farewell evening the day after and I cannot improve on the notes I made at the time to describe our feelings:-

"It was a delightful afternoon with a steady tradewind breeze and the scuddy clouds that come with it emphasized the clean blue of the sky. The way things are planned, tomorrow will be our last evening on Boddam as we aim to move *Vespera* to the lee of Takamaka the day after.

Earlier today *Dawn Treader* delivered a care parcel from

Eric and Robin in Cochin, India. The parcel included a bottle of rum and we escaped the crush of people at the volley-ball court to enjoy a literal sundowner on the western side of the island.

The walk across the island probably took some emotional pressure from the moment as the lovely island path was suffering under the annual population explosion. Thoughtless hands with sharp machetes had 'cleared' the palms that filter the harsh sun, littering the path with browning fronds. Our mood changed from nostalgic sadness to one of anger and we brooded on how we would fit back in society where this sort of callousness was the norm.

But the mood changed again as we emerged from the trees onto the clean white sand of the bay. For months this beach had taken the full brunt of the monsoon with sturdy waves crashing through the coral shelf to swirl and dissipate where the rocks meet the sand. Now it lies in the island's lee and gentle wavelets bumble and swish round the same rocks, caressing rather than pounding them.

The sun had perhaps another ten degrees to fall before meeting the horizon and was playing hide and seek among the clouds, but he wasn't doing very well. His hiding places were outlined in shining silver and brilliant rays spread right overhead arrowing his position exactly. The sea was the deep blue of open ocean water and the surface rippled and swayed, spreading the cloud reflections as far as the eye could see.

We sat on a springy palm log, toppled by God to give us comfortable seats while watching him play, and at first kept our heads tilted away from the intensity of the light. The curve of the bay lent shape to the endlessly changing colours of the bushes and wind, passing high overhead, gently rustled the tall palms to give the scene movement.

As the sun dipped from one hiding place to another the sea changed from blue to green and a school of dolphins moved in close. They also felt the temper of the evening and curved lazily together in the quietness, their movements choreographed for serenity. Then as the sun approached the horizon it burned across the sea, melting it to liquid bronze, and the dolphins retired to play unseen.

So much for anything reducing the emotional load. The

thought of leaving such beauty to rejoin the chaos of crime and thoughtlessness, murderous politics and decay at 'home' was too much to bear and the tears wouldn't stay behind my eyes. Thank heavens the darkness hid the desecration of the path on the way back."

A good night's sleep though established beauty as the predominant memory and quiet reflection put the untidy path in proper perspective. In a few months' time the trimmed fronds would have fallen anyway and the soil wasn't fussy where the leaves decayed, as long as they did. Environmental conservation is, after all, only for mankind's benefit. Mother Nature will adapt and win however much we denigrate her efforts, it's just that we might not like the way she does it.

We were not too happy with Mother Nature when we took the sails and ropes out of storage for the trans-atoll trip. The sails were fine but, unknown to us, the rat had made a nest among the ropes. Our first impression was of catastrophe. The working sheets were bundled together with the anchor warps, mooring lines, tow rope and spare coils, and when we lifted the cover all we could see was shredded fibre.

Fortunately when we shook the shreds off the only real victim we found was the mainsheet. Equally fortunate was that a sufficient length of spare rope of the right diameter had survived unscathed from the salvage operation to replace it, but it cost us half a day coiling and uncoiling string and splicing a new mainsheet.

The farewell evening was lovely. Our friends knew we didn't want a big party and a small group treated us to the best the island could provide. They barbecued a magnificent coral trout and followed it with a breadfruit cake. There was even a jam tart decorated with a mosaic of *Vespera* under sail.

Then, all of a sudden, it was time. Ian arrived early in the morning to help untangle the mooring chains. All through the monsoon transition *Vespera* had swung round like a weathercock, knotting the two chains together like a modern art sculpture. The intention was to retrieve our anchor chain, which was primarily down as a safety measure, and shackle on the anchor while still moored to the other. Leaving would then be a simple matter of dropping the mooring, suitably buoyed for the next visitor, and motoring away.

In principle it was easy, just undo the shackle and pull the loose chain through. In practice it wasn't like that at all as the very rusty chain, the one we'd tied to until it broke, was still there and compounded the tangle into a proper Gordian knot. Eventually we had to resort to bolt-cutters to extricate the anchor chain but from there it was easy.

A few minutes after eleven Glynn came aboard. He was going to accompany us to help with bommie spotting and be on hand if anything went wrong. The engine started on the first try and the conditions were ideal. There was a slight lop on the surface but not enough to hide the bommies, the water was clear and the sky just hazy enough to prevent glare.

Exactly on time we dropped the mooring and moved away. As the gears engaged the propeller shaft groaned loudly but we were now committed to keeping going until clear of the immediate bommies. I had spent a lot of time working the steering from lock to lock while pumping grease into the bearings but it was still stiff, stiffer than I expected.

Despite the shaft noise *Vespera* gained way until the rudder bit and we safely skirted the first danger, only a couple of boat lengths away, to find ourselves exactly on track to miss the next. On board we were too involved with the business in hand to acknowledge anyone but were intensely aware of the eyes on us and the almost tangible good wishes urging us on.

The next bommie slid by a few feet to port and our course changed slightly to take us through the next gap. The shaft noise was audibly less now and I put it down to coral in the outer bearing breaking up and washing out. Now that gap was behind us and a few more yards would see us through the last narrow passage separating us from manoeuvring room.

Vespera didn't hesitate, she just crept along at a stately two knots or so. The coral outcrop on the eastern side of the passage was small enough to be hard to spot and some days earlier we'd anchored a fishing float on it as a marker. We edged up to the float, as close as we dare, to make sure there was plenty of room on the port side, and it was done.

There was room now for *Vespera* to drift to a stop without hitting anything if the engine failed and sufficient space to reverse our course using the self steering rudder if necessary. I was very conscious of my pulse slowing from its staccato tattoo and the tingle of adrenalin draining away.

Gradually the shaft noise quieted and an irritating shudder that accompanied it died away at the same rate. By the time we'd covered a mile there was no trace of either. The steering was also getting easier with use. We checked the operation of all the electrical things that were wired up and were reasonably happy. The wind instruments and log were fine, as was the GPS, but the depth sounder seemed to work sometimes and not others, churning out random numbers like 'Ernie'. However, the most important gadget after the starter motor was the alternator and a voltage check suggested it was working.

The only thing left to discover was whether the gear box would go astern properly. We approached the sandspit with the anchor ready to go but the depth sounder chose the moment the bottom came up quickly and changed to sand to go haywire. For once the crystal clear water worked against us; over the featureless sand there was no way to judge whether it was ten feet or thirty feet deep.

All we could do was guess and *Vespera* eased to a stop pretty much where we chose and the anchor went down with a rush. I slipped the controls to 'astern' and the gearbox kicked in as cleanly as ever, pulling the chain straight until she held. *Vespera*'s phoenix voyage was over and a tot of twelve-year-old Scotch, saved specially for the occasion, rounded off the day.

Actually it would be more truthful to say it rounded off the morning because a later incident rounded the day off more completely. We only reckoned to stay a few days so, like on an annual holiday from suburbia, time was of the essence. As soon as we'd eaten lunch we took a swim over a favourite spot then went ashore for a fresh water shower at Takamaka's well.

What a delightful surprise. The well is located at the back of a large shady glade hidden from the beach by a line of scaevola bushes so it wasn't until we stepped right in that we saw the transformation. At our last visit the glade had been thickly covered with palm fronds, old coconuts and deadwood from the takamaka trees, and access to the well was along a rustic path through it all. Now the whole area had been cleared, to the extent that the sandy ground had been swept, the well shaft cleaned and properly covered and the incinerator hearth repaired and extended to include a barbecue hearth. So it was a rush of goodwill towards our fellows that rounded off the day.

From the boat we were excited to see a pair of black and white wing tips flicking the surface of the water and coming directly towards us. At first we thought it was a friendly eagle ray but as it came closer we realized it was much too big. It changed direction before coming close enough to see clearly and swam lazily along the edge of the sandspit. Whatever it was we hoped this was its regular territory and we would get a better look before we left.

We spent most of the next two days exploring previously unvisited parts of Fouquet and Takamaka or wandering on the reef as the tides allowed, but another sighting of the big wings, this time two pairs, sent us dashing to the dinghy. We'd been told that a group of manta rays visited the locality regularly and were now fairly sure that this must be them. Unfortunately by the time we got to the spot the big creatures had moved off and we still didn't see them.

Over sundowners in the well glade we learnt that several yachties had swum with these mantas and they could usually be found swimming in the stream of rich water flowing into the lagoon. It was very exciting then to see no less than four rays barely fifty yards from *Vespera* while we were taking morning tea the next day.

Our masks and fins were readily to hand and we abandoned the tea to scramble into the water. From the viewpoint of a swimmer they didn't seem nearly as close and for a while we thought we'd missed them. Every few yards we stopped and turned to look around and when we didn't see them stuck our heads out as far as possible and searched the surface for wings. Disappointment was gaining ground but as we crossed the sandspit edge we saw one of the huge beasts flying towards us, looking for all the world like a science fiction space ship.

We simply stopped and hung side by side in the water as the inquisitive creature swam right up to look us over. From head-on the two cephalic fins, which were curled downwards and inwards, looked like a huge mouth and the first close fly-past was quite nerve-racking. As it swerved away it nonchalantly raised a wingtip just enough to pass overhead. I took another all-round look before surfacing and jumped to find another ray hovering an arm's length behind me.

Once the initial nervousness wore off the ensuing half-hour has to rate as the highlight of all our snorkelling. All four mantas swept repeatedly up to us for a good look then drifted away in creative aquabatic manoeuvres; loops, wing-overs, inside-out loops, barrel rolls, the whole gamut. They came close enough, and slowly enough, for us to reach out and stroke their wings.

We were fascinated to see schools of tiny sergeant major fish swimming in and around the funnel of cephalic fins, obviously taking advantage of the food concentration there. We couldn't help wondering if any ever got swallowed, and if they did would they be able to swim out again through the gill vents. Surely they wouldn't swim there if they were natural prey.

I think they would have played for hours but a change in water colour and clarity showed the stream was veering and of course they had to go with their food. We stayed with them until they reached water too deep for us to follow then reluctantly watched as they glided into the shadows. What a finale to our stay in paradise.

This high note took the sting out of cleaning the dinghy. This job is the precursor of stowing it on board and tantamount to pulling up the drawbridge and cutting off communications with the world until the next journey's done. It's as much part of leaving as pulling up the anchor.

We chose to do it in two stages, doing the cleaning in the afternoon and stowing the following morning as this would allow a final sundowner ashore and a last minute freshwater shower before leaving. It was a good job we did as during the evening we received a message that a boat was arriving tomorrow, our planned departure day, with a letter for us from Kenya.

They only had to come from the next atoll so there was a possibility they would be here in time for us to leave, but we couldn't fold the dinghy up until they arrived. As it happened the weather was quite difficult and they only entered the pass in the late afternoon, then made their way directly to Boddam while they could see. Oh well, an opportunity for another sundowner.

Early morning saw us in our squeaky clean dinghy, much faster without its skirt of slimy growth, on our way back to Boddam. We were determined not to go ashore or do the visiting rounds, that emotional hurdle had been crossed already and we had no wish to repeat it, but letters are powerful magnets and, coming from Kenya, this had to be news of last year's helpers. I hope we weren't too rude to the folks on *Imagine*, who'd taken the trouble to deliver this letter, but we certainly didn't stay long as by breakfast time we were already on our way back. It would be a bit of a push but there was still time to grab the treasured freshwater shower, stow the dinghy and leave before the sun was too far over.

There was even time to sneak another 'final' swim so we anchored at another favourite spot and surrendered to the beauty until the skin on our fingers wrinkled up. Then it was back to *Vespera* to drop off the letter, grab fresh towels and make for the well. Half way there the outboard quit!

I suppose it was a good thing it hadn't happened in the middle of the lagoon but even so my morale failed at the same moment. Why should I spend my last hours in paradise working on a recalcitrant engine. There was no real alternative though; it wasn't a good idea to leave with it unserviceable as we may need the dinghy for manoeuvring if anything happened to *Vespera*'s engine before the next landfall.

We paddled back to the boat and while Tina put the kettle on I removed the carburettor. A familiar soup of fuel, water and rust dribbled from the bowl when I turned it upside down so a full strip-down was called for, followed by removal and draining of the fuel tank and hoses.

It didn't delay us long, I don't think it took longer than our earlier swim, but by the time we'd had our showers and lashed down the dinghy the sun was between us and the pass. Visibility was finished for the day and we decided to wait for morning.

The twenty-second of May. One year, three months and two weeks since we anchored on the same sandspit in our second attempt to find Shangri-la. Last night we sat in the cockpit to watch the sun dip behind Anglaise and as it turned the sky red, then gold, it seemed to spotlight the very place where the accident happened and made the attempt so real.

Conversation had been minimal as both of us sifted through memories of the year, glossing over the bad ones, rethinking the merely negative and dwelling on the good. As the incidents popped into mind each could communicate our feelings to the other without words. A distant look in a particular direction or a quiet smile at a reflex action were all that was needed to flood our minds with each other's images. The shipwreck was undeniable, the memories were too fresh and the ramifications still loomed, but had we found our Shangri-la? – Undoubtedly yes.

The morning came gently when the diamonds faded from a clear sky and a five-knot southeasterly greeted the sun. We listened to wild chickens on Takamaka as we hanked on the headsail and tied on the sheets, uncovered the main and reeved the gybe preventers. At last all was ready and we just had to wait for the sun to rise high enough to show the corals.

We were so emotionally charged that our usual response to waiting, of doing so with a relaxing cup of tea, didn't seem appropriate. Both of us fidgeted with non-essentials, tidying and re-tidying the charts on the chart table and checking the rags and pillows stuffed in the cupboards to stop things rattling.

We took our last looks around. Salomon was settling back to its general solitude as many boats had already left. A few more weeks would see it isolated again. But even thoughts like these were not coherent this morning. Too much sadness, too much fear and not enough confidence militated against them.

Ten thirty. The engine had started perfectly a quarter of an hour ago and was warm and ready to go. We hauled up the anchor and snugged it down for the trip as *Vespera* drifted away from the spit. Then Tina took up her station on the pulpit to watch for bommies and I put the controls 'ahead'.

Both of us were grateful for the space between us and that each had to concentrate on what we were doing. Tears were stinging and a moment's eye contact would have broken our resolves. Tina had the most exacting job, interpreting the changing colours in the water through the mist inside her eyelids, while I only had to watch for her signals. But that was enough.

Fortunately Tina controlled the tears long enough to guide us round the only serious bommie en route and shortly after eleven we raised the sails outside the pass in a beautiful ten-knot breeze. Our emotional equilibrium returned as the engine noise died and our world reduced to a clear blue sky, a calm blue sea and the quietness.

BOOK FIVE

VESPERA'S ROUTE PLAN was the result of many hours studying the pilot charts and sailing directions. We could expect southeasterly winds to predominate until we closed Madagascar, where they might become more southerly, and the equatorial current should help all the way except for a north-going burst around Cap d'Ambre.

Consequently we were going to make our way south at the beginning of the trip then go west along a latitude slightly south of Cap d'Ambre, Madagascar's northernmost point. There we would duck round into the lee as fast as possible to reduce our exposure to the hard conditions we believed to prevail off the point. The only thing we had to watch for before entering the Mozambique channel was the Saya de Malha bank, about seven hundred miles from Salomon. We intended to make all our southing before getting there and sail over the huge underwater saddle that separates it from the Nazareth bank two hundred miles to the south.

The conditions as we left the pass were ideal. We had the predicted southeasterly with just enough strength to get us going without interfering with a nice gentle start. Soon we saw the islands fringing the eastern side of Peros Banhos and all seemed set for us to pass safely to windward of the reef. But another hour saw the wind round in the south forcing us to tack back towards Salomon. Not very inspiring but at least it was still gentle.

At sundowner time we were barely a mile from Boddam. We could see a couple of dinghies trawling along the reef in search of supper and the breeze, fading with the sun, was ideal to keep mosquitoes away without disturbing a barbecue fire. The beach, so tantalizingly close, had never been so appealing.

As darkness came the wind died completely and erratic currents pushed us northwards. Without the wind the slight swell played havoc with the sails until eventually I took them down, leaving just enough of the main set to slow the rolling and we drifted through the night. Frustrating on one hand but welcome on the other as both of us got some good sleep on our 'off' watches, most unusual for a first night at sea.

Dawn brought the first southwesterly. The sails went up immediately and we set off to round Peros Banhos but this time to the north. Optimistic hopes of a good start to the south were now history and the best we could do was continue a bit north of west until it changed again.

The breeze was stronger than yesterday's and we made enough speed to start the propeller turning. This was normal and in fact encouraging as it meant the shaft and bearings were now quite clean. Encouraging or not though the noise of an endlessly spinning propeller can drive you to distraction so we always lock it by putting the gearbox 'astern'.

This time it didn't work. No matter what speed the shaft turned at or how crisply we selected the gear the clutches wouldn't take. More concerned at the risk of wearing the clutch plates away with the continuous slipping than with the irritating noise, I wanted to stop it. I didn't think the box had been damaged by the sinking as it worked perfectly under power and I hoped it was simply a problem with the linkages, which were very stiff.

I raised the floor and disconnected the cable from the gearbox lever, and when I shifted the lever by hand the clutches locked up beautifully. If only everything was so easy to solve. But the cable was more problematic. It was stiff from corrosion and salt deposits and all I could do was dribble oil in at both ends, which didn't have much effect, and eventually had to accept that while good enough when the engine was running, the stiffness wouldn't allow us to engage gears normally when it was stopped. Not an insurmountable difficulty.

Having the floor up was a good excuse to inspect the patches. There was an inch or two of water in the bilge but nothing more than I would expect from a dripping stern gland, and that turned out to be the source. All the new cement was dry and clean. So far so good.

Dolphins greeted me as I went topside to wash the oil off my hands and the first red-footed booby adjusted its flight path to land on the solar panels. I was just in time to shout and put him off his stroke before he crashed right into them, then had to do it several more times before he flew away.

Usually it's the wind instrument sensor on top of the mast that attracts big birds. Not only does it look like a reasonable perch but it's sufficiently fragile for clumsy feet to destroy, so it's a natural choice. For this voyage though we weren't using the wind instruments, conserving battery power was too important, so the birds didn't find them so compelling. The solar panels had taken over top spot on the 'where to do most damage' list and the boobies seemed to know.

During the morning the wind swung slowly back to the south and we turned with it to follow a course between Ile Pierre and the Benares shoal, four miles off shore. All was going nicely and if the breeze held and continued to swing we would soon be back on track. At mid-day Tina was at the wheel and called for me to verify our position. She could see what looked like shallow water off the starboard bow.

I hurriedly plotted our position, thanks to GPS, and rushed outside to check that the information agreed with reality; it did. I was then well into my stride explaining that we were three miles from Pierre, which we could see, and on our present course wouldn't get much closer to the shoal when she exclaimed 'What's that then?'

Still well to starboard and some way in front was a bright green patch looking exactly like one of the bommies inside the lagoon. But how could that be? – we were in hundreds of feet of water. Further away the water gave the impression of a change in colour, but nothing specific. I turned on the depth sounder, which I had discovered to work perfectly as long as the engine wasn't running, and it confirmed we were in deep water, or at least in water deeper than the instrument could measure.

We headed up a little to give the 'bommie' a bit more clearance, but in doing so slowed somewhat, and a finger of current pushed us towards it. Suddenly the sounder stopped its 'No Bottom' flashing and showed a string of readings between thirty and fifty feet. It had to be the shoal.

Navigating around it was no longer possible as we had no idea of its size or boundaries. Although it's not unusual to find chart coordinates out by a mile the local details are usually very accurate and I'd taken great trouble to align the GPS with the chart in Salomon, and what was here didn't agree with it. We could only hope that the minimum depth shown was more accurate than the position.

The bommie, and I'm sure that's what it was, slid by with room to spare but now all we could see was light green water, indicating shallow water over sand, spotted all around with black blobs of rock or coral. Steering in any particular direction in preference to another was merely keeping the dice rolling so we just glided over it and listened to the thump of each other's hearts. At one point the sounder showed a mere twenty feet before settling back into its thirty- to fifty-foot range.

Our eyes flickered round the horizon searching for a dark line that might mean deeper water. We were living the nightmare that all everyone had done for us, all the effort to get *Vespera* mobile again and all the plotting and scheming to eke out supplies, were at risk again only hours after leaving.

We didn't dare run the engine even though we might need it in a hurry; if we did we wouldn't know the depth. Eventually, after a half-hour that lasted all day, Tina spotted a distinct dark streak in the water and we steered towards it. The depth sounder took one more heart-stopping excursion to twenty feet before tumbling quickly and starting its regular flashing. No bottom. Mischance had taken us over a shoal where there didn't ought to be a shoal and providence had taken us over it without harm. Quiet prayers were in order.

Neither of us had been particularly hungry yet, a condition we live through at the start of every voyage, and this incident did nothing to improve our appetites. The idea of lunch was abandoned.

In the afternoon the wind increased a little, though the swing in direction had stopped before improving things much, and we were able to set the self-steering gear. This was Fred's first real test since being repaired and he worked perfectly. As we got away from the influence of the islands the wind seemed more stable and the currents less variable so we left him steering as long as we could. Our only concession was to take a reef in the mainsail that night as the wind continued to increase.

While it was pleasant to be relieved of the tedium of steering, the waves that came with the steadier wind were not much fun. Jess was the first victim to seasickness and tucked herself away in a corner of furry misery. Even the excited clicking of dolphins playing under the bow didn't stir her from her torpor.

Vespera's movement was indeed quite vigorous and both hull and rig could be heard working. I really couldn't say if the creaks and groans were more than we would have expected if the accident hadn't happened but we were acutely aware of any new noises. We checked the patches again though and the fact that they were still dry gave us more confidence.

The unplanned trip round the wrong side of Peros Banhos put us several miles north of where we wanted to be and the unexpected winds had made things worse. However, with Fred set to steer as close to the wind as he could the compass showed a gradual change for the better as a bit of east crept in and the gap closed slowly.

But the bit of east in the wind also brought more strength and this was where I missed the wind instruments. I'd always based my sail adjustments on what they showed rather than guess what to do from my senses, so without them I was regularly slow off the mark. Tina had the advantage over me here having learned her sailing without instruments, but she was temporarily out of action with seasickness.

I suppose I wasn't paying the proper attention when I got caught out. I was totally absorbed with a sleeping whale we were bearing down on when I heard a brief staccato zipp… I couldn't see any reason for it and nothing seemed to have changed when I looked, so I returned to my immediate concern.

I called Tina to come up as, seasick or not, she would have wanted to see the whale and it presented something of a hazard anyway. If it woke with a fright or, worse, if we hit it there was no way of knowing what might happen. But its regular blowing, every eight seconds, showed clearly where it was and waves breaking over its back gave us a good idea of its size.

We had a great opportunity to observe him closely as he drifted past, motionless and apparently unaware of our presence. Then, while both of us were staring over the stern at our disappearing companion, there was that zipp… again. On turning we found we had a loose-footed mainsail, all the slides attaching the sail to the boom having pulled out. I had ignored the increasing wind until long after I would normally have taken in a reef.

Too late now. The sail was seriously weakened and it was all my own fault. Fortunately the sail had an unused set of reefing points that would only reduce the area by about fifteen percent so we transferred the outhaul to that position. With a bit of belated wisdom we also took in the next reef, which was more appropriate to the wind now gusting over twenty-five knots. When we finished the sea was too rough to allow our customary deck shower and Tina retreated to her seasick nest.

It was difficult to see why the sea should be so confused. The wind was certainly stronger but the waves didn't really correspond. There was one series of swells coming from ahead and the trade wind set was building up on our port quarter, but the swells alone didn't explain the jumbled, and large, waves.

Before the day was out *Vespera* was taking some hard knocks as she slid down the waves of one train to crash into those of another. Every time a wave hit the side it sounded like an open-handed slap from a giant and we feared for the patches. Most of the bumps, luckily, were landing on the port side, which had suffered the least damage, but we felt every slap as if it had been delivered personally.

One consequence of these big slaps was that each one knocked *Vespera* off course, disturbing the balance between sea, sails and steering gear and we staggered on in a most erratic fashion. It seemed that as soon as we picked up enough speed for everything to work nicely another wave would swat us and stop us dead. In my vanity I thought, having the advantage of anticipation, I could make a better job of steering than Fred, but the moment I took over it was worse. Anticipation meant reasoning with the seas and I wallowed in a morass of indecision while we weaved around like a drunk.

By the time it got through to me that Fred could in fact do it better it was difficult to balance things up again. Then, almost as soon as everything settled down, the wind piped up obliging me to change to a smaller headsail and the performance started over.

During the night Tina's seasickness worsened. I'm sure it was a combination of motion sickness, fear and tiredness and neither of us were sleeping well. We had experienced far worse conditions before, but a boat in which you are entirely confident makes a deal of difference to the way you view things.

Nevertheless next day, with grim determination, she

produced a fine loaf of bread in the pressure cooker and a position plot showing good progress cheered her up a lot. We were still too far north but the wind was steady in the south southeast and we were making up ground.

Not such good news was that the bilge was quite full and the rolling had sloshed water everywhere and made all the surfaces wet, including the new cement, and it was impossible to see where it was coming from. We weren't too concerned as *Vespera* always got her feet wet if she dipped her bow in a wave. There was a long-standing leak from the chain locker that we'd never been able to find, so we contented ourselves with pumping out as much as we could.

Sunday came and the wind relented a bit, though in doing so went back to the south. We discussed shaking out the reef but only decided to do so when the instruments, turned on for a few minutes at a time, showed a steady twenty knots. I even considered putting the bigger headsail on but with the big seas, which were getting steeper despite the falling wind, and Tina still out of commission, thought better of it.

By morning we were taking a lot more water and I found myself pumping the bilge every hour to keep up. Twice during the day I took up the floors and mopped out the forward areas by hand. Cement and general guck from the repairs had blocked the limber holes so parts of the boat wouldn't drain into the bilge. But there was much more water than usually came in from the chain locker and I did my best to dry everything, especially the patches, to find where it was coming from but it was an impossible task. However there was no direct evidence of a failure so we soldiered on.

It's always been our policy to run the engine every few days while at sea, if nothing else just to make sure that it will, but it's a good idea to churn the oil around anyway. I found myself on the horns of a dilemma this trip as one side of me wanted to run it every day while the other realized that every time we started it unnecessarily we put the bodged parts, like the starter motor, at risk.

I compromised on every several days and, the first several days being up, I turned the key that afternoon and it started beautifully. Disappointingly though the alternator played up and at irregular intervals needed re-energizing to start it charging again. At that moment it wasn't important as the solar panels were keeping the batteries fairly healthy but it didn't bode well for cloudy days.

Tina was having a hard time of it doing her deck watch while I was below. She never once missed out on doing her watches but relentless nausea made doing anything a penance, so she wedged herself in a cockpit corner and kept a regular shipwatch for most of the afternoon. Tiredness was another burden and several times she blinked herself awake after nodding off for brief periods.

It was my turn to struggle when the first night watch started. I had barely taken my place, wedged in Tina's corner, when sleep closed over me like a shroud. I woke with a start a few minutes later with the full knowledge that I wasn't going to make a three-hour stint without falling asleep again. We tried changing at one hour intervals but it didn't help as neither of us could stay awake. For the first, and only, time in our cruising we decided not to keep a watch. On the understanding that whenever either of us woke, even if only momentarily, they would have a good look around we both went to sleep.

In the morning the world looked very different. The wind was down to a quiet steady breeze, the sea had eased dramatically and the sun shone from a sky dotted with trade wind clouds. With renewed vitality we hoisted the maximum sail and felt better for our first deck shower in days.

With the easier sea *Vespera* was taking in very little water and we were able to dry things well enough to learn that the decks were the source of the problem. Like the leaking chain locker, deck problems were not new but they'd never let in water before. We'd hummed and hahhed about fixing the existing bad patches while in Salomon when the furnishings were out and we had access, but were too anxious to get ready to leave in August. Of course once it was all covered up again there was little enthusiasm to undo all the work to repair something that had, to date, been benign.

It was obvious now that the impact of the accident had extended the damage in ways we hadn't seen. The deck had failed in several new places and whenever the gunwales went under those failures allowed water in. There was no way to judge whether the structure was seriously impaired, but whatever the case there was nothing we could do about it.

Tina's seasickness was causing more concern as it hadn't gone away with the improvement in the weather. If anything it was getting worse and other symptoms were developing. We consulted the medical books and decided to start treating her stomach ulcer, another old 'friend' that had taken strain in the accident.

In all, though, we were doing well and the pleasant interlude that allowed me to do my watches with a good book and without having to brace myself in a corner was a real tonic. We were almost on track and Fred was able to steer close enough to the wind to keep the gap closing. We were elated that night to see a 'moonbow', exactly like a rainbow but with greys, white and silver in place of the familiar colours. We wouldn't have been so elated had we known the weather it presaged.

The first hints of it were disguised by a succession of squalls that swept over us. Great black rainclouds raged across the sky and turbulent winds under them kept us guessing. In the turmoil the background wind rose steadily and refused steadfastly to swing back towards the east. We marked the end of our first week at sea by reefing down under thirty knots and more. Not at all the easy trip we'd hoped for.

By nightfall I'd taken off even our smallest headsail. Some of the bigger gusts were very strong and I was still unsure of the rig. We couldn't hold such a good course with just the mainsail but I thought that a reasonable trade for the reduced loads. Now we were pleased that the wind direction hadn't changed as the waves, while big, at least all came the same way.

Tina was suffering down below. Her sickness was a round-the-clock personal disaster and the increased movement only added to it. *Vespera* was burying her head under every wave and the side decks were continually awash, so plenty of water was coming in and the depressing surroundings of raised floors, full and sloppy bilges and a wet bed did little to help.

One wave hit us so hard that the improvised locker behind the saloon burst open, strewing bottles and tins all over the galley. Both of us got a serious fright as we thought a patch had given way. The last patch to be done, the one that we floated on only hours after finishing, was under that locker. But it was alright, only a latch had broken.

Twelve hours later we had to face the decision of the bank. The Saya de Malha bank is probably not dangerous at all but with this sort of sea running the shallow water was bound to be uncomfortable and we didn't want to sail over it. The question was whether to keep butting into the waves and pass to the south of it, as planned, or take the easier way, with the waves behind, and go north. If we went north we would lose all the southing already paid for then have to pay for it all again, possibly in worse conditions, so we opted to carry on.

One ramification was that we had to carry more sail. The wind hadn't abated and our inability to hold course with just the main was pushing us northwards, so we needed to balance the boat with some headsail. I suppose it was the only real way to find out if the rig was strong enough, so up went a small jib. Disappointingly, even with the better balance Fred couldn't steer tight enough to the required course so we had to steer ourselves. At least with only one train of waves to contend with this time we could do it better.

But it was a miserable business, hand steering. I've never been terribly impressed with the truthfulness of people who claim to enjoy hard sailing, and every time I have to do it I reinforce my impression. The wind instruments, when I flicked them on, showed not much over thirty so this wasn't hard in the traditional sense but it was thoroughly unpleasant. Every now and then a bigger than average wave would whoosh over the coach roof to land in the cockpit and swirl around your feet. One nasty brute broke right over my head and took part of the cockpit coaming with it as it receded.

Probably because we were carrying more sail than I felt comfortable with *Vespera* broke her daily distance record the next day. It was the third successive day with wind over thirty knots and I suppose we were getting used to it, so it came as a surprise when I plotted the day's run at one hundred and thirty-one miles. Not exactly earth shattering but better than our previous best by a substantial margin, and very good for morale.

This little boost came at just the right moment. Jess had rejoined Tina in the sick-bay and was adding her own aura to the gloom. Miasma would describe it better as one of her trips to the litter box was disturbed by a heavy roll and she peed on my seaberth, then repeated the performance on my oilies. I wasn't too pleased with this, but the good day's run stopped me getting really angry.

It also meant we didn't have far to go to clear the bank. As soon as we had we could change course to due west and the motion should be easier. We had also done well with the direction and Fred was able to steer close enough now so things were looking up.

Then, as well-disguised as the onset, the weather started to break. By the time we were over the saddle there were lengthy spells between gusts when the wind dropped to twenty and it seemed to be swinging a little. However, each time we discussed increasing sail a big gust would blow the idea away and we delayed it until we turned west.

Sixty-one degrees east longitude and at last the bow was aimed at Cap d'Ambre. No longer was *Vespera* scooping water over herself as each wave passed and what a relief not to listen to the endless slamming. We had plenty of sail up now which helped counteract the rolling, the waves from the south were now right on the beam, and in spite of the reduced wind we were going even faster. We were however still getting water on deck and the bilge needed pumping every half-hour, slightly better than the previous couple of days but still demanding.

The changed motion was a relief for Tina who didn't feel nearly so nauseous, but she was very weak. She'd also come out in a rash of red spots that we didn't understand. Another delve into the medical books suggested it was an allergic response and, that being so, we looked for a possible source.

Only two things had changed recently: she was wearing different oilies and was using a previously untried medicine for her ulcer. Here was a problem. She had to wear the oilies to go on watch, which she had to do or I would get no sleep, and the ulcer medicine was the only sort we had. She tackled the oilies first by wearing another layer of clothing underneath them, which was going to be uncomfortably warm but, if it worked, better than itchy spots.

But we were not of a mind to let such things spoil our respite. Even the wind slowing enough to let the sails slat in the rolls was only mildly annoying, and it didn't last long anyway. By late afternoon it was back to twenty-ish and from the southeast; average conditions for the time of year.

It was as well that, for the time being, our course wasn't too critical. With the wind behind him and waves from the side Fred wandered about in all directions, often twenty degrees off one way or the other, but anything was better than hand steering. It was also just as well that he could continue to steer later as the GPS suddenly demanded all my attention.

When I opened the log to make a routine entry I noticed our position, according to the magic gadget, hadn't changed in a couple of hours. Obviously nonsense. All the keys appeared to work and it told me it was tracking enough satellites but it wasn't interested in updating the position. I went through the routine of turning it off and shorting the terminals to earth, but to no avail.

Somewhat reluctantly, because it uses a lot more power, I switched on the old Satnav receiver and was relieved when it came to life normally. Four hours later though it was still scanning the skies without a single bleep, or whatever it listens for, being heard. This was not so good.

As a last resort before digging out the sextant I disconnected the GPS from the boat's system, rigged it as a mobile unit and tried it in the cockpit. Within minutes it had located itself and started updating the position every few seconds, as it should. Thank heavens. If nothing else worked Sue had sent enough batteries to get a couple of fixes a day until we reached port.

My next concern was that maybe the boat's batteries were failing, that being the only thing common to both navigators, but when I checked they appeared okay. Again thank heavens because without them we can't start the engine. Just to make sure I recompromised on my compromise on how often to start the engine and ran it for a short time. It was fine.

There was actually one other thing common to both navigators, both antenna leads ran up the same leg of the canopy frame to their respective aerials, and when I checked I found some of the canopy securing screws loose. This couldn't have any direct effect but obviously the waves breaking over the top had given the structure, including the aerials, a bit of a battering. When I'd done the rounds with screwdriver and spanners, tightening everything that would tighten, both units worked perfectly.

That evening we learned the weather Gods had more hands

to play in their game. It was blustery and rainy and as night approached we reefed down under thirty knots again. Happily Tina was feeling better from the intermission and, as conditions worsened to the point that Fred couldn't cope, we were able to take turns steering. It became so demanding that an hour was about as long as we could concentrate sufficiently and we cat-napped in a one-hour-on, one-off regime.

Morning was grey and miserable, and however carefully we eased *Vespera* into the seas she was slamming as hard as ever. I hadn't been at the wheel long when Tina stumbled out, fully kitted up in oilies when she should have been asleep, and told me she'd come to take over while I investigated a new grating noise coming from the mast.

Before stepping in to listen for myself I scrambled round on deck for a careful check of the rigging and, finding nothing amiss, checked the lashings on the dinghy and fuel drums; nothing there either. Down below, though, something sounded dreadful, like a broken cable scraping over the hull or a fractured support working in the rolls.

With so much background noise it was almost impossible to judge where it was coming from but, like Tina, I eventually tracked it down to somewhere near the mast support. A lot of stuff was stowed there as it's quite a good place to wedge things and I had to move most of it to gain access.

Strangely, the moment I lifted a particularly tin from the pile the grating stopped. Then, when I put it down, it started again. Found. The tin had once been packed tight with Roger's lovely crisp rusks, but now we'd taken some out the remainder were free to slide around inside and the violent motion was shaking it like a baby's rattle. Tina was immediately banished from the cockpit to look after her own noises.

She took her admonishment in good grace and responded by making another loaf of bread, obviously feeling better in spite of things, and in spite of the allergy spots getting worse. Also fairly obvious by the time she finished was that the Weather God's game was coming to an end. A spectacular rainbow against a dark, but lightening, sky heralded a general reduction in wind strength and the sea untangled itself enough for Fred to steer.

This gave us an opportunity to tackle another bothersome occurrence. Our carefully collected and conserved Boddam rainwater was growing 'things' in it. In all probability they'd been there all along but only came to our attention as the boat's motion stirred things up. Our drinking water was no better than a dilute suspension of algae and needed attention.

We had enough bleach to treat what water was left but how do we get it into the tank? Waves still washing over the deck made opening the filler cap impossible and taking the access cover off inside would only let the precious supply splash out. The only other way in was through the breather, but again, how do you pour chlorine down a quarter-inch hole, especially one that's jumping around like crazy?

The solution was among Tina's cooking utensils. She had a plastic squeeze bottle, like a dishwasher dispenser though it originally held distilled water, that she used to measure small quantities. This was commandeered and charged with the right amount of bleach which we simply squeezed down the hole. Whoever heard of a bottle-fed water tank?

The weather respite turned out to be a good one and before long we even contemplated some housework. The periods between bilge pumping had stretched to once a watch and we felt secure enough to put the floors back down. When we did so we gave everything a jolly good clean and were amazed at how much sand was still washing down. We thought we knew every inch of the boat by now but from the amount of coral stones, crab shells and muck mixed in the sand it was plain there were still crannies we'd never seen.

Once everything was neat and tidy and looking more like a home than a battle zone we opted to run the engine. We knew it was out of step with the compromise but wanted to take every advantage of the gentler spell. Once more it started perfectly but the alternator was still playing the fool. Its regulator certainly did its job of limiting the voltage but it kept shutting itself down. It would restart at the touch of a switch but refused to work longer than a few seconds. I would have to think about that.

The evening was a real treat. For the first time since passing Peros Banhos we sat together in the cockpit and enjoyed a civilized meal. Tina's constitution was back to normal for the time being and we had much to be thankful for. We'd come a thousand miles since weighing anchor, almost a third of the way to South Africa and well on the way to the first port.

There was plenty of time for quiet contemplation during the night watches later and I made up my mind to risk shorting out the 'charge' button permanently in an attempt to make the alternator work. It wasn't the real answer but it was the only move I could think of. The risk I was afraid of was starting an electrical fire through ignorance, but I would be much happier with something more than solar panels to charge the batteries.

Next morning I tried it. With Tina standing by ready to disconnect the batteries at a moment's notice I started the engine – very extravagant, two days running – and there was no smoke or glowing cables, but no charge either. Very disappointed, and to avoid any future risk, I disconnected the alternator from the electrical circuit.

One thing we found hard to acknowledge was feeling cold. Ridiculous when you think the temperature hovered around eighty-five degrees during the day but we were further from the equator than we'd been for years and to us it was cold. Blankets, even lightweight ones, were almost forgotten artefacts but when Tina unpacked a couple we found them more than welcome.

We started wearing track suits in the afternoons and the last time we'd done that was such a distant memory the experience felt new. Our thoughts turned to Durban, a place we always associated with sweltering heat, a thousand miles to the south and those thoughts made us pull our collars tighter.

But that was far away. First we had to get past the area with the nasty reputation that we were approaching. Any time now we could expect stronger and more southerly winds that should stay with us until we rounded Cap d'Ambre. Our efforts to get south early were paying us back with interest now as we were well placed to tackle this leg and, as long as the weather stayed 'average', didn't foster too many fears.

True to form, though, when the wind came it was in the south west, not the south, and suddenly we weren't nearly so well placed. Instead of the anticipated long reach we were faced with more days close-hauled into a sea already becoming bouncy. I say we weren't so well placed but on reflection the southing was paying bonuses on top of the interest. Had we gone north of the bank we would have found ourselves in much less friendly circumstances.

Poor Tina succumbed to seasickness again almost as soon as

the motion changed. We still don't know if it was slamming or the fear of slamming that brought her down, but whatever the cause the outcome was a very dispirited lass creeping below to her bunk. Even the successful rescue of a flying fish from among the fuel drums failed to move her, though the discovery that a Boddam crab was alive and well and living under the cap-rail raised a smile.

During the first night watch the following day, sometime between the sun's afterglow and the moon rising, a green flare burst into the sky nearby. To my knowledge the only time a green flare is used at sea is when a submarine issues a warning it's about to surface. Rather hurriedly I switched on the navigation tri-colour light.

It was the blackest of black outside and I could see nothing. The only apparent difference between sea and sky was the absence of stars in the sea. Moments later I noticed the tri-colour had gone off so I turned on the all-round white instead. Another look around and still I could see nothing.

Worried in case it was someone in trouble we made a general call on the VHF but got no response. We searched around with our brightest torch but all it showed was waves. Nothing. Nothing. When the moon rose and lit the surroundings enough for us to see there were no unlit ships or submarines, at least not big ones, in the immediate vicinity so I turned the top light off again. We gave a final call on the radio, but still nothing.

Then, while I was noting this in the log, I found the GPS frozen again. Of all times to happen. We'd had two weeks in the open ocean with nothing to hit and the thing worked perfectly, well almost perfectly, and now we were closing on Madagascar it stopped. To rub salt in the wound when I got back to the cockpit I found the compass light dead.

Tina took over while I fixed a makeshift replacement from the tiny marker light we used in Boddam. It was made from a car instrument bulb mounted in a moulded glass salt cellar and, when hung in the rigging, was clearly visible from a mile. We tried simply hanging it over the compass but, while it let you read the card, it was so bright it destroyed your night vision, so we bound most of it in insulating tape and taped the assembly to the binnacle. The result wasn't ideal as it only illuminated the part of the card that told you where you'd been but it was better than nothing.

Now we could judge which direction we were going in it was time to find out where we were. I suspected that the failure of the two lights had something to do with the GPS glitch and, on investigation, found the light switch burned out. As all the electricals were on the same temporary circuit this was strong circumstantial evidence. I repeated the performance from last time the navigator stopped navigating and by daybreak we had our position again, and a little while later I had the burnt out switch isolated.

While making these repairs we discovered the battery voltage was low; alarmingly so as there probably wasn't enough in them to start the engine. However the sky was fairly clear and the solar panels had several hours of sunshine ahead to do something about it. We would check again later.

Now we could turn our attention back to rounding Cap d'Ambre, and found things looking pretty good. Our intention was to pass the cape as close as possible, within half a mile if we could, and from our present position we could make the necessary course without tacking, just. The wind had come round to the south, where it should be, and was blowing a steady twenty. If we sailed close hauled the combination of course and current should give us the last couple of miles southing with distance to spare and get us to the cape around dawn.

The sea was throwing up hints of why the place had such a poor reputation. So far they were only hints, in the form of very large swells, but we were getting used to that. An east-bound ship pitched and rolled past a mile to starboard confirming our perception of the waves. It was the first ship we'd seen and we debated asking him to report our position on Tony's radio net, but decided against it as we expected to be near a telephone within a day of the next schedule.

Later we felt the reflection waves from the coast and the wind picked up to thirty. In spite of the now very difficult sea we were covering ground quickly, the current was much stronger and we revised our estimate of when we would pass the cape to a little before midnight. The almanac told us a half moon would rise at the same time so, not wanting to make a landfall on an unlit coast in the dark, we hoped we wouldn't go any faster. An extraordinary feeling.

Vespera's motion became extremely uncomfortable and Tina, stoically doing her watches in spite of continuing sickness, gave up on a project to make bread. We ate the last of her castaway cookies, made for such an occasion, instead.

We watched with trepidation the reflection waves impinging on the swells, adding to some and subtracting from others, and relieved Fred of the responsibility of steering in case he steered us straight into an 'added-to' giant. We weren't always successful ourselves but it kept us on our toes trying.

One particular lump gave me microseconds of entertainment that are permanently engraved on my mind. A huge cone of water rose from nowhere leaving a school of dolphins, rising with it, nowhere to swim to and they burst from it in all directions, as stars from a firework. Spray fanned skywards by their flashing tails glittered with rainbow colours to enhance the impression.

We were down to the smallest jib and fully reefed mainsail to suit the stronger wind but still we flew. We'd come seventy miles since morning and peered anxiously ahead for a sight of land, but daylight faded to night before we saw anything. It looked more and more likely we would arrive at the cape before the moon did. Certainly we would make the approach in total darkness.

There were options of course. We could have tacked about and waited for morning, in which case the current would have pushed us far north, or we could simply have passed the cape further offshore. But all the information we had stressed the importance of keeping close in so we pinned our faith on the GPS. Unfortunately there was no indication on our chart of how its coordinates related to those programmed into the GPS, so we eased our aiming point from half a mile to a mile offshore in case. Not a wide margin for error but we would both stay on watch and keep our eyes peeled.

At ten o'clock it was as dark as could be and the navigator, working like a charm, put us eight miles due east of the target and approaching it at seven knots. We weren't going very fast through the water so most of that speed was due to current. Then, shortly afterwards and to our great consternation, we caught a glimpse of a light, far ahead and slightly to the north of our course.

At first it winked and danced, like all distant lights at sea, but quickly settled into a small clump of white spots. If the GPS was telling the truth this had to be a ship as the land stopped a mile south of us, but the lights were not correct for a ship. The horizon all around, especially where we expected land to be, was a flat and unimaginative black with no signs of life or habitation anywhere.

We were boring down on the mark at great speed and indecision descended like a brooding conscience. The lights may be, probably were, a fishing boat exercising its own interpretation of the lighting rules – we'd encountered hundreds like that before; they may even be someone else in the same predicament as us with insufficient power to run the correct lights, or they may be house windows on land!

Decision time. If we were going to do anything we had to do it now. Tina took the wheel while I readied to start the engine, offering up a prayer that the batteries had absorbed enough power during the day, and turned the key. It started. Motor sailing now we turned a little north to give the lights a reasonable berth and soon the GPS showed us covering ground at nine knots – unprecedented in *Vespera*'s history.

In no time at all we lost the day's southing and zoomed past the lights at a mile's distance. Almost at the very moment we made our closest approach, still unsure of what we were seeing, extra lights flicked on like a Christmas tree, including appropriate navigation lights for a working trawler, and the pattern moved off to the east. The GPS was right all along and we'd taken this evasive action unnecessarily.

By coming those few miles north we were right in the middle of an area of turbulent currents where so many of our friends had had frightening experiences, but the Gods let us down lightly. The interfering reflection waves must, for the time being, have been reflecting in another direction as the sea settled to an easy regular swell from our port quarter and we continued to fly under tiny sails.

The moon, when it rose, clearly outlined the landmass well to the south but even with that visual confirmation our adrenalin stayed high and we took turns to enjoy steering in the easier conditions. As we edged into Madagascar's lee and the mouth of the Mozambique Channel both wind and waves reduced steadily and without fuss until a startlingly beautiful dawn found us under full sail in smooth seas and with the gentlest of breezes ghosting us along. The long anticipated, and feared, Cap d'Ambre was behind us.

We had debated at length the relative merits of the two clearing ports available to us. Dzaoudzi in Mayotte had the advantage of being part of a first world community. To all intents and purposes it's part of France, with all that that entails; comparatively little bureaucratic fuss, supermarkets, taxis that work and so forth. But it was two hundred miles away. Hellville, on Madagascar's offshore island of Nosy Be, was only half that distance but the very opposite of first world.

Earlier we tried tossing coins but neither of us were entirely happy with the outcome and delayed making the decision until getting where we were now, and the decider was supposed to be the wind. If it was good to go west we would carry on to Mayotte, if not we would try Nosy Be. In practice it was neither; by breakfast time there was no wind at all. On the spur of the moment we opted for Nosy Be as it was nearer and we were anxious to reach a telephone to let the family know we were safe.

The coastline between the cape and Nosy Be is essentially a huge open bay with a coral bank stretching out to sea, often as far as twenty miles. To us the charts appeared extraordinarily well detailed with myriads of soundings and undersea contours, but each carried the stern warning that the surveys on which they were based were done to locate channels and not to define the bank – 'Shallower soundings than those shown may be encountered.'

Being, as we were, all too familiar with unwanted shallows we opted to do this last bit well to seaward of the bank and use the large ship channel into Hellville. It would cost us a few miles but the peace of mind would be worth it. The pilot also warned of strong tidal currents and we certainly didn't want to feel coral-bound under those circumstances.

Yesterday's prediction that we would be at a telephone before Tony's radio schedule proved woefully wrong. At the time the ship could have relayed a message we were motoring south with four knots on the log and making no headway whatever, such was the current. But in truth we weren't too dismayed. Tina was miraculously better in the calm seas and Jess ate her first substantial meal of the trip. The slow progress was frustrating but splendid views of mountains flanking the shore more than made up for it. It was a year and a half since we'd seen land higher than ten feet.

The light winds persisted, and persisted. Sometimes, when the tides were running with us, we gained a few miles and others, when they ran against, we lost some but three days after rounding the cape the sun rose to reveal the peaks on Nosy Be and we started making ready for our arrival. A big tidy-up of the general clutter, retrieval of our shore-going clothes, preparation of documents, and that sort of thing. In the full heat of the day we took turns for a final shower – a bit premature as it turned out.

I'd just made my way forward, shampoo and dipper bucket in hand, when I clearly saw the sea bottom. This was nonsense as we were far outside the bank, but there was no denying it. The water was so clear and still we could see not only the shapes but types and colours of the coral. The depth sounder, when we turned it on, showed forty feet.

I was faced with a quandary. I wanted the engine running in case it shallowed further as there was too little wind for fancy footwork from *Vespera*. I also wanted the depth sounder to give me a proper warning, but the problem of the sounder not working with the engine running was still unresolved. I chose the engine.

After it started I left it burbling on stand-by while we both took positions at the bow to watch for nasties. The bottom seemed to stay the same distance away, in fact it looked lovely with spectacular fans and clusters, and there were no green giveaways of shallower bommies anywhere.

Tina went below later to do a routine engine check and called, with an edge of alarm in her voice, that it was boiling like mad. A look over the stern showed plenty of cooling water flowing so, not knowing what was amiss, we turned it off to cool down. On the bright side we now had the benefit of a working sounder and before long we watched the numbers creep up then switch to the regular 'No Bottom'. The sea was again a clear and beautiful blue as far down as you could see.

Then the tide turned and what little wind there was faded. The following sunrise brought a repeat performance with the peaks on Nosy Be glowing in nice new colours and almost as far away. But it also brought a fair breeze that clipped us along nicely. As we approached Hellville we chose to use the smaller pass in favour of the main channel as it gave a better angle off the wind.

While Tina sailed us in I gave the engine a little first aid. The only cause of over-heating that came to mind, at least the only one I could do anything about, was a sticking thermostat so I took it out to have a look. I couldn't find anything wrong with it and, when dropped in a pot of boiling water, it worked just fine. We decided to delay testing it *in situ* until almost ready to anchor so that, even if the engine did overheat, we would have time to set the anchor.

The breeze stayed fair all the way in, in fact as we rounded the southern end of the island it swung gently with us. It was such pleasant sailing that Tina was reluctant to hand over the helm until the prospect of a final, final, shower in nice clean water and away from onlookers prized her away from the wheel. We lowered the sails a quarter of a mile outside the port and motored the final stretch with the engine behaving perfectly, and dropped anchor beside a boat belonging to friends from our old club in Durban.

After heartfelt and very intense words of thanks to our Maker for bringing us safely to port we opted for a relaxing cup of tea before snugging the boat down and putting away the sails. Time had flown and it was already four o'clock in the afternoon so we didn't expect the authorities to come visiting today. If they did they could join us for tea.

Tina had no sooner passed up the tea tray when a yachtsman returning to his boat called with a message from an official who could be seen standing at the slipway. 'You must go ashore and report to customs immediately.' Brilliant. There was no suitable dock to take *Vespera* alongside and it was obvious our dinghy was still stowed. Maybe he expected us to walk across the water.

We were obliged to prevail on the message-bearer to give us a lift then return for us when we were finished, an inauspicious start to an episode that didn't improve. It turned out this official's office was the only one still open so we couldn't conclude the business anyway but we made a start by preparing numerous hand-written forms – six copies of each – and were completely taken aback when he confiscated our ship's papers; to be returned only after our vessel was cleared to leave and on presentation of evidence that all fees had been paid. As to what these 'fees' were and how much money was involved he resolutely refused to say. His colleagues would 'work it out' tomorrow.

It was dark by the time we returned to our relaxing 'cuppa' but the cups of cold tea were now just dreary washing up waiting to be done, so we finished off the boat work and quit for the day. The afternoon's proceedings had left such a sour taste we didn't even feel like celebrating our arrival.

In the morning the same official escorted us to the harbour master's office where we wrote out more forms – also six copies – and were advised of 'the fees'. The harbour master was a personable enough sort of chap and at least had the grace to look abashed as he enumerated the charges, but it didn't help. He listed the cost of entry permits, visas and harbour dues plus a large sum, payable to him, for distribution among the police, customs, port health, uncle Tom Cobbleigh and all. In total the equivalent cost of employing a local workman for half a year! Had we the choice we would simply have left but we were trapped. Not only did customs have our ship's registration documents they had our previous port clearance as well.

On the way to the bank to get money for this we tried, without much success, to rationalize the expense on the grounds of gaining access to a telephone, deciding in the end to change just sufficient to pay off the officials, make the calls and buy some vegetables. We were inclined to get away from this greedy society as quickly as possible.

Then the bank presented another difficulty. The teller's face fell when we offered a bundle of hundred-dollar bills for exchange; they wouldn't accept such large denomination notes as they didn't have a verifying machine. We had no other cash. The day was going from bad to worse.

We eventually found a bank, with a much less imposing façade, that was happy to accept our money, albeit at their own 'special' rate, and spent the balance of the morning chasing receipts and trying to get our passports stamped. Another disastrous brush with the authorities as our passports were also detained; not exactly confiscated but 'kept pending signature'. Detained though whatever the excuse.

Then, and only then, did we discover that for the present Nosy Be had no external telephone service. A new international service was being installed and sparkling new booths were in evidence all over, but it wasn't expected to be operational till next month. The old system was 'broken' and the only service available was for local calls on the island. I was starting to get really angry.

At this point we encountered a singularly poisonous character. He summoned us, loudly, as we approached the harbour gate and led us to an office adjacent to the harbour master's. We were never able to figure out quite what this functionary's function was but he'd certainly been recruited from that pool of petty officialdom that attracts ignorance and arrogance. He had the build and demeanour of a junior Idi Amin and presented a great strutting performance in front of his typist, ranting first in his own language then in equally unintelligible English. The outcome of it was we were parted from another week's pay in return for a type-written 'permission' to sail among the local islands.

In the ordinary run of things this sort of hassle is of little consequence, though dealing with a hostile bureaucracy that's confiscated your papers is not so trivial, but we felt Hellville embodied a microcosm of the frustrations we had escaped from, and virtually forgotten, during our sojourn in Shangri-la and we were caught up in it.

Suddenly, overwhelmingly, our idyll was over.

POSTSCRIPT

O F COURSE REACHING Madagascar wasn't the end of it. We were still thirteen hundred miles from the boatyards of South Africa and it would be another three months before the weather in the Mozambique channel would be at its optimum for the trip.

As soon as we could escape the voracious officialdom we took *Vespera* to more secluded surroundings and actually enjoyed the stay, especially after Tony stepped in with his radio safety net and passed on the message that we were safe. Having come this far we were more confident of *Vespera*'s abilities and there were countless interesting places to explore, but we couldn't justify a second and third crop of 'fees' so we only stayed a few weeks.

Mayotte endures the highest cost of living we encountered anywhere but, as they welcome rather than fleece visitors, it proved a more economical place to wait out the weather, and everything there worked. We were able to speak to our family and catch up on the news, to make some positive plans and even start coming to terms with first world living again.

The eventual trip down the channel was pretty ordinary, in the usual sense of the word, and generally uneventful. The only hiccup was tearing the mainsail from leech to luff through sheer stupidity, but fortunately that happened only twenty miles out of Richards Bay.

Of necessity those last miles signified the end of our adventure, for the foreseeable future anyway, and motoring gave us time to reflect on how differently it might have ended if it hadn't been for the unbridled generosity of others. We had gone in search of Shangri-la on uninhabited islands, and found it among the people we met there.

320

ALSO AVAILABLE IN THE REED'S MARITIME LIBRARY

ALL FOR A BOTTLE OF WHISKY
Lying buried on Isle of Arran is a bottle of whisky. On the far side of the world a highly pressurized sales manager decides that the time has come for a change of gear. He wants to return to Europe, and instead of taking the plane he finds himself *Ryusei*, a beautiful 44-ft wooden sloop. Together with friends who form a happy gang of 'Three Men in a Boat,' he sets sails. Taking a long route from Asia via Africa and the Americas they head to Scotland — to dig up the whisky.

Ralph von Arnim, born in 1956 of a German father and French mother, is a metallurgist by training. He was working in Asia's steel industry when he opted to interrupt his career to sail home. His ports of call included many a beautiful island and exquisite cove, but also a handful of industrial sites on which he had worked. He, his wife and son are currently at anchor.

MORUROA BLUES
Moruroa Blues is high action sailing adventure. Fourteen boats sailed at short notice from New Zealand against winter gales through the Roaring Forties to a South Pacific atoll, not to bask on sun-drenched beaches but to join the small but determined flotilla protesting against nuclear weapons testing. For 30 days, *Joie* and crew withstood aggressive intimidation from a hostile French Navy. Like all ships in the New Zealand Peace Flotilla, she also survived gear failures, storms and harassment. In sailing terms alone, this three-month 6,000-mile voyage is an amazing small boat achievement.

While Lynn Pistoll was living on board his yacht in Alaska, fallout from a Chinese nuclear test helped him decide to emigrate from America to the southern hemisphere. He sailed to New Zealand in 1981 and now has three sons and a market consulting practice in Wellington, from where he continues to indulge his love of the sea. In over 50,000 miles of sailing, this was Lynn's first protest voyage.

SAILING IN GRANDFATHER'S WAKE
Here is a seafaring adventure spanning three generations. In 1938, *Caplin*, skippered by Commander R. D. Graham with his daughter Marguerite as mate, set out from England to sail around the world. Sixty years later, Commander Graham's grandson, Captain Ian Tew, bought *Independent Freedom* in New York and, with his aunt's account of the voyage as a guide, sailed in *Caplin's* wake. The side-by-side accounts of their navigation to remote shores provide a fascinating historical perspective against which the calms and storms of sailing are ageless.

Born into a seafaring family reaching back to a notoriously successful 17th century privateer, Ian Tew was learning to sail at the age of seven. He made his career in the British Merchant Navy and then as a salvor in the Middle and Far East but, after returning to the UK in 1991 to run a small business, has put to sea again.

SHERIDAN HOUSE
America's Favorite Sailing Books
www.sheridanhouse.com